Challenges to School Exclusion

Permanent exclusion is the most severe sanction a school can impose on a child and the number of permanently excluded children is rising. Based on systematic observation of exclusion appeal panel hearings, *Challenges to School Exclusion* offers a unique insight into the appeal process. It focuses on:

- mechanisms by which parents and children can challenge permanent exclusion
- the law and current practice on school discipline, including exclusion
- the social context to exclusion
- reforms to the appeal system made by the School Standards and Framework Act
- the DFEE's latest guidance on pupil inclusion.

Challenges to School Exclusion is the first study to examine in detail the legal processes involved in challenging permanent exclusion. The findings reveal serious deficiencies in the appeal system, including a frequent failure to deal fairly with excluded children. The text will be of particular interest to head teachers, local education authorities, school governors, education lawyers and education charities.

Neville Harris is Professor of Law at the School of Law and Applied Social Studies at Liverpool John Moores University. He has written extensively on education law and is the senior editor of the *Education Law Reports*. **Karen Eden** is a research officer at the Trust for the Study of Adolescence based in Brighton. She has also worked as a research fellow in the School of Law and Applied Social Studies at Liverpool John Moores University. **Ann Blair** is a lecturer in law at the University of Leeds. She has worked in the voluntary sector and has served as a school governor.

Challenges to School Exclusion

Exclusion, Appeals and the Law

Neville Harris and Karen Eden

with Ann Blair

ROUTLEDGE / FALMER
Taylor & Francis Group

London and New York

First published 2000 by RoutledgeFalmer
11 New Fetter Lane, London EC4P 4EE

Simultaneously published in the USA and Canada
by RoutledgeFalmer
29 West 35th Street, New York, NY 10001

RoutledgeFalmer is an imprint of the Taylor & Francis Group

British Library Cataloguing in Publication Data
A catalogue record for this book is available from the British Library

Library of Congress Cataloging in Publication Data
Harris, Neville S.
Challenges to school exclusion: exclusion, appeals and the law/
Neville Harris and Karen Eden with Ann Blair.
Includes bibliographical references and index.
1. Student expulsion–Law and legislation–Great Britain. 2.
Student expulsion–Great Britain. I. Eden, Karen. II. Blair, Ann.
III. Title.
KD3628 .H37 2000
344.42'0793–dc21 99-056938

ISBN 0–415–23080–2 (hbk)
ISBN 0–415–23081–0 (pbk)

Contents

Tables

Preface

Not all parents whose child is permanently excluded from school want to challenge the school's decision. Some, for example, feel that their child's needs were not being met at the school from which they have been excluded or in any event believe that a fresh start in another school would be beneficial. However, many others are very dissatisfied with the decision and recognize the inescapable fact that exclusion from school can be a particularly serious matter for the child as well as for the parents themselves, and are prepared to fight it. For those willing to mount a challenge and seek their child's reinstatement there is a two-stage process in England and Wales involving review by the governing body (or its discipline committee) and, if the decision is one not to reinstate, an appeal to an appeal panel. Under changes introduced by the School Standards and Framework Act 1998, the appeal panels have become more independent from schools and LEAs, and in theory parents should now be able to feel more confident that their child's case (or rather theirs, because education law denies the excluded pupil the right to appeal in his or her own right until aged 18) will be dealt with fairly. Yet there are reasons to believe that a much more radical reform is needed.

The appeal system, which was set up in 1987, has attracted some controversy in recent years. The teaching unions, including the NAHT and the NASUWT, have called for its abolition. It seems that, in their view, the more independent the system gets, the more detached it is from the school situation that should inform decisions about whether a child who misbehaves and disrupts the education of others should remain excluded. Other voices, notably the membership of the Council on Tribunals, have called for the appeal system not only to be made more independent but also judicialized, with lawyer chairs. Moreover, at a time when human rights are being enshrined within our national law under the Human Rights Act 1998 and there is ever increasing recognition of the need to acknowledge and protect the independent rights and interests of children, it would seem to many to be inconceivable that this important redress mechanism should be removed, particularly when over 12,000 children each year are currently being permanently excluded from schools in England.

The appeal system has been much criticized by the Council on Tribunals in recent years for its lack of independence and its procedural shortcomings. Reports of investigations of individual complaints by the Commission for Local

Administration (local government ombudsmen), together with deficiencies highlighted in a number of court judgments, have further contributed to a negative, albeit somewhat sketchy, picture of exclusion appeals. What has been absent until now is independent academic research into the appeal system. Our research, funded by the Nuffield Foundation (whose support we acknowledge with considerable gratitude), was the first detailed and comprehensive study of the exclusion appeal system. This book reports the findings, conclusions and recommendations. These are based on observations of nearly 50 hearings in seven representative areas and information provided by nearly 300 parents, almost 100 LEAs, over 100 appeal panel members and a similar number of head teachers, and nearly 70 chairs of governors of schools. There were also interviews with a small number of children who had been to their appeal hearing. They confirmed what a good deal of the research was saying – that the child's voice is not properly heard, if it is heard at all, in the exclusion appeal process. This was just one of the problems with the appeal system we uncovered during the research, the main part of which was completed towards the end of 1998.

This book assesses the importance of the exclusion appeal system and shows how it fits into the overall pattern of redress of grievance in the field of education. It examines the appeal system's accessibility and considers the nature of its procedures, and it looks in depth at the adjudicators who make the decisions. It also discusses the role of governors at the first review stage (the reinstatement meeting). Critical themes running through the analysis include the fairness and impartiality of the system, the participation of and adherence to the rights of the child, and the position of ethnic minorities. The book also analyzes the current law (as at December 1999) on the power to exclude a child from school, including the important changes made by the School Standards and Framework Act 1998. Taking as its context the wider disciplinary framework governing schools under current legislation and guidance, the book also discusses theoretical issues relating to the role of education and the practice of exclusion from school. There is a tension, in that the government wants schools to be well-ordered places in which high standards of education can be achieved, while at the same time is seeking a reduction in the use of the most severe disciplinary measure, school exclusion, because of its association with failure and wider social exclusion.

The main part of the research was based at Liverpool John Moores University (JMU). In addition, we became aware of a small-scale study of the process by which the decision to exclude is initially reviewed by the governing body, being undertaken by Ann Blair at the University of Leeds. Ann agreed to feed her research findings into the book, and they are presented jointly in Chapter 6. We are grateful to her. Ann's findings also contributed to the overall conclusions made in Chapter 10. The other chapters of the book are based exclusively on the JMU research. Responsibility for the writing of individual chapters was undertaken as follows: Neville Harris alone wrote Chapters 1, 2, 5, 7, 8 and 10. The last of these contains the conclusions of the research and reflects the authors' joint views. Karen Eden alone wrote Chapter 4. Harris and Eden jointly authored Chapters 3 and 9. Karen Eden and Ann Blair wrote Chapter 6 (with an input from Neville Harris).

We would like to express our thanks (once again) to the Nuffield Foundation for their financial support. Karen Eden would like to thank her current employers, the Trust for the Study of Adolescence, for giving her time off to complete some of her writing. We would also like to thank Clare Gallagher for secretarial assistance. Particular gratitude is owed to the numerous LEA officials, panel members, head teachers, governors and parents who gave their time and effort to answer our questions and co-operate with our attendance at exclusion appeal hearings. We are also very grateful to the children who tolerated our presence at their hearing and the smaller number who, by telling us about their appeal hearing, agreed briefly to re-live what was for them a daunting and/or depressing experience first time around.

The DFEE's revised guidance on school exclusions – covered within Circulars 10/99 and 11/99 on, respectively, *Social Inclusion: Pupil Support* and *Social Inclusion: The LEA Role in Pupil Support* – was published in July 1999, as we were completing the writing of this book. We were able to make extensive reference to the guidance and, with the express permission of the DFEE, to include an extract on the appeal stage as an appendix. The relevant provisions of the School Standards and Framework Act 1998, to which frequent reference is made in the book, came into operation on 1 September 1999.

Neville Harris and Karen Eden
December 1999

List of Cases

A v United Kingdom (Case 100/1997/884/1096), 23 September 1998, ECHR.
Barrett v Enfield LBC [1999] 3 W.L.R. 79 (HL).
Campbell and Cosans v United Kingdom (1982) 4 EHRR 293.
Cleary v Booth [1893] 1 Q.B. 465.
Costello-Roberts v United Kingdom [1994] E.L.R 1.
Fitzgerald v Northcote (1865) 4 F & F 656.
Goss v Lopez 419 U.S. 565; 95 S.Ct 729 [1975].
Gower v London Borough of Bromley [1999] E.L.R. 356 (CA).
Hunt v Damon (1930) 46 TLR 579.
Jarvis v Hampshire County Council (1999) *The Times* Law Report, 23 November (CA).
Mandla v Dowell Lee [1983] 1 All ER 1062.
Phelps v Hillingdon London Borough Council [1998] E.L.R.38 (QBD) and 587 (CA).
Price v Wilkins (1888) 58 LT 680.
R v Board of Governors and Appeal Committee of Bryn Elian High School ex parte Whippe [1999] E.L.R. 380.
R v Board of Governors of the London Oratory School ex parte R (1988) *The Times*, 17 February.
R v The Board of Governors of Stoke Newington School and Others ex parte M [1994] E.L.R. 131
R v Cambridge University ex parte Beg (1999) 11 Admin LR 505
R v Cobham Hall School ex parte S [1998] E.L.R. 389.
R v Commissioner for Local Administration ex parte Croydon London Borough Council [1989] 1 All ER 1033.
R v East Sussex County Council ex parte T [1998] E.L.R. 251
R v Essex County Council ex parte EB [1997] E.L.R. 327
R v Fernhill Manor School ex parte A [1994] E.L.R. 67.
R v Governing Body of the Rectory School and the London Borough of Richmond ex parte WK (A Minor) [1997] E.L.R. 484.
R v Governors of Bacon's City Technology College ex parte W [1998] E.L.R. 488.
R v Governors of Haberdashers' Aske's Hatcham College Trust ex parte Tyrell [1995] E.L.R. 350.
R v Governors of St Gregory's RC Aided High School and Appeal Committee ex p M [1995]

E.L.R. 290.
R v Head Teacher of Fairfield Primary School and others ex parte W (1997) 18 July (QBD) CO/541/97.
R v Head Teacher and Independent Appeal Committee of Dunraven School ex parte M (1999) 24 September (unreported) CO/1794/99 (QBD).
R v Hopley (1860) 2 F & F 202
R v Incorporated Froebal Educational Institute ex parte L [1999] E.L.R. 488 (QBD).
R v Inland Revenue Commissioners ex parte Preston [1985] 1 AC 835
R v Inner London Education Authority ex parte Ali and Another (1990) Admin LR 822.
R v Kent County Council ex parte C [1998] E.L.R. 108
R v Lancashire County Council ex parte M [1994] E.L.R. 478
R v Laurelhill High School ex parte K (1997) 6 February (unreported).
R v Leeds Metropolitan University ex parte Manders [1998] E.L.R. 502
R v Local Commissioner for Administration for the North and East Area of England ex parte Bradford Metropolitan City Council [1979] 2 All ER 881
R v London Borough of Camden and the Governors of the Hampstead School ex parte H [1996] E.L.R. 360
R v London Borough of Newham and Another ex parte X [1995] E.L.R. 303
R v Neale and Another ex parte S [1995] E.L.R. 198.
R v Newport (Salop) Justices ex parte Wright [1929] 2 KB 416.
R v Northamptonshire County Council ex parte W [1998] E.L.R. 291
R v Rahman (1985) 81 *Crim App Rep* 349.
R v Roman Catholic Schools ex parte S [1998] E.L.R. 304
R v Secretary of State for Wales ex parte Williams [1997] E.L.R. 100
R v Solihull Borough Council ex parte W [1997] E.L.R. 489
R v South Tyneside Education Department and the Governors of Hebburn Comprehensive School ex parte Cram [1998] E.L.R. 508
R v Staffordshire County Council Education Appeals Committee ex parte Ashworth (1997) 9 Admin. L.R. 373 at 395F-G
Ryan v Fildes [1938] 3 All ER 517.
S v Special Educational Needs Tribunal and the City of Westminster [1996] E.L.R. 226
Secretary of State for Education and Science v Metropolitan Borough of Tameside [1976] 3 All ER 665
Sharp v The Governors of Sheene School (1996) (unreported)
W (A Minor) v Education Appeal Committee [1994] E.L.R. 530
X (Minors) v Bedfordshire County Council [1995] E.L.R. 404.
Z and others v UK (1999) European Commission on Human Rights, November 1999.

Abbreviations

CLA	Commission for Local Administration
CRE	Commission for Racial Equality
DFE	Department for Education
DFEE	Department for Education and Employment
DES	Department of Education and Science
ELR	*Education Law Reports*
FE	further education
GCSE	General Certificate in Secondary Education
LEA	local education authority
LMS	local management of schools
NAHT	National Association of Head Teachers
NASUWT	National Association of Schoolmasters/Union of Women Teachers
NVQ	National Vocational Qualification
OFSTED	Office for Standards in Education
PRU	pupil referral unit
SEN	special educational needs
SENT	Special Educational Needs Tribunal
SHINE	Schools Have Inclusive Education
SSFA 1998	School Standards and Framework Act 1998

Note: references in the text to 'the guidance' or 'the new/revised guidance' are to DFEE, Circular 10/99 *Social Inclusion: Pupil Support* (1999) unless stated otherwise.

All pupils' names cited in the book, other than those found in reported cases, are fictitious.

1 Introduction

Background

In the light of the other, wide-ranging, reforms to the education system of England and Wales over the past two decades it is easy to underestimate the importance of the development of statutory appeal rights in respect of various forms of decision. Yet without effective mechanisms for redress of grievance, notions of parental 'empowerment', partnership or participation, which have become a feature of education policy in recent years, would have little meaning. It would be much more difficult, or in some cases impossible, to enforce the individual rights which governments have conferred on users of the education system as a means of reducing the dominance of education providers and contributing to their greater accountability. The only redress mechanism provided by the Education Act 1944, on which the modern education system was founded, namely the right of complaint to the Secretary of State, would have proved inadequate to meet parents' expectations of effective remedies to infringements of individual rights – rights whose increasing assertion formed part of the emergent consumer culture in the education system under the post-1979 years of Conservative government (see Harris 1993).

One of the new redress mechanisms to be introduced post-1979, which are discussed more fully in Chapter 2, is the statutory appeal system in respect of permanent exclusion from school, which is the subject of this book. It commenced in September 1987, exactly five years after the introduction of the school admissions appeal system on which it was modelled. It was and remains confined to cases of permanent exclusion 'in recognition of the fact that permanent exclusion is a very different order of action from temporary exclusion' (DES 1987: para. 5.12.13). The rationale for the new appeal right for parents (and pupils aged 18 or over) was stated in basic terms by the minister, when proposing the amendment to the Education Bill in 1986 introducing the new clause on exclusion appeals:

> [A] parent may genuinely feel that an authority has taken insufficient notice of the pupil's point of view or the difficulties arising through its endorsement

> of a decision to expel. The parent may continue to feel that expulsion is unjustified, or the expelled pupil may be at a critical stage of preparation for school-leaving examinations. An alternative school may pose problems of accessibility, or the parent may be unhappy about the curriculum offered by that school. We therefore propose that … [w]hen an authority confirms an expulsion the parent would have a … right of appeal.[1]

Appeals against a refusal to reinstate an excluded primary, secondary or special school pupil may be brought by the parents or, if aged 18 or over, the pupil him/herself. Now that the relevant provisions of the SSFA 1998 are in force, the power of LEAs to direct the reinstatement of an excluded child and the governors' right of appeal against this decision, which were also introduced under the 1986 legislation, have terminated (subject to transitional arrangements in respect of cases where exclusion occurred before 1 September 1999).[2]

Initially, very few parents made use of the right of appeal. The monitoring system for permanent exclusions (the National Exclusion Reporting System) set up in 1990 on the recommendation of the Elton Committee on school discipline (Elton 1989) revealed that there had been only 92 appeals by parents in England in 1990–91. The following years saw a dramatic increase, which has now levelled out, in both the number of appeals – with over 1,000 appeals in each of the past four years – and the proportion of parents who appeal: see Table 1.1.

The appeal figures in Table 1.1 demonstrate that utilization of the right of appeal has become well established even if only a minority of parents appeal. The reasons for under-utilization of appeal right are explored in Chapter 8. The figures also show the increasing use made by schools of the power of permanent exclusion: 1997/98 was the first year since systematic national monitoring began in which the numbers of permanent exclusions fell. (Note, however, the doubts about the accuracy of the official statistics expressed by Hyams-Parish (1996: 6).)

Within the education system few other decisions taken at school level are

Table 1.1 *Numbers of permanent exclusions from schools and numbers of appeals against permanent exclusion in England, 1990–91 to 1997–98*

	A	B	C
	No. of permanent exclusions	*No. of parental appeals*	*B as % of A*
1990–91	2,900	92	3.2
1991–92	3,833	Not available	
1994–95	11,084	1,242	11.2
1995–96	12,476	1,339	10.7
1996–97	12,665	1,455	11.5
1997–98	12,298	1,287	10.5

Source: *DFE 1992: para. 16;* The Guardian *14 May 1996;* Hansard, *Written Answers, 10 December 1996, col. 115w; DFEE 1997c, 1998b and 1999d.*

Note: *No official figures for exclusion appeals for 1992–93 and 1993–94 have been released*

subject to statutory appeal arrangements. It is therefore surprising that there is so little published information about the operation of the exclusion appeal system. This book offers the first detailed account and evaluation of the work of the exclusion appeal panels. As noted in the preface, it is based on a study of their operation in seven LEA areas, conducted between 1997–1999. It covers all aspects of the appeal process and explores the reasons why parents who could appeal do not do so. It sets the discussion within the broader context of the legal and policy framework to the exercise of discipline within schools, focusing in particular on the respective roles of head teachers and governing bodies. The aims of the research project and the methodologies employed are outlined in the final section of this chapter.

Exclusion Appeals: A Controversial Subject?

Despite their increased independence following the SSFA 1998, and the continuing supervisory role of the Council on Tribunals over their operation,[3] the exclusion appeal panels are clearly perceived by many educators and local administrators to lie within the education system, rather than the judicial system. This perception stems from the fact that the appeal system is administered by LEAs, who also appoint members of panels, and is subject to the jurisdiction of the local government ombudsman (see Chapter 2). Nevertheless, as we shall see in the next chapter, it takes its place alongside the other redress mechanisms that bring access to potential legal remedies to ordinary citizens – in this case parents and (although only indirectly) children – when they question the actions of, and are in dispute with, public bodies such as local education authorities and schools. In this sense, despite its obvious connection with disciplinary aspects of education, the appeal system has a distinctly judicial function (with an associated welfare function, as one sees in family courts) and should not be seen as having a disciplinary role. However, it is one of the contentions of this book that, in relation to their specific role, many appeal panel members in practice fail to appreciate this distinction.

Although the appeal system gives rise to a complex series of issues, explored in this book, the system itself is a relatively straightforward one. As will be explained in more detail in later chapters, parents of children at all state-maintained schools have a statutory right of appeal to a locally constituted appeal panel[4] in any case where their child has been permanently excluded from school – whether as a result of a fixed-term exclusion being made permanent by the head teacher or as a result of permanent exclusion from the outset. This right arises only after the governing body or its discipline committee has met to consider the exclusion, which meeting must normally occur within 15 school days of the decision to exclude permanently. Various parties, including the parent, have a right to attend this meeting and make representations. If the governing body or its discipline committee refuses to reinstate the excluded child, it must inform the parent of their right of appeal and the parent then has 15 school days within which to give notice (in writing) of appeal to the LEA. The appeal panel must convene and hear the appeal within 15 days of the date the appeal was lodged.[5] The relevant parties (they do not include the pupil unless aged 18 or over) have a right to attend the hearing and make representations. The procedure at the hearing is a matter for the panel but it must have regard to the Secretary of State's guidance and to general principles of fair procedure, especially the rules of natural justice.

This kind of procedure is relatively easy to understand and accept. Indeed, as shall be shown, most of those who contribute to the work of the appeal system or whose decisions are at times considered by it agree with the principle that the availability of a right of appeal in cases of school exclusion is fair and appropriate. Only the major teaching unions, most notably the NASUWT, NUT and NAHT, have challenged it. Their opposition stems from a false perception that the appeal system poses a serious threat to the authority and professional autonomy of the education professionals whose interests these unions represent. In October 1996 the NASUWT responded to a government announcement of steps to improve school discipline (which followed a previous announcement in March 1996 of an £18 million programme of pilot projects to identify and promote best practice in managing pupil behaviour). The union noted the improvements that were to be made to exclusion appeal panels, but argued that these were a poor substitute for abolishing them completely, which the union preferred. The panels

> achieve nothing except to turn education into a quasi-judicial procedure in which the parents of violent/disruptive youngsters can exercise their right to insist that their children return to the school of their first choice regardless of their behaviour. ... When they exercise independence and force reinstatement they fatally undermine the authority of the school and Governing Body.
>
> (NASUWT 1996)

At its annual conference in Bournemouth in 1997 the union passed a resolution instructing its National Executive to continue to 'campaign for the abolition of so-called "independent" appeal panels' (NASUWT 1997: 4). Yet not only does the evidence suggest that the appeal system is supported by most head teachers and governors (see below), but it is also clear that panels only infrequently overturn the governing body's decision. In 1997–98 only one in five of the 1,000 appeals brought in England succeeded.[6] This means that schools were ordered to reinstate only 200 of the 12,300 pupils who were permanently excluded in that year.

Such controversy as has attended the operation of the appeal committees has been fuelled by a number of *causes célèbres* in the 1990s. In each of the cases there was an angry reaction from teachers and/or parents to the decision of the appeal panel to reinstate an excluded child. In the first of these cases, in 1993, a boy excluded from a school in Birmingham for fighting and injuring a teacher was reinstated following an appeal. Teachers refused to teach the boy and some parents protested over their decision. The school had to be closed for a two-day 'cooling-off period' (McCarthy 1993). In 1996 a 10-year-boy who had been excluded from Manton junior school in Worksop was reinstated on appeal. Following this decision the NAHT called on the Secretary of State to abolish the parental right of appeal where the school's head teacher, the governors and the LEA agreed that a child was unduly disruptive. The General Secretary of the NUT wrote in the *TES* that the union would sanction industrial action by teachers where appeal panels or governing bodies reinstated pupils against the professional judgement of teaching staff (McAvoy 1996). Local opposition to the reinstatement intensified as a result of the decision to arrange for a personal tutor to teach the child in isolation from other pupils at the school, at an annual cost of £14,000 per annum (Carvel 1996a).

There were similar concerns the same year, following an appeal panel's decision that a 14-year-old boy who had been excluded from a school in the north-east the previous year should be reinstated with a view to reintegration into mainstream schooling, a decision subsequently upheld by the Secretary of State in December 1996.[7] The teachers threatened to take industrial action if the boy should cease to be educated separately and be returned to mainstream classes, but the court refused an order requiring the child's reintegration.[8] There were other local controversies over appeal panel decisions elsewhere: for example, in Oldbury, near Birmingham, 16 NASUWT members agreed to take strike action when a boy who had been excluded for temporarily blinding a science teacher with a laser pen was reinstated by the appeal panel (Charter 1998).

Confrontation between parents/pupils and schools, and attendant publicity, were in fact predicted at the time the Education Bill was before Parliament in 1986. In response to the proposed government amendment introducing the appeal right an opposition spokesperson commented: 'There are likely to be reports in the newspapers and the pupil will be seen as taking on the school or local education authority. We need to design a more effective way of avoiding a high profile confrontation and aim for co-operation'.[9]

Over the past couple of years the high incidence of school exclusion and the growing awareness of its social effects have formed the basis for a number of government initiatives feeding into a broader policy programme aimed at improving levels of social inclusion. These are discussed in Chapter 4. As political and professional attention has focused more closely on the need to reduce the incidence of school exclusion *per se*, the controversy surrounding the exclusion appeal panels has largely disappeared. We found very little opposition to the current right of appeal in our survey of head teachers: despite the NAHT's disparaging views a few years ago (above), 93 per cent of the 106 head teachers in our survey supported the right of appeal and 62 per cent said it did not undermine their authority (only 23 per cent said that it did). Governing bodies were similarly in favour of the current appeal right: 88 per cent supported it and

61 per cent said it did not undermine their authority as governors, although 29 per cent said that it did.

Yet there are several respects in which the appeal system, while intrinsically so important (see below), ought to attract controversy, for reasons which are explored in this book. In particular, the authors' independent research over a two-year period has revealed serious flaws in the way the appeal system operates. We contend that the reforms to the exclusion appeal system under the 1998 Act, which form part of a more general reform of the law governing school exclusion, do not address many of the key difficulties with the present system. Moreover, we argue that the government's recently published revised guidance on exclusion appeals, which is incorporated into the general guidance on 'pupil inclusion' (DFEE 1999a and 1999b), will not overcome the deficiencies in procedural fairness which we have observed in the course of our research. As one possible option for reform, we support the call by the Council on Tribunals for exclusion appeals to be transferred to the jurisdiction of the Special Educational Needs Tribunal (e.g. Council on Tribunals 1993: paras 2.15 and 2.17), a recommendation based on the Council's perception of the panels derived from their visits to hearings as part of their supervisory and monitoring role (noted above). We discuss this and other reform options in later chapters.

Why the Exclusion Appeal System is Important

Exclusion and its Consequences

The appeal system is important because permanent exclusion from a school is a serious matter. In particular, exclusion has potentially adverse consequences for many of the children subjected to it, given the likely disruption to their education and the possibility that, unless and until a suitable school place can be found, an excluded child could remain outside the schools system for some time. In Chapter 4 we cite some of the now considerable evidence that children excluded from school can often spend many months deprived of suitable provision despite the existence of, in the words of Lord Browne-Wilkinson in the *Tandy* case discussed in Chapter 3, 'an immediate obligation [on LEAs] to make arrangements to provide suitable education'[10] (under s. 19 of the Education Act 1996) for any child of compulsory school age who is not attending school due to exclusion or certain other reasons. Despite this duty, the quality of the education that is provided for excluded children varies considerably (Parsons et al. 1996: 8). Both the denial of suitable education and the reduced social contact that result from school exclusion contribute to the alienation and reduced educational attainment of some young people. School exclusion is also associated with problems in relationships, securing employment and avoiding criminality in the transition to adulthood or in later life. There is also a link with entry into child prostitution (Melrose et al. 1999). The association between exclusion and these various problems forms part of the underlying basis to recent government, or government-backed, educational initiatives, such as the development of Education Action Zones to provide flexible patterns of curricular provision in areas of educational under-achievement and above-average levels of truancy or a high incidence of exclusion. The Government's Social Exclusion Unit, in recommending a number of changes in practice aimed at reducing the rate of exclusion, reported that some children receive only three or four hours of tuition per week following exclusion and that 'the wider community suffers because of the high levels of crime into which many truants and excluded pupils get drawn' (Social Exclusion Unit 1998: 1). The government has made a reduction in truancy and exclusions from school a specific target by defining it as an 'indicator of success' in the drive to tackle social exclusion (Secretary of State for Social Security 1999: 57).

Research indicates that the negative consequences of exclusion for the children themselves is often accompanied by a further human cost in terms of the anxiety and tension faced by the parents (Parsons et al. 1996: 31). Furthermore, the wider social costs are matched by an economic cost, in terms of the extra expense resulting from educating children out of school or from agency intervention (for example, it is estimated that 20 per cent of children permanently excluded from school incur a cost to social services) (ibid.: 28). We explore these costs further when examining the social context to exclusion in Chapter 4.

Where the child has been permanently excluded at least once before, the parent loses for the next two years the right to express a preference as regards the admission of the child to a particular school (SSFA 1998, s. 87). Persistent exclusion therefore also limits the power of parents to make decisions about the kind of education they prefer for their child, although the general and difficult to enforce principle that children should be educated in accordance with the wishes of their parents (Education Act 1996, s. 9) is unaffected.

The Nature and Use of the Power to Exclude Permanently

Given the consequences of permanent exclusion for both the children concerned and for society in general, it is important to ensure that any individual exclusion is absolutely necessary. In fact, the test which has come to be applied has been whether exclusion is 'reasonable' in the circumstances. However, now that both the courts and Parliament have declared that schools and appeal panels should have regard to DFEE guidance, the current version of which stresses that exclusion should only be used in cases of serious breach of discipline, when all other strategies have been tried but failed, and if allowing the pupil to remain in school would seriously harm his/her or another pupil's education or welfare (DFEE 1999a: para. 6.2), the legal test is clearly more specific. The legal limits on the power to exclude are explored fully in Chapter 5, but it may be noted here that the head teacher, who alone has the power to exclude a child (SSFA 1998, s. 64), must ensure that the facts support his or her decision (in terms of the culpability of the individual child) and, as already noted, that the punishment of exclusion is justifiable in the particular circumstances. If it comes to an appeal, however, the onus of proof rests with the parent to show that the head teacher's decision was unjustifiable. It has proved a difficult burden to overcome for many parents. The kinds of circumstances which may be relevant to the question whether the head was justified in excluding the child will be discussed in Chapter 5, but it should be noted that they may include a pattern of misbehaviour over a long period as well as one or two very serious acts of violence or other indiscipline. One survey has confirmed that children are 'more likely to be excluded because of a series of minor incidents than a single major one' (Cohen et al. 1994: 16).

Some might argue, as the NASUWT has done (above), that the review of the head teacher's decision by the governing body at its meeting to consider possible reinstatement is a sufficient check on any potential abuse of this power, particularly as the parent may attend the meeting and make representations to the governors. However, our evidence suggests that the governing body is generally reluctant to overturn the decision of the head teacher (Chapter 6). The governors often consider that to do so might prejudice the working relationship between themselves and the head teacher by undermining the head's authority; or they tacitly accept the need to exclude children whose presence might be perceived as detrimental to the interests of the school. There is considerable evidence that the pressure on schools to compete with others in relation to examination results and good discipline has resulted in the power to exclude being used to remove disruptive pupils who undermine their efforts to maintain or improve standards in these areas (Bourne et al. 1994). A MORI survey found that around two-thirds of LEAs regarded this as the main cause of the increase in school exclusions or a major contributing factor (cited in Hyams-Parish 1996: 7). There has also developed a 'culture of exclusion' in some schools, resulting in a disproportionate use of the power to exclude (e.g. Bourne et al. 1994). According to OFSTED, some schools have been 'irresponsibly profligate in the use made of exclusion' (OFSTED 1996a: para. 80).

Even if, as is likely, cultural factors within schools have a relatively modest influence on the power of exclusion, there is a more worrying aspect to it. It is clear that many of the children whose behaviour leads to exclusion have special educational needs. Despite the emphasis within the law and practice of special educational needs over the past 20 years on the integration or inclusion of those with learning difficulties within mainstream settings, growing numbers of such children have been excluded from school, albeit that there was a slight decline in 1997–98 in the proportion of excluded children who had statements of special educational needs – down from 20 per cent of all permanent exclusions in 1996/97 to 18 per cent in 1997/98 (DFEE 1998b: table 5; 1999d: table 5). This still means that pupils with statements are seven times more likely to be permanently excluded from school overall (i.e. including special schools), and nearly five times as likely as other children within mainstream schools only. An OFSTED survey has found that exclusion is rife in special schools catering for pupils with emotional and behavioural difficulties (EBD). The number of exclusions was so high in one in eight schools as to 'inevitably interfere with pupils' education and with the effective running of the school' (OFSTED 1999: 41).

There has also been concern for some time that the proportion of African Caribbean children excluded from school is considerably higher than among other children – five times the average in 1997/98 (DFEE 1999d: table 4). Research suggests that this might well be due to cultural factors such as white teachers' misunderstanding of personality traits, which might be different in young black children compared with their white counterparts (Cohen et al. 1994: 3–4), and negative racial stereotyping of black pupils (OFSTED 1996b). The DFEE's recent draft guidance acknowledges this and recommends that teachers need to 'ensure that they avoid any risk of stereotyping and that they are alert to cultural differences in manner and demeanour' (DFEE 1999a: para. 3.9).

The seriousness of inappropriate exclusion decisions, with all their potential social and economic consequences (discussed in more detail in Chapter 4), is such that there needs to be an effective check against them. It would, of course, be unrealistic to expect a governing body to act wholly objectively given its lack of independence, which is exemplified by the fact that in most schools the head teacher is a governor him/herself (although the guidance says he or she should not be involved in determining reinstatement cases). As noted above, governing bodies are generally reluctant to undermine the head teacher. The appeal process may therefore offer the only hope of an effective safeguard against an erroneous or otherwise unreasonable use of the power of exclusion, particularly as the decision of the appeal committee is binding.[11] The authors' research has examined the operation of the appeal system in order to assess its effectiveness in performing this vital function.

An important point to reiterate here is that we found overwhelming support for the right of appeal among governing bodies and head teachers, who almost universally saw it as providing a degree of natural justice and an objective review of contentious decisions which could have far-reaching consequences (see above). Comments included:

> It is conceivable that governors may be too 'close' to the particular situation to view it sufficiently objectively.
>
> (governor)

> [It is important] in order to ensure due care has been taken by the governing body and that they have not abused their authority.
>
> (governor)

> Permanent exclusion has a potentially devastating effect on the child. This vital interest should be protected through a fair process.
>
> (governor)

> I am not infallible and wouldn't like to give the impression of being so. The appeal process acts as a checking balance.
>
> (head teacher)

> This is a very serious situation for the child and the family. It must be seen as just.
>
> (head teacher)

It is clear that the appeal system is regarded as important even by those whose decisions may be overturned by it. Head teachers and governors recognize the consequences that exclusion can have and so most do not resent the parent's right to a review of the decision. Only a minority of head teachers feel that because they order exclusion only after a careful consideration of the case, an appeal process is unnecessary or undesirable.

The Rights of the Child

With so much pressure felt by head teachers to exclude disruptive pupils, there is a concern that the interests of such children might not receive proper consideration and might not be adequately safeguarded. At the same time, it must be recognized that the interests of the individual children at risk of exclusion have to be balanced against those of other children whose education and social well-being may well be under threat as a result of pupil misbehaviour. The interests of *all* children are the subject of international law on human rights, which prescribes principles relating to rights within the field of state education. In particular, there is a framework of children's rights that seeks to impose basic standards of protection, justice and participation in this context and which has been the subject of considerable academic analysis in recent years (e.g. Fortin 1998 and Bainham 1998).

The European Convention on Human Rights, which will soon form part of national law in the UK under the Human Rights Act 1998,[12] provides (Protocol 1, Article 2) that no one should be denied the right to education – which education must be provided on the basis that (in so far as is compatible with the provision of efficient education and training and the avoidance of unreasonable public expenditure)[13] it conforms to the wishes of the parents in accordance with their religious and/or philosophical convictions. This might be seen to cut both ways. It first connotes an obligation on the state to ensure that a misbehaving child has a right to be educated, taking account of the fact that there is a practical threat to this right as a result of exclusion from school.[14] Second, it could be regarded as placing an obligation on the state to ensure that the right of children in general to education is not undermined by disruption, bullying or other behaviour on the part of a particular child. The most appropriate way of balancing these potentially conflicting obligations is no doubt to ensure that there is an inclusive social and academic culture and an effective disciplinary environment in schools, so that disaffection and misbehaviour, and thus the risk of disruption and exclusion, will be minimized. Where an exclusion nevertheless proves necessary, there is, as in relation to other decisions threatening enjoyment of particular rights, a right to a fair process of adjudication and an effective remedy under the general principles in the Convention governing these matters (Articles 6 and 13). Other parts of the Convention aim to protect religious freedom (Article 9) and freedom from discrimination on religious, gender, racial, language and other grounds (Article 14). Freedom from discrimination is, for example, clearly relevant to school discipline. Thus it has been argued that 'at risk for discrimination would be a school policy of permanently excluding girls who become pregnant or pupils who marry' (Bradley 1999: 11). Racial and sex discrimination in the context of exclusion from school are in any event already largely proscribed under the Race Relations Act 1976 and Sex Discrimination Act 1975, both of which are referred to in Chapter 3.

The UN Convention on the Rights of the Child (1989), ratified by the UK government, also provides for a right to education (Article 28).[15] It stipulates that all parties to the Convention (States Parties) must, in particular, make primary education compulsory and free to all, encourage the development of different forms of secondary education (which should be free and be underpinned by financial assistance in case of need), make educational and vocational guidance available and accessible to all children, and take measures to encourage regular attendance at school (Article 28(1)). The Convention also lays down various principles concerning the matters towards which education should be directed (Article 29). These include the development of the child's personality, talents and mental abilities to their fullest potential;[16] the development of respect for the child's parents, and of his or her own cultural identity, languages and values; and the preparation of the child as a tolerant, peaceful and responsible member of society who respects people of different religions, ethnicity and nationality and those of the opposite gender. This last provision clearly seems to include, for example, efforts to minimize bullying and racial harassment, which are known to be problems in quite a number of schools.

Discipline is dealt with more specifically in Article 28(2): 'States Parties shall take all appropriate steps to ensure that school discipline is administered in a manner consistent with the child's human dignity and in conformity with the present Convention.' The first part of this obligation is concerned not only with physical or corporal punishment but also with any act of punishment that is humiliating or degrading, a matter also covered by Article 3 of the European Convention on Human Rights. Unlike the European Convention, which at present (the system is under reform) has a Commission and a Court of Human Rights, the UN Convention on the Rights of the Child does not provide an enforcement machinery. This means that judicial interpretation of the UN Convention is confined to national courts and only in the context of disputes arising under UK law. The jurisprudence of the European Court of Human Rights on the European Convention is, however, available. It holds that while corporal punishment is not unlawful *per se* (after 1987 under UK law it was only sanctioned in independent schools and even then only for wholly privately supported pupils), it would conflict with Article 2 of Protocol 1 (the right to education) or Article 3 ('no one shall be subjected to torture or inhuman or degrading treatment'), respectively, if given in conflict with parental religious or philosophical convictions or if it is too severe or protracted or administered in circumstances giving rise to factors such as humiliation or undue mental stress.[17] The SSFA 1998 has in any event now removed legal authority to administer corporal punishment in independent schools (see s. 131, which came into effect on 1 September 1999). The general principle that school discipline must conform with human dignity and not be degrading remains operative and is certainly relevant to all sanctions including exclusion.

In considering the second part of the obligation in Article 28(2) of the UN Convention two key principles are relevant. First, Article 3(1) of the Convention provides that 'In all actions concerning children, whether undertaken by public or private social welfare institutions, courts of law, administrative authorities or legislative bodies, the best interests of the child shall be a primary consideration'. This important 'best interests' principle again highlights the potential for conflicting rights noted above when applied to school discipline and exclusion in particular: whose best interests prevail where one child is threatened with exclusion from school (with all the potential consequences that might flow from it) and the other pupils might benefit from such removal? In practice, as we shall see, the decision to exclude is often taken primarily in the best interests of the school's teaching staff and management. If any children's best interests are being considered it is, and as a secondary consideration only, those of the children who will remain at the school.

The best interests principle is not, in fact, incorporated into the Education Acts. In contrast, the Children Act 1989 s. 1(1), makes the welfare of the child the 'paramount consideration' for a court in determining questions relating to the upbringing of the child and certain other questions. Indeed, the UN Committee on the Rights of the Child, in its monitoring report in January 1995, was critical of the absence of the principle in the UK's education legislation (UN Committee 1995: para. 213). There is little evidence that the best interests principle is applied in practice in the exercise of the power of exclusion, so this gap in domestic law needs to be filled if there is to be proper adherence to this important principle in the UN Convention. Unfortunately, education appeal bodies cannot be relied upon to compensate for this deficiency. Freeman (1998: 343) reminds us that 'there is a vast range of tribunals dealing with matters affecting children which are in no way bound by the "best interests" principle. … Tribunals in the education system, hearing appeals on such matters as school choice, school exclusions and special educational needs are not so bound.' In practice, exclusion appeal panels, free of such an obligation, pay little regard to this principle.

The second key principle that is relevant to the proper exercise of school discipline within the terms of the Convention concerns the need to engage with the views of the child in all decisions on matters affecting him or her. Article 12 provides that:

1. States Parties shall assure to the child who is capable of forming his or her own views the right to express those views freely in all matters affecting the child, the views of the child being given due weight in accordance with the age and maturity of the child.
2. For this purpose, the child shall in particular be provided with the opportunity to be heard in any judicial and administrative proceedings affecting the child, either directly, or through a representative or an appropriate body, in a manner consistent with the procedural rules of national law.

Article 12 contemplates that the views of the child of appropriate maturity should be given due weight and be heard, but it is a moot point whether it guarantees the child him/herself a right to present those views in person to an adjudicative body. The Convention as a whole clearly contemplates that children's rights will often be exercised through an adult, usually a parent. This is exemplified by the right of parental direction and guidance in Article 5 of the Convention:

> States Parties shall respect the responsibilities, rights and duties of parents or, where applicable, the members of the extended family or community … to provide, in a manner consistent with the evolving capacities of the child, appropriate direction and guidance in the exercise by the child of the rights recognized in the present Convention.

However, this does not detract from, but rather supports, the principle in Article 12 that the views of a child of sufficient maturity should be given due weight; and it should also be noted that the right in Article 12 is not subject to a specific parental right of direction, unlike the right to freedom of thought, conscience and religion under Article 14 (see Barton and Douglas 1995: 42). Article 12 clearly contemplates that any child capable of forming a view should have an opportunity to express it. Nevertheless, neither the Convention, nor the European Convention on the Exercise of Children's Rights 1996 (not at present ratified by the UK government and in any event concerned with family cases)[18], gives any right to be a party to such proceedings.

So far as school exclusion is concerned, the SSFA 1998 in effect provides[19] that a young person may not bring an appeal in his or her own right until aged 18. Here, as in most other areas of education decision-making, it is assumed that the interests of the child will be protected by the parent. The contrast between education law and the Children Act 1989, which at least goes a good way towards recognizing the autonomy of the child, has been much commented upon (Harris 1993; Barton and Douglas 1995; Bainham 1996; Fortin 1998;

Freeman 1998). The possibility that the child's and parent's views might conflict is not acknowledged by education law. For example, if the child wishes to appeal against his or her exclusion but the parent does not, the latter's view will clearly prevail. This epitomizes the potential for conflict between protective rights (exercised by others on the child's behalf) and the child's right to self-determination, a conflict which is a 'central concern in the recognition of children's rights' (Masson and Oakley 1999: 11).

Freeman (above) argues that the Children Act 1989 should adopt the requirement in section 6 of the Children (Scotland) Act 1995 that a person, in making any major decision which involves 'his fulfilling a parental responsibility ... or ... exercising a parental right', shall 'have regard so far as practicable to the views (if he wishes to express them) of the child concerned, taking account of the child's age and maturity'; under the 1995 Act a child aged 12 or over is legally presumed to be of sufficient age and maturity to form a view. Of course, the Children Act 1989 does not in any event apply to exclusion appeals. However, if this general principle were also adopted by education law it would at least mean that the parent would be under a duty (albeit one that would be difficult to enforce) to consult the child over the question whether an exclusion appeal should be brought. As things stand, education law fails to ensure that decision-makers or parents elicit the child's view although authorities in Scotland will soon have to do so in exclusion cases.[20] The UN Committee on the Rights of the Child expressed concern that specifically in relation to the parent's right to withdraw his or her child from sex education at school and 'other decisions, including exclusion from school', 'the child is not systematically invited to express his/her opinion' (UN Committee 1995: para. 216). The Committee recommended that 'children's right to appeal against school exclusions be assured' (ibid.: 6). As things stand, the pupil has not even a right to attend an exclusion appeal hearing unless aged 18 or over.[21] Yet, as one commentator has noted, those aged 18 or over 'must surely be a very tiny proportion of the school population' (Hyams-Parish 1996: 18). The most recent national exclusion statistics for England, covering the year 1997/98, show that only 6 of the 12,298 pupils permanently excluded from school were aged 18 or over, compared to, for example, 6,000 who were aged 14–16 (DFEE 1999d: table 3). Most children aged 14–16 would be well capable of expressing a view and the denial of an explicit right to do so in the context of school exclusion seems contrary to the idea in Article 12 that rights of participation should be acquired progressively with advancing age and maturity. The government's limited response to the UN Committee's criticism has been to acknowledge the appropriateness of the child being able to address the appeal panel in most cases (HM Government 1999: para 9.25.1) and to reflect that view in the guidance to panels (see Chapter 9).

The extent to which children do in practice participate in appeal hearings is discussed in Chapter 9. It should also be stressed that this is but one aspect of a much broader issue relating to the participation of children in education decisions and processes (see generally Sinclair 1996). It has been argued that the development of parental rights in respect of redress, choice, access and participation over the past 20 years and the promotion of the idea that parents are consumers of education, have tended to hinder the development of individual children's rights in the education system (Carlen et al. 1992: 59; Harris 1993: 19–22; Savage and Rae 1994). Certainly there has been a failure in respect of a wide range of decision-making processes, including choice of school, access to parts of the school curriculum (such as sex education) and, as we have seen, exclusion from school, to recognize independent children's rights to participation (see generally Fortin 1998: Chapter 6). Even where such recognition occurs it is often weak. For example, while parents are to be encouraged to sign a home–school agreement spelling out a range of matters, a child may be invited to sign (where the governing body considers he or she has 'sufficient understanding of the home–school agreement as it relates to them') merely as 'an indication that he acknowledges and accepts the school's expectations of its pupils'.[22] Children's participation will be considered further in later chapters.

Children as Witnesses: Special Considerations

Special considerations apply to any adjudicative body that is concerned with the interests of children and before which children regularly appear as witnesses. Although, as noted above, the excluded child is not a party to the appeal and has no right to attend the appeal hearing,[23] our research found that the child attended in approximately 40 per cent of cases and in nine out of ten of those cases was asked questions. The child attends as a witness and has no right to independent representation. This contrasts with care proceedings under the Children Act 1989, where, although the child's attendance is at the discretion of the court (s. 95), the child is named as a party to the proceedings and the court appoints a guardian *ad litem* (under s. 41 of that Act), who in turn is expected to appoint a solicitor to represent the child (see Sherwin 1996 and Masson and Oakley 1999). In exclusion appeal cases, although the child is not independently represented the parent's representative might well consider him/herself to be acting also for the child. However, as we explain in Chapter 9, only a minority of parents are represented at their hearing and few have legal representation.

Even if children did have representation, there would be no guarantee that it would always be effective. Research into representation in care proceedings has revealed that it tends to be 'largely based on shielding them from the process rather than assisting them to participate' (Masson and Oakley 1999: 144). Adjudicators in any case involving a child can aid participation by interacting with the child in an enabling way. In exclusion appeal hearings, given that the child is not independently represented, it is all the more important that the panel is able to ensure that participation by children who are involved in the proceedings is effective.

A number of initiatives designed to aid children's participation in legal proceedings are under way, primarily concerned with criminal proceedings – where, for example there are special problems in respect of child witnesses in cases of alleged child abuse and where children often feel intimidated by the justice system (see, for example, Brown 1998). Most children in exclusion appeal hearings are in the 12–15 age group and, as commented above, would be well able to understand and respond to basic questions about factual events and to recall thoughts or conversations. Indeed, the courts have expressed the view that the exclusion appeal panel should hear from the child if he or she is present, on the grounds of fairness.[24] Such a view, coincidentally, reflects a general presumption in criminal proceedings that children's evidence should be heard by a court: 'A child's evidence shall be received unless it appears to the court that the child is incapable of giving intelligible testimony' (Criminal Justice Act 1988, s. 33A(2A)). In *DPP v M*, Philips L.J. explained that 'A child will be capable of giving intelligible testimony if she or he is able to understand questions and to answer them in a manner which is coherent and comprehensible'.[25] This contrasts with the Children Act 1989 (s. 96) which actually imposes a higher burden in respect of evidence not given on oath – that the court must be satisfied that the child understands that it is his or her duty to speak the truth and is of 'sufficient understanding to justify his evidence being heard' (see Spencer 1998). There is no such requirement in the case of exclusion appeal hearings. Arguably, the kind of test articulated by Philips L.J. would be appropriate, although the potential distress that might be caused to the child in certain cases is also a relevant consideration.

We were therefore concerned to assess the effectiveness of exclusion appeal panels in treating children appropriately and especially in involving them in the hearing. We took account of the fact that approximately half of the children whose parents appeal have special educational needs and that the child's age, gender and race, and emotional factors associated with him or her, would also need to be taken into account.

The Issues and How They Were Researched

In a previous study by one of the authors it was suggested that there was a common set of criteria by which the effectiveness of an appeal body operating within an area of social welfare law could be judged. These criteria were concerned with the accessibility, suitability and fairness of the tribunal in question:

> Effective access to justice in the context of a public welfare dispute demands that cost, complexity, formality, inequality of the parties, delay, inconvenience of location and other matters which could stand in its way should be minimized; at the same time, all aspects of the appeal process should be as fair as possible. Impartiality is vital.
>
> (Harris 1997: 26)

Certainly these criteria formed the basis for the project design and evaluation in the study of exclusion appeals. In addition, there were a number of specific questions that needed to be explored. In relation to access to the system, we needed to find out why relatively few parents appealed. In some cases it might have been because an appeal was unnecessary because the dispute was resolved to the satisfaction of the parent at an earlier stage. On the other hand, there might have been particular barriers to bringing an appeal. Ignorance, due to lack of information, or cultural barriers could have been factors. Parents' access to advice about their rights and about the appeal process was a further issue that needed to be investigated. As far as suitability was concerned, the nature of the appeals procedures and the appointments to appeal panels themselves needed to be examined. It was important to find out about the membership of the panels – for example, members' ages, social backgrounds and how they were recruited. We also needed information on their training for their role. The role of the clerk also warranted exploration.

In assessing the fairness of the appeal system a particularly important subject of the study was the way appeal hearings were conducted and the extent to which parents were able to participate effectively. We also investigated whether parents were represented and, if so, by whom and how effectively. As noted above, we were also particularly concerned to ascertain the involvement of the excluded children in the appellate process. We were especially interested in their participation in the hearing and in finding out how appropriately the panel dealt with them. We also needed to look for evidence of impartiality or bias on the part of panels, particularly as the majority of panel members were people with a background of one sort or another in education. We wondered whether the low success rate for parental appeals was in any way due to conscious or unconscious bias on the part of panel members. We were concerned to discover whether, and to what extent, the school's case for exclusion was properly tested by the panel.

In exploring these issues we undertook observations of 48 appeal hearings in six LEA areas and one diocesan authority. These comprised: one largely rural county; three cities; two mixed urban/rural authorities; and a diocese comprising a city, several large towns plus various rural communities. All those authorities agreeing to assist us were in England – three in the north-west, two in the north-east, one in the West Midlands and one in London. We also elicited views and other information from a large number of parents of permanently excluded children (a minority of whom had appealed against the exclusion), appeal panel members, school governors, head teachers and LEAs. The total numbers of those who responded to postal questionnaires, which contained open and closed questions, and the response rate in each case (shown as a percentage), were as follows: 289 parents (17 per cent), 99 LEAs (67 per cent), 111 appeal panel members (57 per cent), 106 head teachers (48 per cent) and 67 school governors (30 per cent). The response rates were relatively high and even the lowest return (from the parents) was very respectable for a postal survey of ordinary members of the public. The parent and panel questionnaires were administered in five of the LEA areas and the head teacher and governor questionnaires in four of those five areas. The researchers were also granted permission to interview a small number of excluded children whose parents had appealed.

We were very fortunate to have received the full co-operation of the LEAs and diocesan authority in whose areas the observations were carried out. These authorities also provided us with very helpful insights into the organization of their appeal arrangements and useful statistical and other information. Our only regret is that although we saw some good practice, albeit as part of a variable pattern across the authorities concerned, the evidence overall does not enable us to paint a very positive picture of their exclusion appeal arrangements as a whole.

2 Education and Redress of Grievance

Introduction

This chapter explains how exclusion appeals panels fit into the overall pattern of redress of grievance in the field of education. The aim is to provide a broader context to the exclusion appeal system, enabling comparison to be made between it and other mechanisms for resolving education disputes. A further objective is to explain the alternative or further avenues of redress that are available to parents and children who challenge exclusion decisions, particularly the possibility of applying for judicial review and of complaining to the Secretary of State or the Commission for Local Administration (CLA) (the local government ombudsmen). These avenues are increasingly being utilized in exclusion cases; many 'parents ... see appeals as only one part of a longer process' (ACC/AMA 1992: 14). The chapter will include an overview of developments in relation to judicial review and the CLA's jurisdiction in the field of school exclusion, and particularly cases concerned with the procedures adopted in the exercise of the power of exclusion and in reviewing an exclusion decision. Judicial decisions of particular relevance to operation of exclusion appeal panels will be discussed further in later chapters.

There is clearly scope in exclusion cases for ensuring that disputes are avoided or minimized: for example, as discussed in Chapter 8 (p. 136), there is less likely to be a dispute if the LEA provides effective support for excluded pupils. An informal resolution of the disputes that do still arise will have a number of benefits. It is widely accepted, and acknowledged for example by the reforms to the civil justice system initiated by Lord Woolf, that an informal resolution of a dispute can bring benefits to the complainant, in terms of speed, access and reduced financial and emotional cost, and to the administration, in terms of improved efficiency and reduced cost. Nevertheless, while informal negotiations can proceed in a somewhat unstructured manner, even an ostensibly informal dispute procedure, such as characterises most of the complaints arrangements, and to some extent the review and appeal process, in the field of education, needs to have a basic defined structure to help to ensure procedural fairness.

Complaints, Reviews and Appeals: An Overview

In relation to education matters there is a distinction to be drawn between three types of redress mechanism: complaints, reviews and appeals. All such mechanisms have had a growing caseload over the past decade as parents have become increasingly prepared to challenge decisions over their children's education. This is undoubtedly a product of the government's policy of promoting parental choice and involvement and raising expectations, so that parents are less likely to accept decisions which conflict with their wishes. Indeed, in part the rights of consumer culture in this field has developed from the provision of information to parents about their opportunities for redress if dissatisfied. Generally there is a duty on decision-makers to inform parents of specific rights of redress, such as appeal or complaint, either when communicating a decision (as in the case of the right of appeal over exclusions, admissions and special educational needs) or as part of general information (such as the right of complaint about the performance of statutory duties relating to the curriculum, which must be included in the information to be set out in a school prospectus).

The distinction between complaint, review and appeal rests with the procedures rather than the grievance itself, for it is possible for the remedy to a single dispute to lie within more than one of these processes. For example, a person dissatisfied with their child's exclusion from school may complain to the head teacher over the decision, while his or her grievance must in any event be subject to a second-tier review by the governors or their discipline committee. Similarly, the parent might appeal over the exclusion while in the meantime complaining to the CLA, the LEA or indeed the Secretary of State over, for example, the failure of the LEA to make suitable provision for the child, although in fact the CLA could refuse to investigate a complaint in any case where it is felt that it would be reasonable to expect the complainant to bring an appeal.[1] And ultimately some aspects of the decision (e.g. a question whether the LEA has fulfilled its statutory obligations) might prompt an application for judicial review. The panoply of overlapping mechanisms might well justify suggestions for a more integrated system of administrative justice (see Thompson 1999), although this might reduce the complainant's choice of weapon in the fight for justice. From the point of view of the organization (see Page 1999: 93), the availability to the citizen of a complaints procedure where other avenues of redress are also possible will have the advantage of reducing the likelihood of the organization being subjected to another form of challenge that might, for example, make the cause at issue more public.

Table 2.1 (p. 22) lists the principal redress mechanisms operating in the field of education (each of which is discussed further below). Only four of the thirteen that are listed pre-date the 1980s: complaint to the Secretary of State, which dates from the Education Act 1944 (under ss 68 and 99); the Parliamentary Commissioner for Administration (1967); the CLA (or local government ombudsmen) (1974); and of course judicial review, which in one form or another is over 200 years old.

It can be seen that, as is a common feature of administrative justice in the United Kingdom (see generally Harris and Partington 1999), redress is available in this field through a combination of mechanisms of general application (the CLA and the courts) and ones which are specific to education. What should also be borne in mind is that there are often alternative or diverse routes for redress of grievance in relation to education matters. Challenges can take a number of different courses.

Complaints

The development of complaints mechanisms has been one of the key elements in opening up public services to greater accountability, particularly in respect of the quality of service to the public. It was a fundamental tenet of the *Citizen's Charter* (1991) that providers of public services should have complaints procedures that are clear, well-publicized and effective (see Lewis and Birkenshaw 1993: 81–83). Although complaints procedures do not always match up to these standards and are not always entirely independent of and external to the public body concerned (the most obvious exception being the CLA), they are of considerable importance. Mulcahy (1999) rightly argues that what she describes as 'low level justice systems' such as complaints procedures need to be taken more seriously by lawyers. They are widely used – far more so than traditional judicial mechanisms, although this is not entirely true of education complaints procedures (see below). The importance of procedural rights and aspects of natural justice might be underplayed so that more emphasis can be placed on ensuring that decisions can be made more quickly and cheaply than if formal, judicial, processes were involved.

One of the problems with complaints procedures, however, is that they tend not to place much emphasis on the participation of the complainant. This means that once the complaint is initiated there may be little or no opportunity to respond to the points made by the respondent public body. The benefits of participation are clear: 'Participation can be seen as an important way of complainants experiencing process and promoting accuracy in the investigatory process. It transforms service users from passive recipients or resisters into active co-operators in decision making' (Mulchahy 1999: 81). Although opportunities to participate are not always available, there is at least some evidence that the *Citizen's Charter* initiative has led to greater assertiveness on the part of dissatisfied public service users (Goriely and Williams 1997: 18).

The burgeoning complaints procedures in relation to public services and the utilities (see generally Goriely and Williams 1997) have led to the publication of various guidelines designed to ensure that the procedures conform to minimum standards, meet the expectations generated by the *Citizen's Charter* (HM Government 1991) as well as reflecting legislative and other attempts to promote remedial rights. In particular, the CLA in England (CLA 1992) and the Citizen's Charter Complaints Task Force (1993) identified broadly common principles

Table 2.1 *Principal education redress mechanisms, England and Wales*

	Remit
A *Complaints*	
1. Secretary of State	All issues
2. Local procedure	A. Curriculum and information duties
	B. Matters not covered by A
3. Local government ombudsman	LEA provision; and appeals re: exclusion and admission; *not* internal school matters, e.g. discipline. Must relate to 'maladministration'
4. Parliamentary Commissioner for Administration (PCA)	Central government (e.g. DFEE) decisions and action where there is 'maladministration'
B *Reviews*	
1. Adjudicator	Objection to proposed school admission arrangements and school organization plans
2. Governors (pupil discipline committee)	Review of head teacher's decision to exclude a child permanently
3. Judicial review	Review by a judge of a decision of a school or LEA
C *Appeals*	
1. Exclusion appeals	Non-reinstatement of permanently excluded child
2. Admission appeals	Refusal to admit child to school parent prefers. Or direction by LEA to governors to admit child excluded twice
3. Special educational needs (SEN) appeals	Statements of SEN; Assessment
4. School inspectors registration tribunal	Appeals re: registration as an inspector of schools
5. Independent Schools Tribunal	Appeal against Secretary of State's 'notice of complaint' on proprietor of independent school
6. School governing body	Appeal over access by parent or child aged 16-plus to school record

Notes:

[a] *There have to date been no appeals since this new tribunal was established under the*

[b] *There was only one case in 1995; there was one in both 1996 and 1997: Council on*

Description	*Source*
Power to issue directions to school or LEA that is acting 'unreasonably' or in default of its duty	Ed. Act 1996, ss 496 and 497
Three-stage procedure: (1) Informal, (2) and (3) Formal (governing body LEA). No enforcement power	Ed. Act 1996, s. 409
Procedure to be established by governing body under regulations (not yet made)	SSFA 1998, s. 39(1)
Investigation and report by Commission for Local Administration (CLA). Finding of maladministration with or without injustice possible. Recommendation, including one of compensation	Local Government Act 1974, s. 26 and Schedule 5
Parallels the CLA (above) with same basic powers. Complaint must be referred to PCA by complainant's MP	Parliamentary Commissioner Act 1967
Adjudicators are appointed by the Secretary of State. They are under the supervisory jurisdiction of the Council on Tribunals. In some instances the Secretary of State may have this jurisdiction instead	SSFA 1998, ss 25, 26 and 90; Scheds 5 and 6
Pupil discipline committee must consider whether permanently excluded child should be reinstated. Can confirm head's decision or reinstate	SSFA 1998, s. 66; Education (School Government) (England) Regs, and (Wales) Regs, 1999
Limited to question of legality of decision – whether decision-maker acted within the scope of his or her powers (*intra vires*) or whether the decision-making process was fair (e.g. failure to consult could constitute breach of natural justice)	Supreme Court Act 1981, s. 31 and Common Law
Appeal to panel of 3 or 5 convened by LEA. Panel's decision binding. Can confirm or overturn non-reinstatement	SSFA 1998, s 67 and Schedule18
Appeal to panel of 3 or 5 convened by LEA. Panel's decision (e.g. reinstatement) binding	SSFA 1998, ss 94 and 95 and Scheds 24 and 25
Appeal to Special Educational Needs Tribunal, chaired by lawyer, organized by national office of President. Tribunal's decision binding	Ed. Act 1996, Part IV
Appeal to Registered Inspectors of Schools Tribunal chaired by a lawyer[a]. Can confirm, reverse or vary registration decision or remit the matter	School Inspections Act 1996, s. 9
Appeal to Independent Schools Tribunal chaired by a lawyer.[b] Powers include striking school off the register of independent schools	Ed. Act 1996, ss 470 and 476; Schedule 34
The governors must make the arrangements for the appeal. They can delegate a committee to hear the appeal	Ed. (School Records) Regs 1989, reg. 8

Education (Schools) Act 1992.
Tribunals (1996) Appendix H; (1997) Appendix F; (1998) Appendix E.

that should underlie any effective complaints system relating to public services such as education. The procedures should be easily accessible and conspicuous to service users (through appropriate publicity). They should be clear, simple, fast and informative (in the sense that complainants should be kept informed of the progress of their complaint and that complaints in general should inform management of services in order to stimulate their improvement). The procedures should also operate impartially and maintain confidentiality. The CLA suggested that complaints procedures should begin with an informal stage followed by two more formal stages. This is actually the model adopted in relation to local curriculum complaints procedures (below).

Ensuring effective utilization of the complaints procedure is clearly the most important aspect of these guidelines. There is no point in having a well-constructed and efficient complaints system if it is not used. There are various barriers to be overcome, including ignorance on the part of service users, low expectations concerning the outcome of a complaint and cultural factors. So far as complaints about education decisions are concerned, one of the factors is parents' fear of prejudicing their child's interests: '[W]orries about how complaints may affect a continuing relationship are raised by many kinds of people. Parents may be reluctant to raise complaints with a school because they are worried about causing problems for their children' (Goriely and Williams 1997: 32). These barriers are discussed more fully below.

One of the limitations of complaints mechanisms, as opposed to appeals, concerns the available remedy. The fact that a complaint has been upheld does not necessarily mean that the decision is being reversed. The investigator generally has a discretion as to the most appropriate remedy and indeed whether, even if the complaint is upheld, it should be granted. Moreover, as shown below in relation to education complaints, the enforcement mechanisms for complaints adjudications are cumbersome and involve initiating a separate redress mechanism. This is less of a problem in relation to the CLA (see below): its decisions take the form of recommendations only, but according to the CLA, very few of the ombudsmen's decisions are not implemented (Thomas 1999: 144). Complaints to the Secretary of State that are upheld may be enforced by directions issued by the Secretary of State which, if disobeyed, can in turn be reinforced by court order in some cases.[2]

We now turn to the specific education complaints procedures. We shall also include the CLA here, because education complaints form a significant part of the CLA's caseload. It should be noted that local authorities also operate separate general or service-related complaints procedures which are relevant to their functions concerning, for example, provision of education awards or school transport. We shall not consider the Parliamentary Commissioner for Administration (see Table 2.1) here, because complaints may relate only to the DFEE (comprising just 49 cases out of over 1,500 which were referred to the PCA by MPs in 1997/98).[3]

Complaint to the Secretary of State

Procedures first established under the Education Act 1944 and now governed by the Education Act 1996[4] enable anyone with a complaint that a local education authority or school governing body has acted or is proposing to act 'unreasonably' (as judicially interpreted)[5] or is in default of its legal duty may refer their complaint to the Secretary of State for Education. This complaints jurisdiction may also be used where an appeal decision has not been implemented. The Secretary of State may also act on his own initiative (i.e. without a complaint having been made). There are believed to be thousands of such complaints made every year (National Consumer Council 1992: 5), but many representations made to the DFEE are not classed by it as formal complaints, so the true figure is difficult to determine. Although a procedure for complaining is not prescribed, generally a letter setting out the points at issue will suffice.

In many cases the Department will merely advise the complainant to take the matter up at local level first, if this has not already been done. Indeed, if the complaint concerns the way that the authority has performed its duties concerning the curriculum, the Secretary of State may not entertain it unless and until it has first been investigated under the local complaints procedure prescribed for such complaints under the Education Act 1996 (see below). The Secretary of State (like the CLA – see below) will also generally refuse to interfere unless or until any right of appeal has been exercised – and particularly where an appeal is in progress. If he or she upholds the complaint, the Secretary of State has the power under the statute to issue directions to the authority.[6]

This avenue of redress has the advantage of having a very broad remit: it would seem to extend to complaints about almost any form of educational decision – from the closure of a school to the nature of religious education provided to pupils or alleged over-use of the practice of excluding pupils. The drawbacks are that complaints can take many months to be investigated and that often the Secretary of State will defer to the original decision-maker and refuse to overturn his or her decision. Although the Secretary of State's refusal to intervene does not preclude an application for judicial review in the courts, the court will take account of this refusal when deciding whether, if it finds the authority's decision unlawful, it should grant a remedy[7] (such remedies being at the discretion of the court). The courts have in any event interpreted the scope of the Secretary of State's default powers under these provisions somewhat restrictively, which is one reason why they are not used all that frequently (see Harris 1993: 31–37).

Local Complaints Procedures

The Education Reform Act 1988 set out a new legal framework for the curriculum in schools in England and Wales, including the national curriculum. The reforms also included provision for a new local complaints procedure in each LEA area, which became a legal requirement (section 23) with effect from

1 September 1989. The procedure had to be prepared by the LEA and needed the approval of the Secretary of State. The scope of the procedure was confined to complaints that the LEA or governing body of an LEA-maintained school had acted or were proposing to act unreasonably[8] with regard to the exercise of a power, or the performance of a duty, under a 'relevant enactment'. Enactments covered were those relating to the curriculum in schools, including religious education and collective worship. The statutory complaints procedure did not apply to nursery schools. The 1988 Act provided that, as noted above, no complaint that fell within the scope of the local complaints procedures could be taken to the Secretary of State under his or her general education complaints jurisdiction unless or until it had first been adjudicated under the local procedure.

The *Citizen's Charter* initiative of the early 1990s (above), which included a *Parent's Charter* (1991, and revised version in 1994) relating to education services, might have been expected to prompt an extension of this complaints procedure to other aspects of education. This extension would have been consistent with the broader aims of the *Citizen's Charter* that all public services should have clear and well-publicized complaints procedures (above: see also HM Government 1991: 42). It would also have prevented the confusion that arose among governors and LEAs about the limits to the scope of these procedures, despite the publication of DES guidance (DES 1989) intending to clarify the matter (Harris 1992). However, no substantive change has been made; the only alteration to the legislation since it was first implemented ten years ago has been the consolidation of the existing provisions into section 409 of the Education Act 1996.

A research survey confirmed that a majority of parents were ignorant of the complaints procedure in their area (Harris 1992). One reason for this was the fact that nearly one in five schools had not complied with the legal requirement (under the Education (School Curriculum and Related Information) Regulations 1989) that each school prospectus should make reference to the complaints procedure. It should be noted that although the Act did not prescribe that parents alone would have a right of complaint, the DES guidance (DES 1989) and most LEA complaints procedures have assumed that children will not be making complaints. This issue is discussed below.

The DES guidance indicates that the procedures should be in three stages. The first (stage 1) is an 'informal' stage, where the complainant would take the complaint to the head teacher. It was expected that most complaints would be resolved at this stage, and this has proved to be the case. The next two stages (stages 2 and 3) are 'formal' and must be made in writing. Unless the complaint is about the governing body's action, it will lie to the governors (stage 2) and subsequently to the LEA (stage 3). As a complaints adjudicator the governing body is hardly in a position to act entirely independently and would clearly be unwilling to undermine the head teacher, who has already investigated the complaint and either rejected it or has in any event decided not to respond to it in the way the parent would like. That said, the governing body would have an interest in ensuring that problems which could damage the reputation of the school would be identified and dealt with. Either way, official statistics indicate that only one-third of complaints that reach stage 2 are upheld (Harris 1993: 250).

If the complaint is about the governing body, it must go straight to the LEA. This means that formal complaints about the governing body undergo a relatively independent investigation whilst a complaint about the LEA is investigated by one of its own officers (designated for this purpose) and then determined by a panel of three LEA members, generally drawn from members of school admissions and exclusions appeal panels. Very few complaints that reach this stage are upheld (Harris 1993: 250). There were only 73 formal complaints across the whole of England and Wales in 1991–92, according to DES statistics (ibid.).

Although the upholding of a complaint may well result in the making of recommendations, there is no machinery to enforce their implementation other than further complaint to the Secretary of State (see above). This is, unfortunately, a common feature of various kinds of complaints procedure. On the whole the evidence suggests that these procedures are under-utilized and inherently flawed.

A good illustration of the problematic nature of these procedures is a case reported by Neville Harris in the report of his above-mentioned research survey (Harris 1992). This case is also helpful to our discussion of redress of grievance in respect of school exclusion. The complaint arose out of the exclusion of a boy from a secondary school. The boy had been admitted to the school with some other children following the closure of their previous school which had been in an area of social deprivation. The new pupils were kept in a separate teaching group for a year and were then integrated into the rest of the school. It was alleged that some of the new pupils had been engaging in intimidatory conduct towards other pupils, and the head teacher excluded three of them for an indefinite period. The parent of one of the excluded pupils brought a formal complaint under the above procedures. Her principal allegation was that her son had been victimized and that her complaint had been mishandled by the school. The head teacher considered that because the complaint concerned a disciplinary matter it fell outside the scope of the legislation. The LEA, however, felt that because the complaint arose out of the integration of the pupils from the other school, and thus touched upon the treatment of pupils and the organization of classes, it was within the remit of the relevant statutory provision (then section 23 of the 1988 Act, above). The complaint was heard by the governing body (at stage 2). After a hearing lasting more than four hours it was rejected.

The case clearly highlights the artificiality of the distinctions necessitated by the parameters set for the procedures. It is true that the disciplinary issue was the central feature of the dispute; but often such an issue is tied to broader questions relating to curricular provision in a school that might fall within the scope of the section. A more general complaints jurisdiction could avoid the need for such distinctions. As it happens, there is no longer a power to exclude from school for an indefinite period as occurred in this case and some challenges to exclusion might in any event need to come before the governing body for review (see below).

The lack of a general local complaints system at school level is, in fact, now being rectified. As shown in the table earlier, the School Standards and Framework Act 1998, section 39(1) (when fully in force), will require a governing body to establish procedures for dealing with 'all complaints relating to the school other than those falling to be dealt with in accordance with any procedures required to be established in relation to the school by virtue of any other statutory provision'. This new duty is to be supplemented by requirements under regulations which, at the time of writing, have yet to be made. At this point it seems fairly clear that curriculum complaints will continue to be covered by the section 409 procedures (above). However, it would make sense at school level to merge the two sets of procedures in order to ensure a coherent complaints system. It is unfortunate that LEAs have not been included within the scope of the new (i.e. s. 39(1)) provision, although it is possible that the government would like LEAs to be involved and will include them in the regulations or any guidance issued. Either way, the new complaints procedures will clearly cover school exclusions. A merger of statutory arrangements would potentially avoid any troublesome demarcation issues such as arose in the exclusion case referred to above. Indeed, in this regard it would be important to bring within the scope of the general complaints procedure any specific procedure for complaints about special educational needs matters. The way that the requirement on the new general procedure has been set out in the 1998 Act is such that it is broad enough to cover special educational needs complaints procedures, as they are not currently 'required to be established'. (The only duty is one to publicize them if they exist.)[9] As a high proportion of the children excluded from school have special educational needs (see Chapters 1 and 4), there might be issues relating to the school's special educational needs policy and special educational provision to be considered in addition to those concerned with discipline.

There is no specific provision for complaints about the exclusion appeal process; this contrasts with the internal complaints procedure which operates in the Special Educational Needs Tribunal. Nevertheless, exclusion appeals are within the remit of the Commission for Local Administration (below).

Complaints Investigated by the Commission for Local Administration (CLA)

There are three Commissioners for Local Administration in England and one for Wales. The caseload of each Commissioner (who is often referred to as a local government ombudsman (LGO)) always includes a number of education complaints. In 1997/98 there were approximately 1,000 education complaints, although this only represented just over 7 per cent of the total number received by the CLA (CLA 1998: Chapter 6). Complaints arising out of exclusion from school are among the most common, together with admission to school and special educational needs assessments, statements or provision. As shown in the table earlier, complaints about exclusion or admission appeals fall within the jurisdiction of the CLA. This was acknowledged by Woolf L.J. in *R v Commissioner for Local Administration ex parte Croydon London Borough Council*[10] in granting an application for judicial review of the LGO's findings concerning an education appeal panel. However, this jurisdiction did not extend to appeal panels (whether relating to exclusion or admissions) in voluntary aided, special agreement or grant-maintained schools, because the organization of appeals was the responsibility of the school's governing body, not the LEA. This gap was closed by the Education Act 1993.[11] Nevertheless, the decisions which give rise to exclusion appeals are not within the CLA's jurisdiction at present (see below). Note that grant-maintained status was abolished in September 1999 under the SSFA 1998.

One of the three English Commissioners has reported that 265 (or 5 per cent) of the complaints she received in 1996/97 were about education appeals (admissions or permanent exclusions) and they were the subject of 16 (13.5 per cent) of her reports (Thomas 1999: 142). Given the wide brief of the CLA these are quite large numbers. Some examples of complaints investigated are given below.

The CLA must not investigate if the complainant has a right to take the matter to an appeal body which could resolve the matter. Other grounds for not investigating are that the complainant has a right to refer the matter to the Secretary of State or has a route to a potential remedy by way of court proceedings. But in any of these cases an investigation would nevertheless be possible if an LGO were satisfied 'that in the particular circumstances it is not reasonable to expect the person aggrieved to resort or have resorted to it'.[12] Approximately one in twelve of the CLA's decisions in 1996/97 was not to investigate because there was an alternative avenue of redress (Thomas 1999: 141). However, the CLA is conscious of the need to exercise its discretion to permit an investigation, at least where court action is the alternative, because the CLA offers a more accessible remedy for the ordinary citizen (ibid.: 143).

Complaints about the exercise of the power of exclusion itself are not within the Commission's jurisdiction. Schedule 5 to the Local Government Act 1974, specifying matters not subject to investigation by the Commission, includes (para. 5(2)(b) as amended) 'Any action concerning … conduct, curriculum, internal organization, management, discipline, in any school or other educational establishment maintained by the authority.' There have been suggestions that this restriction should be removed (e.g. CLA 1995). Lewis and Birkenshaw (1993: 136) argue that 'it is curious that a child may complain about treatment in a local authority home, whereas a child cannot complain about treatment in a state school'.

The CLA's jurisdiction in any event extends only to complaints concerned with injustice resulting from 'maladministration' – interpreted to include such matters as bias, neglect, inattention, delay, incompetence and turpitude, but not a complaint about the merits of the decision.[13] Typically, a complaint concerning a school exclusion might relate to a delay in making suitable arrangements for the child's education following a permanent exclusion or might concern misinformation on the part of the LEA. In relation to exclusion appeals, the CLA has found maladministration (and in some cases an injustice) in relation to complaints: that a parent or carer was not informed of the right of appeal when it was required under the statute (Reports 92/A/3573, 7 July 1994, 93C/0824, 17 January 1995 and 93/C/3220, 6 June 1995); and that there were procedural deficiencies in relation to the hearing of the appeal, such as the absence of a trained clerk and a failure to provide the parent with a copy of the school's evidence (Reports 96/C/729, 21 October 1996 and 97/C/5075, 29 October 1998) or to ensure that the appeal panel had the full written submission from the parent (Report 97/B/1981, 6 April 1999). The CLA has also published a large number of reports of investigations into complaints concerning admission appeals (see Harris, N. 1999 for a review of these cases).

Quite a high proportion of complaints fall by the wayside or are resolved without a full investigation and report by an ombudsman (CLA 1998: Chapter 6, from which the following figures are taken). In 1997/98 23.6 per cent of complaints across the CLA's jurisdiction were settled locally and 63 per cent resulted in a finding of no maladministration. If the ombudsman finds that there was maladministration he or she must also determine whether there was an injustice as a result. Only 2.5 per cent of the complaints (256 in total) in 1997/98 resulted in a finding of maladministration plus injustice whilst in 1 per cent (88) there was found to be maladministration only.

Reports by the CLA are very thorough, although the downside to this is that an investigation can sometimes take several months to be completed. In 1997/98 less than half were completed within ten weeks and over one-quarter took longer than twenty weeks. If injustice is found, the CLA's recommendations to the authority can include the payment of compensation. Although the CLA has no enforcement powers most recommendations are acted upon, as noted above.

Reviews

Internal and External Review Distinguished

Reviews of decisions of public authorities may be internal or external. An internal review occurs when the decision-taker, or the administrative body he or she represents, takes a second or fresh look at the issue. Michael Harris (1999: 43) sees this as 'a continuation of the primary administrative decision-making process'. The review may be informal or formal. An informal review could occur at the instigation of the decision-taker him or herself (as under the arrangements introduced under the Social Security Act 1998 for officers to have a 'second look' at decisions on entitlement to a welfare benefit), or it could be prompted by a complaint or request from the complainant. This is often regarded as an administrative rather than adjudicative process, although where there is also provision for an external review the overall model of review is adjudicative. Informal internal review is not always part of a legislative scheme of review, unlike (in most cases) a formal review. M. Harris (1999) distinguishes a formal from an informal internal review with reference to the fact that the former generally operates as a pre-requisite to an external review or appeal. An informal review is not generally linked to access to an external review.

In the case of school exclusion, the head teacher could conduct an informal review of the decision to exclude permanently – or, indeed, of a fixed-term exclusion, which is not subject to a right of appeal. This could be the result of having second thoughts, perhaps triggered by additional evidence communicated by another pupil or by a plea in mitigation by a parent on receipt of the head teacher's written notification of the exclusion decision. At the same time, a formal process of review occurs automatically where the exclusion would result in the pupil being absent from school for a total of more than five days in any term or losing an opportunity to take a public examination, or where the exclusion is permanent, including where it was originally fixed term but has been made permanent following the head teacher's further investigation of the incident.[14] As explained more fully in Chapter 6, this formal review is conducted by the governing body or rather by its pupil discipline committee. The degree of formality is emphasized by rights to make representations and to attend with (or without) a representative a meeting which forms part of the review. It is still an internal review because it is conducted within the provenance of the school's disciplinary process. The formal nature of the review is confirmed by the fact that in the case of permanent exclusion the right of appeal does not lie in respect of the head teacher's initial decision to exclude but rather against the decision of the pupil discipline committee on its review of it.

There is an ongoing debate about the value, in administrative justice terms, of internal reviews. Harris, M. (1999) sees a number of advantages to internal review. He claims that in high volume areas (such as social security cases, where hundreds of thousands of decisions are made each year) internal review, by acting as a filter, ensures that many or even most cases are resolved more speedily and cheaply than if they went to external review. It also ensures that the review is conducted by those with a closer connection to the area of decision-making. Thus, it would be argued, in the case of school exclusion the governing body or its discipline committee would be better able to conduct an effective review of the head teacher's decision because it would have a close appreciation of the school's disciplinary environment and policy.

The essential argument against internal review is that while an informal review can have benefits in terms of enabling decisions to be changed quickly and with minimum fuss, and without compromised appeal rights for those who remain dissatisfied, a formal internal review can present barriers to the exercise of the appeal right. Concern arises from the fact that internal reviews lack the independence and often the thoroughness that an external review can provide. Complainants might find that the experience of going through a formal internal review is such a negative one that they do not perceive there to be any value in taking their case further. Alternatively, they might be deterred by further delay or strain. We explore these problems further in the context of exclusion cases later in the book. With so few reinstatement decisions on review going in favour of parents, it would not be surprising if parents see little value in taking their case further, particularly if they fail to distinguish the internal from the external review/appeal processes.

Judicial Review

> The purpose of judicial review is to challenge public bodies ... the little man versus the big man.

These are not the words of Lord Denning, the avowed champion of the 'little man', but of Sullivan J in a judgment in a recent case brought against the University of Cambridge by a student who was disqualified from admission to his degree on the grounds of plagiarism.[15] Judicial review embodies the long-standing inherent power of the courts, acting on behalf of the Crown and at the instigation of the individual citizen, to question the legality of executive actions by public bodies, including ministers of state, local authorities and state schools. As such, judicial review is concerned with abuse or misuse of power. It contrasts with the courts' role in private law civil cases of compensating the victim of a wrong (under the law of contract or tort). Under the judicial review jurisdiction the courts will only be concerned with questions such as: did the education authority have the power to act the way it did, or did a school governing body act so unfairly as to take its action or decision outside the scope of the power conferred upon it by the legislation? In relation to the latter, the unfairness could result from the way the power was exercised, particularly the procedure adopted. As the court said in a case which involved a challenge to an exclusion decision:

> [A] pupil at a State-maintained school does have a right in an appropriate case to apply to this court to enforce the principles of fair play in action if he or she is expelled from school without fair procedures having preceded his or her expulsion.[16]

Cases have, for example, examined whether the governors, other authorities or appeal body investigated with sufficient thoroughness the events which prompted the exclusion, or whether they took proper account of the guidance on exclusion issued by the DFEE in coming to their decision.[17] The court will *not* therefore act as a general court of appeal to consider the merits of a case; and this in turn has an effect on the remedy which is available. In any event, in most cases the dispute must be first adjudicated by the Secretary of State or appeal body under the statute before a court would be prepared to consider the matter. This is the principle of exclusivity of statutory remedies. 'Judicial review should not be granted where an alternative remedy is available'[18] is a principle applied in a raft of education cases. However, in one exclusion case where an appeal had not first been brought the court nevertheless granted leave to apply for judicial review: this was because the dispute concerned alleged procedural unfairness (not permitting the parent an opportunity to make representations to the governing body about the child's fixed-term exclusion), which was more appropriately dealt with by a court.[19]

The scope of judicial review may be illustrated with reference to a hypothetical exclusion decision. A child is permanently excluded from a school for violent behaviour and his parent brings an appeal when the governing body refuses to reinstate the child. When reaching its decision, the local appeal panel fails to take account of the published guidance on exclusion issued by the DFEE. Yet the courts have held that regard should be had by appeal panels (and others) to this guidance and this has recently been made a statutory duty.[20] A child may apply for judicial review in his or her own right. In the present case the child asks the court to quash the appeal panel's decision, primarily on the grounds that the failure of the panel to have regard to the guidance made its decision unlawful. The court upholds the child's application. In doing so the court does *not* have the power to decide that the child's violent behaviour justified his/her exclusion from school. It is, therefore, merely saying that the decision was reached unlawfully. The only suitable remedy that the court can provide is to set aside the decision of the appeal panel and remit the case to the panel with an order that it should give proper consideration to the official guidance on exclusion from school. The appeal must therefore be heard again by the local appeal panel. Second time around the appeal might succeed, but there is no guarantee that it will: even after taking account of the Department's guidance the panel might (justifiably, dependent on the facts) reach the same decision as before.

Decisions which have been subjected to judicial review in the past couple of years (see Harris 1998) have included, in addition to several on school exclusion,[21] decisions concerned with closing a school,[22] reducing the funding for home tuition,[23] not awarding a university degree with honours,[24] and refusing to pay for transport to school.[25] However, despite its relatively wide scope, there are several limitations to judicial review from the point of view of the litigant. First, judicial review is confined to the actions of public bodies and is not available therefore if the dispute centres on the action of an independent school. In *R v Fernhill Manor School ex parte A* [26] Brooke J held that although natural justice had not been followed when a 15-year-old girl was excluded from an independent school for alleged bullying and intimidatory behaviour and neither she nor her parents were informed of the allegations against her or given any opportunity to respond to them, the decision was not justiciable under the court's judicial review jurisdiction. The basis for the relationship between a private school and its pupils and their parents was a contractual one. Thus the only recourse was to sue for breach of the contract, which involves an entirely different procedure and remedy. Curiously, one judge recently suggested that even the exclusion decisions of a head teacher of a state school might not be amenable to judicial review.[27] The judge, Mr Nigel Pleming QC (sitting as a Deputy High Court judge), said that 'although... there is some statutory underpinning for the role of the head teacher in the exclusion process, and, of course, it is his decision and only his decision which can result in exclusion, I am not satisfied that the head teacher is engaged in the discharge of a public law function such that the High Court has jurisdiction to review and quash, if necessary, his decisions'. In contrast, the governing body and appeal panel were 'the true public bodies' whose exclusion decisions could be judicially reviewed (see further part 7 of the chapter, below). This is a contentious view and it is not certain that other courts would follow it. In any event, as noted above, a court would hardly ever entertain an application where the statutory remedy (a review meeting with the governing body followed by an appeal to an appeal panel) had not first been pursued.

Another limitation to judicial review is the fact that the court will not re-examine the merits of a claim, as has already been mentioned. In addition, judicial review must be applied for speedily (normally within three months), the applicant must have a sufficient legal interest in the dispute (or 'standing' (*locus standi*)), and a judge must in any event grant leave to bring the application. Leave will be denied where the matter is outside the remit of judicial review or where the case has no reasonable prospects of success in any event. Also, the court is not bound to grant a remedy even where the claim succeeds: the remedies are all discretionary. This is illustrated by the decision in the recent case of *Cram*, noted briefly in Chapter 1.[28] A boy aged 14 who was alleged to have struck a teacher was excluded from school. The appeal panel ordered that he should be readmitted. Teachers at the school were opposed to this and threatened to go on strike if the boy returned. The school therefore decided not to comply with the appeal panel's decision. The boy's father applied for judicial review. The court held that the school had acted unlawfully. However, Ognall J exercised his discretion and refused to make an order that the school should readmit the boy. The main ground for this was that if the industrial action by the teachers went ahead it would damage the education of a large number of pupils and this was an overriding concern.

If the outcome of a judicial review application would be of no practical benefit to the applicant regardless of his or her success in the action the court might also refuse to rule on the matter. This happened in a case where the application was for an order to quash the head teacher's decision merely to issue a verbal admonition where a primary school pupil had broken another pupil's arm while the two pupils were waiting in the lunch queue at school. The case came before the judge on the last day of the school year. The two pupils were due to go to secondary school the following term. Scott Baker J said that the dispute had 'ceased to be of practical significance and, therefore ... it is inappropriate to hear the judicial review application'.[29]

The special nature and peculiarities of judicial review are the result of its public law character. Although, in theory, individual rights have been infringed in these cases, the actions of public bodies have such a wide social importance that the court's role is primarily to ensure that such bodies act fairly and that they are legally accountable in a constitutional sense for the way they act. Decisions on judicial review send important messages to all administrators and other decision-makers, not just those involved in the actual case decided. This is the result of 'the radiating effect of court decisions and their role in the setting of regulatory frameworks' (Mulcahy 1999: 73). As we saw above and shall see further in later chapters, the power of exclusion from school has been the subject of judicial consideration on a number of occasions in recent years, albeit that the courts are not over-willing to interfere. As the judge said in one case where the head teacher, governing body and appeal panel had made or accepted a rather dubious identification of an alleged culprit, who was then excluded:

> Nothing could be more inhibiting to the difficult task of maintaining the welfare of all pupils by a sensible and realistic system of discipline than for the court to intervene too readily and to import too eagerly the techniques and formalities of courts of law. I hope that a reminder of the dangers of identification evidence with which the courts are more familiar does not impose an unreasonable burden, voluntarily assumed, on governors and those who serve on appeals committees.[30]

The court in this judicial review case wanted to offer guidance to the relevant bodies (which would 'radiate'), but was doing so cautiously.

Involving, as it does, court proceedings, judicial review might be regarded as a somewhat cumbersome and not particularly accessible way of challenging an education decision. It is clear that, save where it is not feasible to pursue other avenues of redress – such as in emergency cases where a definitive order is needed quickly or in a case outside the scope of the statutory redress mechanism – judicial review will in fact operate more as a long-stop provision or procedure of last resort. Nevertheless, education cases have featured prominently in the growing judicial review caseload in the courts in recent years, and education's share of these cases has increased (Bridges et al. 1995: 15). The fact that the child can apply for judicial review is a significant factor: a child may be awarded legal aid in his or her own right without account being taken of his or her parents' means. Judicial review also enables the decisions of education appeal bodies to be called into question, if for example they are based on an error of law or made in breach of natural justice.

In the absence of a right of appeal against an appeal panel's decision, judicial review provides a vital checking mechanism in respect of procedural shortcomings and legal errors by these lay adjudicators. As a postscript it should be noted here that since the Education Act 1993, members of appeal panels may be indemnified by LEAs (or, prior to the 1998 Act, governing bodies) in respect of legal costs reasonably incurred by them under an order of costs arising out of a successful judicial review application.[31] Grant-maintained schools in particular had become anxious about such costs (Council on Tribunals 1993: para. 2.23).

Appeals

Local appeal panels adjudicate on disputes over choice of school or over a decision not to reinstate a child who has been permanently excluded from school. Parents have become increasingly aware of and prepared to exercise their right of appeal in recent years. For example, the total number of school admission and exclusion appeals made in England and Wales increased from approximately 18,000 to 72,000 between 1990 and 1997 (Harris, N. 1999: 297). The most recently established appeal body is the Special Educational Needs Tribunal (SENT). Unlike the other appeal bodies, which are local, the SENT is a national body. It has been in operation since 1994[32] and it hears appeals by parents who disagree with certain decisions taken about their child who has special educational needs, especially about the kind of education the local education authority proposes for the child in a statement made under the Education Act 1996. The tribunal has the power to order the authority to change its arrangements for the child's education or to think again, but not to award compensation.

Although an appeal takes the form of an external review of a decision, the terminology used here is intended to reflect the distinction frequently made between the two concepts in legislation. This usage is particularly necessary in relation to exclusion cases, where we can distinguish between a review of an exclusion decision undertaken by the governing body's pupil discipline committee (above) and an appeal to an exclusion appeal panel. But the distinction can also be found in other areas such as social security law (although curiously housing benefit appeals lie to a local 'housing benefit review board' whereas other social security appeals lie to an 'appeal tribunal') (see Sainsbury 2000).

The terminology used here is also intended to distinguish between independent appeals on the *merits*, on the one hand, and independent review by the courts in respect of the *legality* of a decision, on the other. However, somewhat confusingly to many non-lawyers, access to the courts will in some instances be via an appeal. In particular, in the case of appeals in special educational needs cases decided by the SENT (see above) there is a right of further appeal to the High Court against the tribunal's decision, on a point of law. Judicial review, as a distinct procedure, would in special educational needs cases therefore be confined to decisions which do not fall under the jurisdiction of the SENT (see Harris 1997). In the case of exclusion appeals and those concerned with school admissions, both of which lie to local appeal panels established under the SSFA 1998 (see table above, pp. 22–23), there is no right of further appeal to the court; but an application for judicial review, subject to the various limitations noted above, would be possible. Unlike special educational needs cases, where there is a hierarchical appellate structure through the tribunal to the courts, in these exclusion and admissions cases appeal and judicial review are separate and mutually exclusive avenues of redress. However, as noted above, generally the courts will not intervene via judicial review unless and until the avenues of redress available under statute have been exercised.

The reason for having single-tier appellate structures for some kinds of case and two-tier systems for others is less than clear. Examples of the former include school exclusion appeals and those concerned with school admissions, which have already been mentioned, and housing benefit reviews. Two-tier systems include those for special educational needs appeals (as noted above) and social security appeals. As the appeal bodies in the two-tier group have legally qualified chairs, the rationale for the further right of appeal is presumably the same as that for having lawyers on the panel – that points of law are more likely to be at issue, not least because the legislative framework is on the whole more complex. There are of course exceptions to this: in particular, housing benefit law is very complex yet there is no requirement for a lawyer chair. In the past the main reason given for not having lawyer chairs of exclusion appeal panels has in fact been the risk that the hearings might become too formal. This issue is considered further in Chapter 7, but it may be noted that the DFEE's guidance now recommends that panels be chaired by lawyers, although this is still not a formal statutory requirement.

Appeals in exclusion and admissions cases centre on the merits of the case. It is in the nature of an appeal that the matter is considered *de novo*. This means that, in the case of an exclusion appeal, while the appeal lies against the governing body's committee's decision not to reinstate the child, the appeal panel will be considering whether the original decision to exclude was justifiable in the circumstances and whether the facts, based on the evidence as found by the head teacher and the said committee, were fully made out. The decision will therefore be based on a combination of fact and law.

Children as Complainants or Appellants

Issues surrounding children's participation, including appeal rights, were discussed in Chapter 1. A particular focus was Article 12 of the UN Convention on the Rights of Child. It was noted that the child's lack of an independent right of appeal against an exclusion decision, or even to attend the appeal hearing,[33] conflicted with the spirit and almost certainly the substance of Article 12. The child also has no independent right under education legislation to make representations to the governing body when it conducts its review of the head teacher's decision to exclude. That right is confined (by section 66 of the SSFA 1998) to 'the relevant person', defined as the parent or, only if aged 18 or over, the excluded pupil. But there are anomalies. For example, a child may apply for judicial review in his or her own right, as noted above, and yet the courts have rejected the right of the child to be a party to an appeal to the High Court against a decision of the Special Educational Needs Tribunal (SENT), on the grounds that a child was not (and cannot be) a party to an appeal to the tribunal itself.[34]

The anomalies extend to the area of complaints. Children have an independent right of complaint under s. 26 of the Children Act 1989 in respect of local authority services provided under Part III of that Act, whereas there is no specific right for a child to complain under the statutory education complaints mechanisms discussed above (see p. 26). There are barriers to the effective utilization of the right of complaint by children, such as the fear of repercussions (Goriely and Williams 1997: 32). Nevertheless, there is an important issue of principle at stake: the recognition of the child's independent rights to participate and particularly to seek redress where he or she asserts an infringement of substantive rights and interests.

As noted in Chapter 1, in the context of education, the subjugation of the rights of the child to those of the parent presupposes that the parent is able to protect the child's interests. In the context of redress, it would often be left to the parent to decide when intervention is necessary. This might well reflect the protective role envisaged by the UN Convention on the Rights of the Child itself (see Article 5, set out in Chapter 1) and in a practical sense might well mean a greater likelihood of redress being sought in any individual case. On the other hand, as we shall see (particularly in Chapter 9), the lack of an independent right of appeal has an arguably adverse effect on the treatment of the child within the appeal process itself by giving the child a lower status than would otherwise be the case. Moreover, it fails to recognize another important principle in the Convention (see also s. 1(3) of the Children Act 1989), that with advancing age and maturity children would be expected and should be given the opportunity to participate more fully and take more responsibility for decisions. The lack of a duty on those within the education system to ensure the primacy of the child's best interests (as per Article 3 of the Convention: see Chapter 1) reinforces the weakness of children's rights in this context, particularly in the light of the remedial issues referred to here.

Private Law Remedies

In recent years there has been a growing emphasis on using private law remedies, in the form of ordinary actions for breach of contract or tort in the courts as a means to redress in education cases. It is clear that court action in respect of a child's exclusion from a private school would have to take the form of a claim for breach of contract,[35] as judicial review only lies against public sector schools,[36] although if the exclusion resulted from the withdrawal of a state-funded ('assisted') place by the school there would be a sufficient public law element to bring the matter within the scope of judicial review.[37] City technology colleges, although classed as independent schools, receive public funding and are operated under an agreement with the Secretary of State; they are classed as part of the public sector, so an exclusion of a pupil from such a college could be challenged via judicial review.[38] There is no contract with a school in the public sector; any thought that a home–school agreement might give rise to legal obligations in contract should be quickly dismissed, not least because the SSFA 1998 Act removes any doubt by providing (in section 111(6)) that 'a home–school agreement shall not be capable of creating any obligation in respect of whose breach any liability arises in contract and tort'.

The law has long held that unjustifiable exclusion does not give rise to a right in tort.[39] On the other hand, although this is as yet a matter of conjecture, it might be possible in the future to bring a successful claim arising out of a *failure* to exclude. This is because a pupil whose education or well-being suffers as a result of a school's failure to control bullying, racial abuse or other forms of psychologically damaging behaviour by another pupil towards him might be able to succeed in arguing that there has been negligence on the part of the head teacher, who has a responsibility for standards of behaviour. Indeed, the SSFA 1998 (in section 61(4)(b)) now imposes a specific responsibility on head teachers to determine measures within the school with a view to, amongst other things, 'preventing all forms of bullying among pupils'. Hopes of private law actions succeeding were raised by an out-of-court settlement in a bullying case in 1996[40] (see O'Leary 1996), but the chances of success had receded until recently.

In 1995 the House of Lords had accepted in *X (Minors) v Bedfordshire County Council*[41] that there could be a common law duty of care on head teachers, advisers and educational psychologists to take proper steps as regards assisting those with special educational needs and in advising their parents, but later doubt was cast on this by the Court of Appeal's decision in *Phelps v Hillingdon London Borough Council*.[42] This case concerned alleged psychological damage and reduced career prospects due to the failure by an educational psychologist employed by the LEA to diagnose dyslexia. The action had succeeded in the High Court[43] but was subsequently struck down partly on public policy grounds by the Court of Appeal. The appeal judges seem to have adopted the position that, in the absence of any clear evidence that the professional had assumed a duty not only towards his/her employer but also a parent, it would be contrary to public policy to permit such actions to succeed, often in respect of events long in the past, given the potential cost and disruption to the education system as a whole. Even if the public policy barrier had not arisen (and it might change when the further appeal which has been brought in *Phelps* is determined by the House of Lords in due course), it would still be difficult for these actions to succeed because of the need to prove a causal link between the alleged negligence and the psychological and other problems experienced.

It is important to note that in the *X (Minors)* case (above) the court drew a distinction between decisions involving the exercise of 'statutory discretions', which were non-justiciable, and others which were part of ordinary professional duties. In 1999, in *Barrett v Enfield LBC*,[44] the House of Lords applied this distinction to the question whether a local authority should be liable in respect of the harm a child who had been in local authority care suffered due to the authority not seeking his adoption, placement in a foster home or reinstatement with his mother. The decision was taken in the exercise of the statutory discretion of the authority, but court held that such decisions were not necessarily non-justiciable. The question whether a duty of care existed and whether it was broken had to be considered in the overall context of what the statute was providing in terms of the service in question: it was necessary to balance the delicate and difficult task that was involved in performing the social services function with the interests of the individual child.

Applied once again to the context of education, this issue led subsequently to a reassertion by the Court of Appeal of the potential negligence liability of education professionals, in *Gower v London Borough of Bromley*.[45] Here a boy with a degenerative physical condition argued that due to the professional incompetence of the head teacher and other teaching staff of the school he was not provided with the computing, teaching or aids necessary to enable him to communicate adequately or to make the educational progress he could have made. He claimed he had suffered psychologically. The Court of Appeal accepted that in the light of the *X (Minors)* case there could be a duty of care in such circumstances and referred the matter back to the High Court to consider on the facts. The Court of Appeal felt that *Barrett* (above) had shown the policy considerations in relation to such cases to be not as limiting as the court had suggested in *Phelps* (above). A subsequent case, *Jarvis v Hampshire County Council*,[46] arising from the alleged negligence of an educational psychologist employed by the LEA and others, was dismissed on a similar basis to *Phelps*, but this decision is distinguishable from that in *Gower* (above), where the Court of Appeal had felt that it was 'an error' to rely upon the Court of Appeal's decision in *Phelps* 'as an authority for the proposition that a local education authority could not be responsible for the quality of education that its teachers provided' (at 362G-H). Pending any guidance given by the House of Lords in *Phelps*, this seems to leave open the potential for successful negligence claims arising out of ordinary educative duties, including those relating to discipline matters (subject to the question of causation in any individual case, as referred to above). Moreover, there is even a question mark in the long term over the limitation set by the House of Lords in *X (Minors)* concerning the non-justiciability of decisions/actions undertaken as part of the statutory discretions of local authorities or LEAs. The European Commission of Human Rights has concluded (*Z and others v UK*) that that limitation constitutes a breach of Article 6 of the European Convention on Human Rights on the basis that the court applied an exclusionary rule protecting authorities from negligence actions in respect of their statutory duties to protect children.

Conclusion

A wide range of redress mechanisms is available to those dissatisfied with an education decision. Most are available in cases of exclusion from school. The standard (statutory) procedure in permanent exclusion cases involves an automatic review by the governing body followed by an elective appeal to an exclusion appeal panel. As there is no right of further appeal, further challenges would normally take the form of either an application for judicial review, which would focus not on the merits of the punishment but on whether any illegality resulting from unfairness or errors of law had occurred in the decision-making process; or a complaint of maladministration could be brought to the CLA. The seriousness of exclusion from school as an immediate term problem for a child and his or her family is such that if parents wish to challenge the decision they are less likely to resort to the generally more lengthy process of formal complaint, particularly as it might well be perceived as less potent and conclusive than an appeal or review. In the case of local complaints procedures, parents may well be deterred (at least in an exclusion case) by the procedure's lack of independence.

Education redress mechanisms, although concerned with decisions affecting children, tend to be parent-centred. This is particularly true of the exclusion appeals system. This gives rise to theoretical concerns over matters of principle relating to the independent rights and status of children, discussed more fully in Chapter 1. It also raises doubts about the practical ability of the appeal system to engage fully with the child's perspective and interests which, under other legislation, including the UN Convention on the Rights of the Child, ought to be the central focus of attention.

3 Discipline in Schools

Social Theory and Law

Introduction

Since the general election in 1997 the topic of school exclusion has become inextricably linked with the more general issue of social exclusion, now the subject of a number of policy initiatives. The first report of Labour's Social Exclusion Unit made strong associations between these two types of exclusion and urged a target for reductions in the number of school exclusions: principally a 'reduction of one third in the number of both permanent and fixed term exclusions from the current level' by 2002 (1998: para. 5.3; see also HM Government 1999: para 9.27.3). Yet at the same time, Labour's education policy stresses the need for schools to operate in an appropriately disciplined environment: 'Most schools are well-ordered communities but it is vital, in the interests of all pupils, that standards of behaviour are improved where they are not satisfactory' (DFEE 1997a: Chapter 6, para. 13). Exclusion from school is an important sanction used to maintain discipline. So if its use is to be minimized there is a balance to be struck. This is recognized in the revised guidance on exclusions, which states:

> Schools must maintain discipline and good conduct to secure an orderly learning environment so that teaching and learning can take place. Schools will therefore need to adopt a range of strategies, including exclusion, to ensure they are providing a sound learning environment for all pupils. But many pupils excluded from school never get back into education and risk exclusion from mainstream society later in life. The number of exclusions from school is unacceptably high, and national and local targets have been set to reduce the number of school exclusions by one third by 2002.
>
> (DFEE 1999a: para. 6.1)

Clearly, there are competing objectives. To increase discipline, exclusion may need to be used readily, but to decrease social exclusion the use of school exclusion must be contained and reduced.

It is therefore the purpose of this chapter to examine exclusion in the context of these two, competing ideals. Since Labour took power over two years ago, education has been one of their main target areas for reducing social exclusion among disadvantaged sections of society. Although their ideas are not entirely new, the ideology and driving force behind them are. The disciplinary context will be examined by highlighting the socializing role of the school, in a theoretical context, and considering the availability of sanctions and other means of controlling behaviour under the law.

Sociological/Theoretical Perspectives

Schooling is not solely preoccupied with providing the child with a suitable education for entry into employment. It is also concerned with a broader process of socialization – with developing and moulding the child into a respectable, law-abiding 'social being'. Thus, school plays a significant part in the development of a child's personality, morals and values. Although school does not have an exclusive influence on these matters, it has an important and well-recognized socializing role. One aspect of the school's influence is as a social control mechanism, that is as a means to regulate a society/community – in this case the school community. Not only is the school an educating environment, it also uses the tool of discipline against those who transgress its rules. Some pupils will be subjected to the punishment of exclusion, which as research has shown (see Chapter 4), may begin a downward personal spiral and result in social exclusion from not only the child's peer community but the social world in general. In a sense school discipline mirrors social control in the wider society: those who disobey the laws of the land may find themselves controlled by the sanction of punishment. Limiting the most potent sanction, school exclusion, might be seen to undermine the social control that schools need to employ to the greater good of the pupil community as a whole, even though the social control message is at the same time strongly being transmitted from another source, namely the policy emphasizing the need for schools to be well-ordered communities.

Within the sociology of education there are obviously many theoretical perspectives. Particularly relevant to our discussion are the consensus (functionalist) approach of Durkheim, the conflict perspective taken from the works of Karl Marx, and the theories developed by Foucault with regard to disciplinary power.

Durkheim and Education

Durkheim believed that individuals consist of two parts. One part comprises individuality – 'made up of all the mental states which apply only to ourselves and to the events of our personal lives'. The second 'is a system of ideas, sentiments, and practices which express in us, not our personality, but the group of different groups of which we are part … their totality forms the social being. To constitute this being in each of us is the end of education' (Durkheim 1968: 124). According to Durkheim, for society to exist harmoniously individuality and individual gain have to be subjugated to the needs of society as a whole. Thus the individual is sacrificed for the better good of society: 'it is society that has taught us to control our passions, our instincts, to prescribe law for them, to restrain ourselves, to deprive ourselves, to sacrifice ourselves, to subordinate our personal ends to higher ends' (ibid.: 76). Society only exists if there is in place a homogenizing code of thought and conduct which prevails over and above all other ideals and ideologies within society. This code of thought and doing is what Durkheim named the 'conscience collective': it is a set of moral beliefs above and beyond general life, which is instilled in individuals at an early age and which all members of society have to obey if society is to exist. Thus, 'Society can survive only if there exists among its members a sufficient degree of homogeneity; education perpetuates and reinforces this homogeneity by fixing in the child, from the beginning the essential similarities that collective life demands' (ibid.: 70). According to Durkheim, if a conscience collective did not exist, neither would society. We would live in a world of constant conflict, without rules and regulations, in which a state of anarchy would ultimately prevail. Although morality changes in relation to developments within society, there always exists a conscience collective.

For Durkheim, school reflects the wider society which the child will later enter and in which he or she will form social relations. It is therefore of great importance that the child learns at an early age to distinguish right from wrong; school seeks to perpetuate this process through school rules and discipline. Education is viewed as a primary tool to socialize the child, instilling the norms and values of its given society (conscience collective), so that the child will be ready once leaving school to enter the world equipped with the required moral standing and appropriate social values. According to Durkheim, the school plays an essential function in the maintenance of the social structure – education is merely one part of the superstructure which exists to maintain social order and social solidarity.

Within the Durkheimian analysis of the sociology of education the state plays an integral role. The state cannot be separated from the education process, as it is the state which needs to ensure through the school and its teachers that the collective conscience is being instilled in the pupils' basic teachings. Yet the state's role is to maintain, rather than define, the social order. Prescription is socially driven and based partly on what has been learnt from our history and historical developments. The principles which have evolved are 'implicitly or explicitly … common to all … the role of the state is to outline these essential principles, to have them taught in its schools, to see … that nowhere are children left ignorant of them' (Durkheim 1968: 81).

The influence of the state in upholding the conscience collective is highly visible in, for example, the national curriculum and more recently in the proposals for citizenship education to form 5 per cent of the national curriculum in the future. Another example is the introduction of 'personal and social education' (PSE; now 'personal, health and social education'). Thus it can be seen that much of the ideology behind the schools system today is based on a

Durkheimian perspective – that education is of benefit to society and furthers social solidarity, which under a functionalist perspective is an essential pre-requisite to a harmonious social co-existence. Within the terms of policy development, the socializing nature of the school has been recognized in recent years within the initiatives set out in official reports such as *Better Schools* (DES 1985); the Elton Report (Elton 1989); *Misspent Youth* (Audit Commission 1996) and the White Paper *Excellence in Schools* (DFEE 1997a). All of the reports speak of the role schooling can play in reducing social exclusion through socializing the child into a 'rounded' social being, which can be achieved partly through better discipline in schools.

Marxism and Education

The traditional social aims of schooling fit neatly into the Durkheimian perspective of the sociology of education; yet we can also see that to facilitate the process of creating 'social beings' social control mechanisms are adopted. Notions of welfarism and paternalism give way to social control ideologies. Meighan (1981: 247) offers a clear distinction between the Durkheimian (consensus) and Marxian (conflict) theories of the sociology of education:

> What distinguishes Marxian analysis of education, is that schooling is seen not as a process which serves to socialize new members of society into the collectively established, consensual moral order, simply as the outcome of the rule-governed creative interaction of local groups of social actors, but rather as a phenomenon which is related most profoundly to the distribution of resources and opportunities in a society.

The theories offered by Marx[1] which can be related to education centre on the forces of production, which the school can be seen to reflect. According to Marxist theories, a product of capitalism is the inevitable alienation of workers in the workplace from the product they are producing. Although when a worker produces/makes something, part of the worker becomes imbued in the final product, because of the nature of capitalist enterprise and the formation of employment the worker now becomes dissociated from the final product, and work is no longer a means of expression and personal satisfaction. Instead it becomes a means to existence – the worker is paid for their work and without wages the worker would not be able to buy food, shelter and clothing. The means of production have now become dehumanized.

School and education is seen to be a reflection of the same processes which occur in the workplace, of alienation and dehumanization. As Sarup (1978: 129) notes:

> education is a mode of production involving pupils, teachers, and knowledge is both private property and cultural 'capital'. Schools are factories …

> education is conducted in such alienating circumstances that it becomes a process of dehumanization.

Sarup continues by conceptualizing school pupils as workers and commodities that are produced through the education system, demonstrating how a pupil's product is their educational attainment which is rewarded through grades, certificates, and so on, analogous with the factory worker's wage. Certificates and qualifications are then 'cashed in' when leaving school for employment with wages. Pupils are socially judged or valued 'only in terms of certain characteristics that ideal pupils should possess: interest, discipline, ability, intelligence' (Sarup 1978: 140).

According to conflict theorists, education is used as a social tool to repress the working classes whilst advancing the position of the upper classes. Education is, therefore, merely seen as a reflection of the class divisions that exist in our society. However, class is not the only division: there is also the issue of gender and race (discussed in Chapter 4).

According to Bowles and Gintis (1976) the division which is recreated in the education system is partly generated by the 'hidden curriculum'. The hidden curriculum reflects the underlying ideology of schooling and education. It is not visible or a set of recognized school practices, such as the national curriculum, but is instead a hidden set of beliefs, values and practices which are extremely influential on the school population – perhaps more so than the official subjects taught. The hidden curriculum according to Bowles and Gintis is what prepares and produces a subservient workforce, whilst encouraging the acceptance of a hierarchical society, as the school can be seen to reflect the hierarchical adult society which the children will later enter (ibid.: 37). The hidden curriculum exerts social control through, for example, building design, surveillance, streaming, placing disruptive children into separate classes, excluding persistently disruptive pupils, and behavioural reward and punishment systems in general.

The hidden curriculum reinforces subordination and the maintenance of capitalism in various related ways. It operates to control the teachings and behaviour of the 'lower' classes – the maintenance of class division. According to Bowles and Gintis, educational reform of the nineteenth century was a far cry from egalitarian reform. There existed instead a hidden agenda behind the pretence of such equality. Reformists, whilst recognizing the huge division of labour, as between the social classes, that existed in the factories, sought through education to normalize placing within society. Specialist training was given to the poor to reflect their general social standing (Bowles and Gintis 1976).

The hidden curriculum can inculcate the acceptance of authority and seek behaviour modification: 'the concept of discipline has itself changed ... the teacher has become part of the bureaucratic structure of the modern school ... the aim of discipline is no longer mere compliance: the aim is now behaviour modification ... the internalization of behavioural norms ... equipping the child with a built-in supervisor ...' (ibid.: 39). Thus, school produces a subservient workforce which is needed for capitalism to exist. The school would instil subordination and compliance to a hierarchical organization. This is achieved through grading, with those children who conform to the school environment receiving higher rewards than those who do not: 'students are rewarded for exhibiting discipline, subordinacy, intellectually as opposed to emotionally oriented behaviour, and hard work independent from intrinsic task motivation' (ibid.: 40). Conformity to the social order of the school and for demonstrating a personal motivation to succeed within the dictates of the social order would also bring rewards. Thus conformity combined with scholastic behaviour are rewarded, whereas creativity and independence of thought are not. Education therefore reinforces and perpetuates the social relations and hierarchy which exist in capitalist societies.

With the increasing recognition that exclusion from school often leads to involvement in crime, there is a greater emphasis now more than ever on the need for social control within the school, to curb the threat of young children becoming tomorrow's criminals. The idea of using education as a form of social control mechanism is not new. It can be viewed as a facet of social or community crime prevention methodology. Those people who are viewed as being at risk of offending will be targeted through, for example educational initiatives. As will be expanded upon within Chapter 4, the Audit Commission report *Misspent Youth* (1996) found that one factor predicting those most at risk of offending is truancy or exclusion from school. Therefore, the idea of using community crime prevention initiatives is to instil in children at an early age the importance of schooling and the immorality of crime. So, whilst the Labour government may be seen to act via a welfare ideology concerning the desire to prevent truancy and exclusion from school and thus social exclusion in general, they are in many ways using school as a social control mechanism to prevent future anti-social and/or criminal behaviour.

Despite the government's desire to reduce the use of the sanction of school exclusion, a strong emphasis on an effective disciplinary environment within schools continues to be advocated. But what form will this discipline take? How does it sit with the welfare ideology reflected in the policy of social inclusion? Is it in fact a form of social control and a tool that will enable a finer tuning of the social body and the technologies of power, so advocated by Foucault in his discussions of bio-power? Through taking a Foucauldian perspective it can be seen that punitive measures relating to disciplinary power can in fact result in a closer mapping of the social body – what in neo-Marxist terms would be seen as another form of social control. However, for Foucault this power is enabling and facilitating in developing individual identities.

Foucault and Education

In *Discipline and Punish*, Foucault highlights the emergence of capitalism and the changing structures of society by describing different power relations in terms of:

sovereign power; bio-power; and disciplinary power. In relation to this chapter, disciplinary power is perhaps the most relevant. Although Foucault did not write specifically about the interplay of school and power relations within society, he did in describing discipline as a technique of power cite the school as one of the many apparatuses needed through which to exercise power. Thus the discussion which follows will focus upon disciplinary power in relation to the importance of the school in creating a disciplined society.

Within discipline a new modality of power was created. Foucault cites this as the birth of a 'political anatomy': 'the human body was entering a machinery of power that explores it, breaks it down and rearranges it' (Foucault 1991: 138). However, it was not just power over the body which emerged in a suppressive sense, as Marxists would suggest, but instead a power which was also enabling and facilitating to the individual, creating active and independent citizens needed for modern society:

> Discipline 'makes' individuals; it is the specific technique of a power that regards individuals both as objects and as instruments of its exercise.
>
> Discipline increases the forces of the body (in economic terms of utility) and diminishes these same forces (in political terms of obedience). In short, it dissociates power from the body; on the one hand, it turns it into an 'aptitude', a 'capacity', which it seeks to increase; on the other hand, it reverses the course of the energy, the power that might result from it, and turns it into a relation of strict subjection.
>
> (Foucault 1991: 138 and 170)

According to Foucault, there are a variety of techniques through which disciplinary power is maintained: hierarchical surveillance; normalizing judgement; and examination (each of which will be discussed in turn). For these forms of power to be made possible the setting has to first be established through four prerequisites: enclosure; partitioning; analytical space; and ranking.

'Enclosure' is the 'specification of a place heterogeneous to all others and closed in upon itself' (Foucault 1991: 141). Thus, through *enclosure* of children, within individual schools, it is possible to maintain a form of control over the younger generation.[2] This control or power through the school is made possible through *partitioning*, in which it is easier 'to establish presences and absences, to know where and how to locate individuals, to set up useful communications, to interrupt others, to be able at each moment to supervise the conduct of each individual, to assess it, to judge it, to calculate its qualities or merits' (ibid.: 143). In the case of the school, children are *partitioned* according to ages and abilities – supervision over a class is therefore more easily defined. Through creating *'analytical spaces'* within the school it is possible to map children's progress, *'rank'* them accordingly, and collate files upon them, through easily managed spaces, as well as creating an arena in which surveillance of individual movements and gestures is facilitated. Thus what has been created is an analytical/functional space:

> The organization of a serial space was one of the great technical mutations of elementary education. … By assigning individual places it made possible the supervision of each individual and the simultaneous work of all. … It made the educational space function like a learning machine, but also as a machine for supervising, hierarchizing, rewarding.
>
> (Foucault 1991: 147)

Now that an analytical space has been created through enclosure, partitioning and ranking, the three tools – hierarchical surveillance, normalizing judgement and examination – which make up disciplinary power can be set in motion:

Hierarchical surveillance

Hierarchical surveillance is a combination of seeing and installing power simultaneously. In the case of the school it can be achieved, for example, through: seating arrangements; building design; and the use of school prefects. Classes are arranged in such a way that the teacher can gaze across and see every individual movement and gesture. The constant gaze by teachers or school prefects made available by various apparatuses instils in the pupils a disciplinary self-control; thus the idea that they are possibly being watched makes them behave, through fear of being punished.

Normalizing judgement

Through surveillance a normalizing judgement is cast across the school population, made possible through the ranking of pupils according to age and ability. Through ranking it is possible to identify an 'expected norm' which all pupils can then be judged upon according to this standardized ranking system, as well as being judged individually against their own recognized ability. Thus those who do not meet a school's expectations or who transgress the rules and misbehave contrary to the norms of the school may find themselves punished; likewise those who do behave are rewarded – 'The power of normalisation imposes homogeneity; but it individualises by making it possible to measure gaps, to determine levels, to fix specialities and to render the differences useful by fitting them one to another' (Foucault 1991: 184).

Examination

The third tool used is examination, made possible through observation and normalizing judgement. Examination allows individuals to be categorized and examined according to what is classified as 'normal' and acceptable. Foucault mentions three characteristics of disciplinary power which are a cause of examination. First, power over the individual has now become invisible: accepted into our daily routines it has become disguised within normal daily practice. However, the object of power – the individual – is now more visible, as everyone is using examination as an everyday technique to categorize society through daily encounters. Second, the collation of files upon individuals through categorization makes it possible to examine society in minute detail. Within the school it is possible to produce detailed records on each child – to follow not just their educational progress but also their behaviour. It also allows individuality to flourish through resources being easily targetable at those who need them most. Thus collation can be seen throughout the school in the guise of: examinations; awards; certificates; the establishment of the national curriculum which makes assessment of individuals easier and precipitates the normalizing of acceptable educational attainment; and league tables which act as a form of surveillance and examination over the whole school population including teachers and school governors. The third cause of examination involves individualization: 'the formation of a whole series of codes of disciplinary individuality that made it possible to transcribe, by means of homogenization the individual features established by the examination … the educational … code of conduct or performance … marked the first stage in the formalization of the individual within power relations' (Foucault 1991: 189) Through this new power every individual is targeted: 'the child, the patient, the madman, the prisoner, were to become, with increasing ease from the eighteenth century … the object of individual descriptions and biographical accounts' (ibid.: 192).

The creation of disciplinary power and individualization has paved the way for various professionals to enter the personal lives of individuals. This can be seen through the emergence of social workers, the professionalization of policing, psychology and psychiatry, and so on. Specifically, in relation to the school, we have inspectors, educationalists, the new managerialism currently being brought into the role of teachers, and the increasing involvement of parents within the management of schools and pupils. These are prime examples of disciplinary power being dispersed throughout society. The law has reinforced and legitimated the ideological and social trends that precipitated these changes. Below we discuss the impact of the law on disciplinary power within the school.

The Discipline Environment in Schools: The Legal Context

We have already seen some examples of how the disciplinary environment within schools can be seen to contribute to the broader socializing function of education and as an instrument of control. It may also exercise a prominent place within the discourse of power. Foucault's techniques of surveillance and examination, and the practice of normalizing judgement, have become increasingly apposite to analysis of the regulatory framework governing pupil behaviour in schools in this country. The use of authority to regulate individual freedoms is seen to be necessary in order for the school to promote the required basic values and fulfil its broader social reproduction roles. Even parental choice over the content of education and disciplinary issues may have to give way to collective social goals. As Sutherland (1988: 166) says, 'where it is believed that education must make children into good members of society, greater emphasis will be given to the right of society to make decisions and such decisions may involve overriding parents' preferences and wishes'.

At the same time, educational policy has adopted a general aim of maximizing individual opportunity. This has been seen as a key to securing 'social justice', but without centrally or popularly directed redistribution of wealth and power. It has, however, created a tension in the traditional disciplinary approach to education, as described in the introduction to this chapter. Providing a well-ordered environment in a school should enable individual potential to flourish, but not necessarily the potential of those individuals who do not conform to prescribed or implicit behavioural norms. In the past, the latter individuals have been the casualties of a failed socialization process and the most serious offenders have faced exclusion from school and in some cases from mainstream society. This problem has increasingly received official acknowledgement in recent years, such as through the Social Exclusion Unit set up by the Labour government to look at this issue and make recommendations. It has involved not only putting an emphasis on ensuring that those who are excluded receive suitable educational provision and are reintegrated into school as quickly as possible, but also seeking to minimize the risks of exclusion from school by providing proper support (for example through LEA duties to operate behaviour support strategies) and tackling bullying, racism and disaffection (DFEE 1997a: Chapter 6 and DFEE 1999a). At the same time, control mechanisms have in some ways been strengthened – for example through the requirement for schools to adopt home–school agreements (although parents do not have to sign them, there will clearly be social pressure to do so), through the widespread use of 'behaviour contracts' (under which excluded pupils and their parents agree behavioural norms as terms for the child's reintegration)[3] and through the power of detention being placed on a statutory footing (see below). The need to control pupil behaviour is reinforced by the fact that although it is not specifically referred to in the statute as a matter on which registered inspectors of schools must report following an inspection, it is implicit within the statutory criteria[4] and is referred to in the guidance on inspections.

The current legal framework governing school discipline is based on the Education Act 1997 – in some cases amending parts of the Education Act 1996 – and the SSFA 1998 (referred to below as, respectively, the 1996 or 1997 Act and the SSFA 1998, as appropriate). What follows is merely an outline, in order to illustrate the principles underlying the legal provisions and to provide a context for the discussion of school exclusion in the next two chapters.

General Disciplinary Functions

General disciplinary functions are specified in section 61 of the SSFA 1998. The governing body must ensure that 'policies designed to promote good behaviour and discipline are pursued at the school'. This requirement, first introduced via the 1997 Act,[5] sets within the law a clear disciplinary ethos for schools. In furtherance of this duty the governing body must make (following consultation with the head teacher and parents of registered pupils), and from time to time review, a written statement of the general principles to which the head teacher is to have regard in connection with the exercise of his or her own functions as laid down in the legislation. The statement may be amended, but again there needs to be prior consultation. In addition, the governing body is empowered to notify the head teacher of any particular measures which should be taken or particular matters that it considers should be brought to his or her attention, and may give guidance to the head.[6] The governing body must itself have regard to guidance issued by the Secretary of State.[7]

The governing body is certainly able to exercise a major influence over the disciplinary ethos of the school; but it is likely, and indeed probably expected, that the statement of general principles made by the governing body will be fairly broad, leaving the head teacher to devise strategies and systems for the management of discipline (again in line with the Secretary of State's guidance, plus any guidance on specific matters determined by the governors). The Act directs the head teacher towards a particular approach to the management of discipline within the school. He or she must determine the measures to be taken with a view to achieving prescribed objectives, namely:

(a) promoting, among pupils, self-discipline and proper regard for authority;
(b) encouraging good behaviour and respect for others on the part of pupils and, in particular, preventing all forms of bullying among pupils;
(c) securing that the standard of behaviour of pupils is acceptable; and
(d) otherwise regulating the conduct of pupils.[8]

The reference to the prevention of bullying in (b) was not in the previous version of this section, specified by the 1997 Act. The government says it 'attaches a high priority to helping schools prevent and combat bullying' (HM Government 1999: para 9.33.2). The question of what amounts to an 'acceptable' standard of behaviour, for the purposes of (c), is left to the head teacher, but only 'in so far as it is not determined by the governing body' (s. 61(6)).

The effectiveness of behaviour management in ensuring that pupils conform and that parents reinforce the school's efforts must obviously depend on awareness of the basic code determined by the head teacher. Prior to the 1997 Act the head merely had to make the disciplinary measures he or she had determined 'known within the school'. The 1997 Act extended this duty so that the head also had to make the measures generally known to parents and, at least once in every school year, take steps to bring them to the attention of all pupils, parents, and persons employed at the school.[9] The 1998 Act extended this list to include persons engaged to provide services at the school.[10]

Home–School Agreements

The expectations of pupils as regards behaviour can be further reinforced and communicated via home–school agreements, referred to above, for which the SSFA 1998 also makes provision. Although it is not compulsory for a parent to sign the declaration attached to the school's adopted agreement, most parents are in practice likely to sign. In fact, had the relevant provisions of the Education Act 1997 been implemented, school admissions arrangements could have made it a pre-condition to admission to a school that a parent signed up to the agreement.[11] The 1998 Act contains no such power. Section 110 requires governing bodies of maintained schools and city technology colleges to adopt an agreement but they may not tie the agreement to admission as the 1997 Act would have done.

The document itself must, in addition to stating the school's aims and values and its responsibilities as regards the education of the child, specify the parental responsibilities concerning the education of the child at school and 'the school's expectations of its pupils, namely the expectations of the school as regards the conduct of such pupils while they are registered pupils there'.[12] Parents and others to be prescribed must be consulted before an agreement is adopted and where a revision is proposed. Although the governing body will be required to seek signatures from all parents, it will be able to grant an exception. In any event, as noted in Chapter 2, the Act states that a home–school agreement shall not create obligations under the law of contract or tort.[13] Moreover, no person may be excluded from school or be subjected to any other 'adverse consequences' (as the Act puts it) as a result of a failure to sign the parental declaration.[14]

When the legislation was before Parliament an agreed amendment conferred a duty on the governing body to invite a pupil who is considered to have 'sufficient understanding of the home–school agreement' to sign the parental declaration 'as an indication that he acknowledges and accepts the school's expectations of its pupils'.[15] While this could be seen as a recognition of the child's right of participation as enshrined in Article 12 of the UN Convention (see Chapter 1), it is somewhat unfortunate that the child's signature is narrowly directed towards acknowledging his or her behavioural responsibilities rather than, for example, also acknowledging the school's responsibilities towards the child. Indeed, although, as noted above, the school's broad obligations and values are to be stated in the agreement, the principal function of the agreement is clearly to reinforce the (non-negotiable) key responsibilities of parents and children concerning attendance, behaviour and performance of schoolwork. In this sense the agreement in some ways constitutes a repressive tool (see Blair and Waddington 1997).

The value of these agreements has been called into question. Some argue that the lack of enforceability and the unavailability of sanctions for breach combine to weaken the potential effectiveness of these agreements in the case of defaulting parents, and that they are unnecessary for the many parents who are fully committed to ensuring that their children behave and succeed at school. Moreover, the lack of true mutuality in these agreements means that they fail to give real substance to the partnership ideal that the government has been keen to promote as a means of improving discipline and helping to raise levels of academic achievement in school (Blair and Waddington 1997). It has been suggested that rather than promoting partnership, the home–school agreement as provided for in the Act will in fact be more likely to 'set up an antagonistic and litigious atmosphere from the moment a child sets foot in school'.[16]

The LEA's Role

The 1997 and 1998 Acts have given LEAs a range of new responsibilities for discipline in schools. In addition, their reserve power to prevent a breakdown, or continuing breakdown, of discipline in schools, first introduced under the Education (No. 2) Act 1986, continues in section 62 of the SSFA 1998. This power enables the LEA to take any steps it feels are required for this purpose if pupils' education is likely to become, or is, severely prejudiced as a result of pupil behaviour or action taken by parents. The power is linked to the new power in the Act to issue a warning notice to a school where management has broken down or pupil or staff safety is threatened by a breakdown of discipline.[17]

LEAs also have various other enforcement and support roles. These are outlined in Circular 11/99 (DFEE 1999b) and it is not proposed to deal with them in detail here. The main areas concern the enforcement of school attendance and the provision of education outside school for excluded pupils and others (for example in pupil referral units) (discussed in Chapter 4). A further role involves the preparation and administration of behaviour support plans under section 527A of the 1996 Act (which was added by the 1997 Act). The behaviour support plans must outline the arrangements to be made by the authority for the provision of advice and resources to schools with a view to helping with 'the promotion of good behaviour and discipline on behalf of their pupils' and 'general behavioural problems and the behavioural difficulties of individual pupils'.[18] LEAs also have specific responsibilities under Part IV of the 1996 Act for children with special educational needs; and these needs might arise from emotional and behavioural difficulties. In the past, schools and LEAs have not always brought within the special educational needs framework, as they ought to, some of the pupils who misbehave and cause disruption. The DFEE's guidance (DFEE 1999a: paras 3.1 and 3.2) urges early identification of needs and intervention in relation to such pupils.

School-based Sanctions

School-based sanctions should be specified by the head teacher within the disciplinary code he or she has determined, but either way they need to be in compliance with the law. The power of exclusion, whether for a fixed term or on a permanent basis, is discussed at length in Chapter 5. In addition, statutory limits, introduced by the Education Act 1997, are set on the power of detention outside school hours and the use of force to restrain pupils (but not for the purposes of corporal punishment). The power of detention[19] may only be used where the head teacher has expressly included it within the disciplinary measures to be used in the school and has previously made its potential use known both within the school and, so far as possible, to parents. Only the head teacher or a person authorized by him or her to do so may use the power of detention. The parent must be given at least 24 hours' notice in writing of his or her child's detention, but there is no provision for a parental veto. Detention may only be given where it is 'reasonable', and what is interesting about the way the power of detention has been set out in the statute is that the legislation prescribes the factors that must 'in particular … be taken into acccount' in determining whether detention is reasonable. First, the detention must constitute a 'proportionate punishment in the circumstances of the case' – in particular it must be proportionate to the misbehaviour involved. Second, consideration must be given to any special circumstances relevant to its imposition on the pupil which the teacher knows about (or ought reasonably to know about), including the pupil's age, special educational needs (if any), religion and travel arrangements. Given these criteria, it is perhaps surprising that appropriate statutory criteria have not been specified in relation to the power of exclusion. However, as we shall see in Chapter 5, the requirement in the SSFA 1998 for the Secretary of State's guidance on exclusion, which includes such criteria, to be taken into account by schools has a broadly equivalent effect.

The power to use force[20] rests with teachers and others who, with the authority of the head teacher, have lawful control or charge of pupils. It may be exercised whether there is a risk to pupil safety or of damage to property or in order to prevent a pupil from 'engaging in any behaviour prejudicial to the maintenance of good order and discipline at the school or among any of its pupils, whether that behaviour occurs during a teaching session or otherwise'. The aim of introducing this provision on the use of force was claimed to be that of restoring some balance between the powers of teachers and the rights of pupils, in the face of evidence that teachers felt unable to intervene in situations of danger or severe disruption due to fear of litigation or accusations of child abuse. When the legislation was before Parliament, the minister was keen to stress that not only was the power expected to be used in a proportionate manner, it was also not expected to sanction restraint when a pupil was committing 'trivial misdemeanours' but only to be used 'as a last resort to prevent seriously bad behaviour'.[21] Nevertheless, the law has been expressed in somewhat repressive, authoritarian terms as well as being widely cast.

The authority to inflict corporal punishment was abolished in respect of pupils in maintained schools and state-funded pupils attending independent schools by the Education (No. 2) Act 1986. The 1998 Act has extended this ban to all pupils.[22]

Anti-discrimination Legislation

The Sex Discrimination Act 1975 and the Race Relations Act 1976 prohibit direct or indirect discrimination within schools or most other educational institutions on the grounds of sex or colour, race, ethnic or national origins or nationality. Both Acts specifically refer to discrimination in relation to access to benefits, facilities or services or in subjecting a person to 'exclusion or other detriment'.[23] As noted in Chapter 1, international human rights law is also relevant in this context. The DFEE's guidance stresses the importance of avoiding racial or gendered stereotyping of pupils which might lead to inequality in treatment in the disciplinary or broader context. We explore the issue of inequality further, in the specific contexts of race and gender, in Chapter 4, noting the disproportionate incidence of exclusion among boys and black children.

Conclusion

The message conveyed by recent education legislation is that schools must continue to strive for higher standards of achievement among pupils, but with additional support to help them in this mission. At the same time they must continue their traditional role, variously described in theoretical terms as socialization, social reproduction or even social control.[24] Citizenship education and sex education (the latter required to be provided to secondary school pupils (see Harris 1996) and the former likely to be elevated from a cross-curricular area to part of the national curriculum) are expected to contribute to this. The national curriculum itself exercises a disciplinary effect, in a broader sense, through its emphasis on assessment and performance. Indeed, good discipline is clearly regarded as integral to the success in achieving the objectives set by the government, expressed baldly in terms of targets for improved standards of literacy and numeracy and a 'zero tolerance of underperformance' (DFEE 1997a: Chapter 1, para. 19 and Chapter 2, para. 21). Discipline in a more direct sense, in terms of behaviour control through rule-making and the exercise of authority, also plays its part. One way or another discipline constitutes one of the key elements of the hidden curriculum of the school, as the various theoretical perspectives outlined above suggest.

Despite the ban on corporal punishment, which has now been in operation in state schools for over 12 years, disciplinary authority within schools has been strengthened over recent years. The law has reached into many areas of this authority traditionally implicit within the professional and social roles of the teacher and school but which, in a modern democratic state, is considered to need legislative underpinning. Regulation of disciplinary authority has offered protection to the pupil (and parent) by setting more carefully defined limits; at the same time it has further legitimated the exercise of discipline at a time when the actions of professional élites are more readily called into question by ordinary citizens. It has also acknowledged the social control dimension to collective educational provision. Yet when the ultimate sanction of exclusion of a child from school is employed, the institutionalization of discipline can be seen to weaken rather protect the social fabric. In the next chapter we examine the price that often has to be paid by the child and by the community as a whole when exclusion from school takes place.

4 Exclusion in Practice

The Social Context to School Exclusion

Introduction

School exclusion has been much examined in recent years by researchers and policy-makers and has been the subject of numerous policy initiatives. This is not surprising: with over 12,000 pupils permanently excluded from schools in England during each of the last two academic years, compared to just 3,000 in 1990–91 (see Chapter 1), explanations have been sought for the propensity of head teachers to use with considerably greater frequency than in the past the most severe disciplinary sanction open to the teaching profession as a whole. Moreover, as the costs of exclusion have become better understood, so means of reversing the trend have been sought. Renewed impetus has resulted from the present government's preoccupation with raising school standards and all pupils' levels of achievement, especially in the case of those from disadvantaged backgrounds who have traditionally under-achieved in educational terms and who are more at risk of exclusion than others. These groups include black (especially African-Caribbean) children, those with unstable and economically disadvantaged backgrounds and children with special educational needs.

It is beyond the remit of this book to seek to provide a comprehensive analysis of the problem of exclusion from school and ways of tackling it. This book is concerned with the role of review and appeal in exclusion cases. But it seeks to place these matters within a broader context. Indeed, in order to ensure a proper understanding of the issues arising from the decisions to be made in these processes it is necessary to explore the social dimension to exclusion. This chapter therefore aims to provide a contextual overview of exclusion from school by considering the backgrounds of the pupils who are excluded and the implications of exclusion for the children, their families and society. We also examine the provision made for children who are excluded from school, including children who are unable to be reintegrated back into the schools system. Finally, the chapter takes a very brief look at the initiatives undertaken by the government and other agencies to reduce school exclusion generally and among particular groups. (Note that legislation to limit the scope of the power of exclusion and restrict the use made of it are discussed in Chapter 5.) We should stress that it is not within our remit here to propose solutions to the problems we describe.

Reasons for Exclusion

The reasons given by schools for a child's permanent exclusion can range from accumulative misbehaviour to specific incidents involving violence or the possession of drugs. A report by the Social Exclusion Unit (1998), drawing on a range of published research findings, cited violence, whether physical or verbal, as the most common reason for permanent exclusion, followed by disruption, other misconduct and, towards the end of the list, drugs. Parents in the authors' survey cited similar reasons for their child's exclusion: violence was referred to in 175 out of 227 responses as either the sole reason or one of the reasons for permanent exclusion, compared with disobedience and/or insolence in 128 cases and drugs in 17 cases. Often there was more than one reason for the exclusion.

Violence in schools has attracted considerable media attention in recent years. Newspaper headlines include: 'Head closes pupil-row school' (MacLeod 1996: 1); 'Weapons carried at 1 in 10 schools' (Smithers 1997: 4); 'Teachers may strike over pupils caught with gun' (Charter 1997: 2); 'Parents threaten revenge for primary school rape' (Lee 1997: 9). Cases like the fatal stabbing of head teacher Philip Lawrence have rightly given the issue a high public profile. While the media may exaggerate the scale of the problem, research nevertheless confirms that it is real. An Exeter University project found that 31 per cent of 15-year-old boys admitted to carrying a weapon (Carvel 1996b). According to a DFEE (1997c) report, 1 in 35 school assaults involve a person being hit with a weapon or an object used as a weapon. A report by the NASUWT (cited in Carvel 1997: 13), based on a survey of 1,000 schools, found that weapons carried by pupils included machetes, knives, air pistols and objects close to hand, such as a chair. However, school violence does not only involve pupil assaulting pupil, but can take the form of a pupil or parent assaulting a member of staff. Researchers at Keele University found that pupil assaults on staff ranged from verbal abuse and theft to harassment in their own home (cited in Thornton 1998). In the academic year 1995–96, in a sample of 2,303 schools, over half of the staff had experienced verbal abuse from parents (Gill and Hearnshaw 1997).

Just under two-thirds of teaching staff surveyed believed violence in schools had increased over the last three years (NASUWT cited in Carvel 1997: 13). Research commissioned by the Suzy Lamplugh Trust (Gill and Hearnshaw 1997) found that assaults by pupils on staff were occurring in roughly one in five schools and that in one in ten schools pupils had been found carrying weapons on the school premises. Action to prevent such occurrences were, however, rarely put into practice by school management, with 40 per cent of the schools in the NASUWT survey lacking safety procedures and many of the schools failing to have in operation a reporting system for acts of aggression. (Note that the DFEE issued guidance on school security and violence in December 1997: DFEE

1997d.) There have been many cases of teachers threatening to strike or actually striking over the reinstatement of pupils who have been permanently excluded for some form of violent act, or because of the governors' decision to reinstate in such a case, as noted in Chapter 1. Although research does suggest that there has been an increase in violence within schools, the reasons for this increase are uncertain.

In many individual cases exclusion seems to be an inevitable consequence of the fact that the child's needs cannot be met in the school. This is especially true of pupils with special educational needs (see below). Moreover, some children become alienated due to bullying or racism. Others simply have difficulty conforming to the behavioural standards required or in coping with the pressures of school life, or simply do not fit in. Within the authors' research comments from parents included:

> School couldn't cope with the demands Scott made – Scott could not cope with the demands school made.

> Normal schooling was no good for my son.

> Unfortunately Luke could not or would not adapt to the classroom situation or conform to normal school behaviour.

> The school could not cope with Robert's special needs and Robert could not cope with the pressure from such big numbers.

The reasons for school exclusion may be more fully understood by looking at the pupils who are most at risk of exclusion.

Pupils Who are Most at Risk of Exclusion from School

The main area of concern has been the over-representation of ethnic minorities among those who are permanently excluded. The overall exclusion rate for the academic year 1998/99 among all pupils was 0.18 per cent of the total school population (DFEE 1999d). The highest exclusion rate was among black Caribbean pupils (0.76 per cent), followed by black other pupils (0.70 per cent) and black African pupils (0.30 per cent). The exclusion rate for black Caribbean pupils currently stands, therefore, at four times the average. In contrast, the exclusion rate for white pupils was (0.17 per cent), which roughly corresponds with the average rate for pupils in general. Indian, Pakistani, Bangladeshi and Chinese pupils all have exclusion rates below the average.

A number of explanations have been given for the high percentage of African and Caribbean pupils in the exclusion statistics, such as cross-cultural misinterpretation through mistaken interpretations of black pupils' body language by white teachers (Gibson and Barrow cited in Blyth and Milner 1993), racial stereotyping, difference in dress and racist attitudes of teachers (Mac and Ghaill 1988 in Blyth and Milner 1993; Bourne et al. 1994; Sewell 1997). This has occurred despite government guidance warning strongly against it and despite the continuing operation of the Race Relations Act 1976 (see Chapter 3). Racist banter can also indirectly increase the risk of a child from an ethnic minority being permanently excluded. A child may retaliate after racial harassment by another pupil, and as a result may find themselves not just a victim, but a double victim – of racism and of permanent exclusion – particularly when a full and thorough investigation has not been carried out by the school. The authors observed instances within the independent appeal hearing where a child or the child's parent explained behaviour, noted on the child's record, as retaliation to racial harassment from another child. Yet such instances still appeared on the child's record as examples of misbehaviour without such a clarification. These types of cumulative misbehaviour may lead to a child being unfairly excluded (see Bourne et al. 1994: 33–34 and Cohen et al. 1994).

In general, members of ethnic minorities who have been excluded from school tend to be of average or above average ability, but under-achieving in school (OFSTED 1996b; Social Exclusion Unit 1998). For this reason some ethnic minority children have in the past been wrongly placed in special schools.

As noted in Chapter 1, children with special educational needs are also over-represented in the exclusion statistics. Those with statements are around seven times more likely to be permanently excluded than pupils without special educational needs (DFEE 1999d: table 5). Within the authors' research 35 per cent of parents said that their child had special educational needs; two-thirds of these children had a statement. Research by the Advisory Centre for Education (ACE 1992) found that many parents believed their child had been excluded because the school could not cope with their special educational needs. According to ACE, if a child with special educational needs is excluded this often reflects the fact that the LEA has not met its statutory duty to identify and meet such needs (under Part IV of the Education Act 1996).

The inclusion of children with special educational needs in mainstream schooling has been advocated through policy initiatives since the Education Act 1981. However, other legislation, notably the Education Reform Act 1988, has brought education into the arena of competition and 'market forces', making schools concerned about their performance in examination league tables and, in some cases, less accommodating towards children with special educational needs as a result (Harris 1993; Cohen et al. 1994; Hayden 1994; Hyams-Parish 1996). Changes are planned in the way that performance data is presented in the future so that this disincentive towards retaining pupils with special educational needs is removed. Note that exclusion rates in special schools vary according to the type of school. Schools catering for children with sensory impairment or specific learning difficulties are less likely to exclude than those for children with moderate learning difficulties or emotional or behavioural difficulties (OFSTED 1999:41).

So far as gender is concerned, males are much more likely than females to be excluded (OFSTED 1996a; Hayden 1996; Cohen et al. 1994; Hyams-Parish 1995). In the academic year 1997/98, 84 per cent of excluded pupils were male (DFEE 1999d). So far as age is concerned, DFEE statistics show that in 1997/98 only 1.8 per cent of children permanently excluded from schools in England were aged 16 or over, whereas 67 per cent were aged between 13 and 15, 12.7 per cent were aged 12 and 19 per cent of children were aged 11 or under; but between 1994/95 to 1996/97 there has been a 15 per cent increase in primary school exclusions and this is an area of concern (see Hayden 1994 and 1996).

The majority of excluded children come from difficult home backgrounds. Research conducted by Barnardos and the Family Service Unit (Cohen et al 1994), investigated the exclusion of 30 children. The findings, which mirror those of many other studies (Bourne et al. 1994; Cohen et al. 1994; Hayden 1996; Parsons et al. 1994; Parsons 1996), show that just over half of the children were from lone parent families, and 15 per cent were in care. The relatively high numbers of excluded children who are in care was also confirmed by a recent study conducted by the Children's Society (Smith 1998).

A longitudinal study conducted between 1974 and 1980 by the Commission for Racial Equality (CRE) (1985) into Birmingham LEA's use of exclusions and suspensions, concluded that 46 per cent of those suspended from school, and 69 per cent of those referred from school to special educational centres, had home circumstances which were viewed as contributory to the child's exclusion. Difficult home circumstances were also raised by parents or carers within the authors' study:

> My son was under a lot of pressure from outside school which the school knew about but didn't take into consideration.

> I was a social worker for a child subject to a care order, the child had multiple family problems which precipitated her bad behaviour.

> She was in need of a psychological service, social work service December last year when [her] dad had radiotherapy … it made him ill in many ways. He had to go to hospital and hospice, he was going to kill himself, you can see [he] was in need [of] help but there was no help at all.

> We were experiencing a terminal illness in the family and I was on the edge of a breakdown.

> His mother and I have been divorced for 7 years. In the last two years he has been surrounded by a lot of upset.

Economic disadvantage is another, related, factor. Cohen et al. (1994) found that the majority of children in their sample came from low income families. Similar findings emerge from the authors' research (see Chapter 8, Table 8.1). Economic disadvantage is also one explanation offered for the over-representation of black pupils being excluded from school.

Thus all evidence points to a high percentage of excluded children coming from low income families (a factor which also explains the higher exclusion rate in many poorer districts in socio-economic terms), with other familial problems encroaching upon the child's life. Family circumstances often seem to have a detrimental effect on the child's behaviour which can result in permanent exclusion from school. It is a vicious circle, because permanent exclusion generally increases the problems at home, through financial pressures for parents in finding day care for their child or the emotional stress of having a child that needs specialist care at home, twenty-four hours a day.

Home circumstances are particularly important in the discussion of exclusion. DFEE Circular 10/94 stated that schools needed to consider outside influences that could have played a contributory role in the child's behaviour, identifying home circumstances in particular – 'any particular circumstances unique to the pupil which might sensibly be taken into account in connection with the behaviour, e.g. strained or traumatic domestic circumstances' (DFE 1994b: 10). The new guidance, which replaces this, also acknowledges family stress (DFEE 1999d: paras 3.13 and 3.14):

> As teachers are well aware, family stress can affect children's emotional and educational development at school. Unemployment, bereavement, the loss of one or more parents through divorce or separation, and new adult partnerships can all have a significant effect on children.
>
> Home circumstances need to be taken into account when considering pupils' needs.

This new guidance is welcome and schools, LEAs and governors will have to have regard to it.[1] In the course of our research we became concerned at how lightly these bodies and the independent appeals panels took such troublesome and often tragic home circumstances into account.

The Cost of Exclusion to the Child

There are two fundamental, interrelated questions that need to be addressed in assessing the justification for exclusion as a disciplinary measure open to schools. One concerns the social costs of exclusion and the other whether the alternatives to mainstream schooling are satisfactory. These questions raise the issue of whether the benefit to the school and its pupils of excluding a pupil outweighs the cost to the child, the child's family and society as a whole. From the perspective of the school, the benefits will include security, safety and the maintenance of a conducive educational environment. For the child, exclusion could in theory mean that the child has an opportunity to reflect upon and modify their behaviour, with the ultimate aim of eventually returning to full-time education suitable to their needs. On first glance the theory appears cogent; however, the costs of exclusion are considerable.

As would be expected the largest cost to the child is the lost education whilst he or she is permanently excluded and waiting for suitable alternative arrangements to be made. The processes surrounding exclusion can be slow. Regardless of the procedures laid down in DFEE Circular 10/94 and now the revised guidance (in Circulars 10/99 and 11/99) that try to keep the time the child is out of school to a minimum, there needs to be sufficient time for assessment, planning and administrative and judicial procedures to take place, although these things can to some extent run concurrently rather than consecutively. Under the revised guidance there can be up to 15 school days (in effect three weeks) from the date of a permanent exclusion before the governing body's pupil discipline committee needs to meet to consider possible reinstatement (see Chapter 6). The parent has a further 15 days to appeal if the decision is not to reinstate; and the appeal panel has of meet within a further 15 school days of the date on which the parent lodges notice of appeal. The decision of the appeal panel must normally be notified within two days of the hearing. The procedure is much streamlined compared with the previous arrangements. The guidance now stresses that arrangements for the continuation of the child's schooling should be put in place while the process continues (see Chapter 5). However, there is still the task of finding another school to take the child, or making alternative arrangements (see below), which can prove onerous. Within the time the child is out of school, he or she is still on the school register (where exclusion is fixed term or where permanent exclusion is under review or appeal: DFEE 1999a: 43), thus the school is still receiving funding for the child; but in most cases the child receives no school work from the school (Hamilton 1997: 228) – hence the new guidance. Although, in theory the excluded child should now re-enter the education system reasonably quickly, past experience shows that there needs to be a considerable improvement if this is always to happen in practice.

There have been various estimates of the average length of time excluded children spend out of school: according to one survey it was 115 days in 1990–91 and 161 days in 1991–92 (Mitchell in Blyth and Miller 1996). Another survey showed that the average time out of mainstream schooling was 145 days, but could range from 17 to 360 days (Parsons et al. 1994). A DFE study showed that in 1995 only 27 per cent of primary school and 15 per cent of secondary school children returned to mainstream schooling at all, although the researchers believed this could be an underestimate (DFE 1995). Regardless of the many reforms emphasizing inclusive education and the need for a quick return of excluded children into mainstream schooling, little seems to have changed today compared to Galloway's research 20 years ago (Galloway 1982). The government's response has been to require LEAs to ensure that all children excluded for more than 15 days receive suitable full-time education – a requirement to which LEAs must operate fully by 2002 (DFEE 1999b: para 5.1).

Since the Education Act 1993 LEAs have been under a specific statutory duty (now in s. 19 of the Education Act 1996) to make arrangements for the provision of 'suitable full-time or part-time education at school or otherwise' for children of compulsory school age who, by reason of exclusion (or other reasons), may not otherwise receive suitable provision. Research has shown that even when excluded children do receive some alternative form of education it is rarely full time and is often erratic. Many of those receiving education in the form of home tuition receive under 10 hours teaching per week (OFSTED 1993: para. 14; Parsons 1996). The CRE (1996) calculated that a child who has been permanently excluded from school for a year on average receives only 10 per cent of full-time education. This was attributed to inadequate resources and the long waiting period for full-time education to commence. Not only will this cause long-term problems in relation to the child's learning, it will also make it harder for the child to cope with the full-time educational environment. (We discuss alternative forms of education for excluded children further, below.) The Social Exclusion Unit's (1998) report on truancy and exclusion found that those children who miss schooling are likely to gain fewer or no qualifications and thus have lower chances of gaining employment (see also Cohen et al. 1994), becoming more at risk of homelessness.

The authors' research found similar patterns to those revealed by the above-mentioned studies. The majority of parents who responded said lack of education was the most pressing concern. Typical comments included:

> [I]t has been 11 months since he has been in full time school.
>
> Paul is only getting 9 hours of education a week now.
>
> My son was not allowed to take any of his exams ... and is now finding it very difficult to get a job or any money.
>
> He is now getting hardly any education and hasn't had any for nearly two years. He is going worse because he is not in school.

The effects of this educational limbo can be serious for some excluded children. For one thing, the emotional pressures of exclusion can become unbearable. A child's life is centred on the education environment at least until the age of 16. It forms the backcloth to their social relationships and contributes much towards their self-identity. It can be devastating for children who find themselves permanently excluded from school, with no structure to the day and no contact with their friends or other adults. This may result in longer term consequences that could affect the rest of their lives. Excluded children often enter an insular and isolating environment, feeling bored and frustrated – not just excluded from school, but also from society and the typical lifestyle of other children their age. Typical comments from parents within the authors' sample illustrated the effect of exclusion on the child:

> He was off school for months, he got depressed and almost took his own life. It was so traumatizing for him, he was locked in the house whilst I was at work.
>
> [H]is self-esteem was pretty low after being excluded from school.
>
> [The] stress on [him] was too much.
>
> David was so upset by the way he had been treated.
>
> He is still punishing himself now. He is very embarrassed by it all.
>
> [He] has to carry the stigma of excluded pupil.

Excluded pupils often portray an image and air of self-assurance, but are in many cases hiding behind a façade that masks low self-confidence and a lack of belief in themselves (John, cited in Blyth and Miller 1996). This self-image may have repercussions, with a vicious circle of bad behaviour and rejection through the processes of labelling and self-fulfilling prophecy. Excluded children may experience the need to build a new identity for themselves. This new identity may emerge from the label that has now been placed upon them. A destructive label of 'excludee' or 'disaffected child' can cause delinquency to emerge in a new form – criminal activity (Cullingford and Morrison in Blyth and Miller 1996). Through marginalization of the 'misbehaved' child from mainstream schooling and their social world, the child is being stripped of their citizenship. Their social environment has been taken from them (cf. Blyth and Miller 1994) and instead, they may find themselves in the unfamiliar territory of an educational void.

Although the authors did not specifically ask parents of excluded children whether their child had been involved in criminal activity since being permanently excluded, some parents did touch upon this subject:

> My son is on drugs, burglary, shop lifting since he has been out of school.
>
> [But for exclusion] he would probably not be facing his second custodial sentence.
>
> Once he was permanently excluded from school he became more difficult to control and got himself into more trouble and ended up in jail about two months ago.

> When my son was excluded he started to get into serious trouble with the police and has since served a custodial sentence.

Even when the parents did not report that their child had been involved in criminal activity, there was often a hint that it could happen. There was serious concern that their child had too much time on his/her hands and was often left at home alone or was wandering the streets. The prospect of excluded children entering the world of crime is real: a report by the Metropolitan Police (cited in Social Exclusion Unit 1998: section 3.5) showed that 748 excluded children were arrested in London between 1995 and 1996.

According to the study *Misspent Youth* (Audit Commission 1996: 66), truanting and excluded children, as well as young people who grow up in areas of deprivation with lack of parental supervision and meaningful contact with both parents, are more likely to enter a life of crime than others of their age. *Misspent Youth* found that in one LEA area children aged 11 years plus who had been permanently excluded committed 50 per cent more crime in the year after exclusion than they had the previous year. The report stated that 42 per cent of young offenders who had come to the attention of the youth courts had been excluded from school. Excluded pupils were around 50 per cent more likely than other children to have offended.

The Cost of Exclusion to the Child's Family

It is not just the child that experiences the emotional pressures of exclusion, as great a strain is also placed on the child's family. Some siblings may resent the child's apparent luxury of staying at home. The excluded child may cause difficulties at home due to behavioural problems. If both parents are working, who is to look after the child? Thus, we are not only talking about exclusion for the child, but in many cases exclusion for the parent(s) in the sense that they may even have to contemplate resigning their employment if the child's full-time education is not resumed, in order to look after their child. Research has highlighted this as a problem and concern for families (Cohen et al. 1994; Parsons et al. 1994). The added pressures resulting from the child's exclusion from school can even precipitate the breakdown of the family and the child being placed into social services care.

Replies to the parent surveys in the authors' research confirmed the emotional problems within the family which can arise from their son's or daughter's permanent exclusion from school:

> As a result of Sean being excluded I was ill for months with depression because I got no help at all from the school. I also ended up in hospital as a result of an overdose.

> Susan was uncontrollable I felt very ashamed and still do.

> My child is badly behaved at home. He was the same in school they couldn't do nothing with him. I can't do nothing with him myself and can't get any help from any one about it.

During the course of the research the authors were contacted on a number of occasions by parents desperate for help in finding a way of putting their child's education back on track and thereby ease some of the strain.

The Cost of Exclusion to Society

In addition to the cost to the child and family that can result from permanent exclusion from school, there are also costs to society – not only in terms of criminality (above) but also the need to provide welfare and social services, medical and psychological intervention, law enforcement and crime prevention.

Parsons et al. (1994) developed a typology to estimate the costs of exclusion, distinguishing between direct costs, indirect costs and hidden costs. Hidden costs are those which were discussed earlier in this chapter – the emotional costs to the child and the child's family. Direct costs involve social services support, where agencies become directly involved with the family. Indirect costs include costs that immediately affect the family, such as child care, loss of earnings, extra heating and food bills. Through the examination of one case study Parsons et al. (1994) found that social services provision, which included family therapy and social work involvement, cost £591.72. The cost to the LEA, which involved home tuition and travelling expenses, was £6,724. Finally, the child had been involved in car crime, costing the police service £82.56. Thus the total cost for this one child out of school for just a 360-day period was calculated at £7,398.28. The researchers went on to compare the estimated cost of excluding the child with the costs that would have been incurred if the child had remained in mainstream schooling. For an academic year's schooling the cost would have been an estimated £3,904.65. The results therefore show that this one excluded child cost nearly £2,500 more than they perhaps would have if they had remained in school.

The most recent investigation into the financial cost to society of school exclusion has been carried out by the CRE (1996). The study calculated the cost of excluding a child for the year 1994/95, then forecast the cost of exclusion for the year 1995/96 for those children still excluded. Parsons et al's. (1994) finding that the cost of excluding a child was nearly double that of keeping them in mainstream education was confirmed by the CRE study. A permanent exclusion would result in a cost of £4,300 per child compared with the normal cost of £2,500 per child in mainstream schooling. Through an examination of spending procedures across six LEAs, it was discovered that home tuition and PRU amounted to 66 per cent of the cost involved, while 17 per cent comprised administrative costs; and support services such as health and social services also amounted to 17 per cent of the total cost. The cost for children who were still excluded for a second academic year averaged £5,134. The CRE (1996) estimated that 20 per cent of excluded children incur an average cost to social services of £1,100. Health services were used by 10 per cent of excluded pupils, at an average cost of £100. Costs to the police service were estimated at an average of £2,000. It was estimated that on average 70 per cent of costs other than educational costs were incurred by the criminal justice agencies.

A New School and Alternative Provision

Through the early identification and involvement of the various agencies it would be possible to put into action preventive initiatives to reduce the need for exclusion. The revised DFEE guidance (DFEE 1999d) emphasizes this strongly, while also stressing the important role of the school in particular. However, there will always be those children who fall through the net and for whom the system fails. For these children an alternative provision may need to be found, whether on a temporary or permanent basis.

Following the child's exclusion the LEA will normally seek a place for a child at another school. This can take time, although the LEA does have a power to direct a school to admit a child who has been excluded from school if the new school can provide him or her with a suitable education.[2] The parent can in any event seek a school place for the child and could invoke the parental preference provisions in section 86 of the SSFA 1998 (replacing section 411 of the Education Act 1996), under which the school would in effect be obliged to accept the child unless specific admissions criteria apply (e.g. religion in the case of a denominational school, or if the admission of the child would 'prejudice the provision of efficient education or the efficient use of resources', which might well be the case if the school is physically full). However, section 87 of the 1998 Act provides that if a child has been permanently excluded (not including cases where the child was reinstated) from two or more schools, and the most recent exclusion was within the past two years, the rights under the parental preference provisions in section 86 do not apply. This is a punitive measure which, although ostensibly aimed at protecting schools from having to take particularly difficult children – 'if a school deems that it is not in the interests of the child or the school to meet parental preference in such circumstances, the clause supports its right to make that judgement'[3] – seems also intended to sanction parents who 'allow' their child to misbehave and be excluded more than once. It could compound the problems of a child who is already experiencing difficulties.

It can prove difficult to find a suitable school place (delays of several months are common). While this is happening the LEA remains under a duty to arrange suitable educational provision for children excluded from school, as noted above. The House of Lords has held that this is a mandatory duty and that an LEA cannot avoid its responsibility by making decisions to cut provision to a child in the face of financial constraints: the resources of the LEA are not a legitimate factor by which to determine the suitability of the educational provision.[4] Suitable is defined as 'efficient education suitable to the age, ability, aptitude and to any special educational needs the child (or young person) may have'.[5]

DFE Circular 11/94 advised that this alternative provision 'is always to be regarded as a short-term alternative to mainstream education' and the new guidance says that 'ideally, permanently excluded children should rejoin a mainstream school within days or weeks', stressing that 'The longer a young person is out of school the more difficult it can be for them to re-integrate' (DFEE 1999d: para 7.1). There are three options available to the LEA: home tuition, either carried out by the parent or a home tutor arranged through the LEA; placement in a PRU; and arranging for a child nearing the compulsory school leaving age to begin a course at a local college, normally a vocational course. It was estimated in 1998 that 25,000 children were receiving alternative education (Social Exclusion Unit 1998: para 2.23).

Under revised guidance (DFEE 1999b: part 5), LEAs are now expected to convene reintegration panels, comprising education welfare officers, social services, educational psychologists, PRU or further education staff, head teachers and representatives of ethnic minority communities, to devise suitable arrangements for the child's return to mainstream schooling (see further Chapter 5). This multi-agency approach, although already in use in some areas, represents a welcome step forward in assisting excluded children. Research suggests that it works and should be developed also as a preventive strategy (see The Children's Society 1997 and Smith 1998, reporting on multi-agency projects which produced positive results, with parents and children feeling actively involved within the education system and the scale of exclusion or referral diminishing). Normington (in Blyth and Miller 1996) discovered that in many cases the biggest barrier to ensuring successful help for a child was conflicts between the various welfare and educational institutions. Although all of the agencies have the ultimate aim of helping the child, they were often working against each other rather than working effectively together as a team. Within a case conference situation all relevant agencies are brought together to discuss the needs of the child.

The authors observed three case conferences in which the LEA had the final decision but the different agencies present discussed the best available option for the excluded child. The parents and child were invited to discuss the child's future. Also present were teaching staff from the school who had had direct contact with the child, an education welfare officer, a member of the school's governing body and, in one case, a social worker. One conference resulted in the LEA agreeing to find the child an alternative school on the condition that the current school withdrew the permanent exclusion, which meant that the child was not left with such an exclusion on her school record. All concerned viewed this as the best option. In the second case, the exclusion was upheld, and with the parent's agreement the child was sent to a PRU. In the third case, it was agreed that the permanent exclusion should be upheld and an alternative school found. These cases suggested that a case conference is helpful in planning the child's educational future. Such a process will have to occur at an early stage, however, as the guidance contemplates. If agreement cannot be reached, the parent would still be able to pursue an appeal.

We now turn to the different forms of alternative provision for excluded children.

Home Tuition

In 1993, approximately 45 per cent of those being educated outside a mainstream school were receiving home tuition (DFEE press release 126/93). Home tuition involves the child being educated at home either by a teacher arranged through the LEA or a person suitably qualified arranged through the parents' own initiative. Occasionally, home tuition is provided by the parent him/herself. In most cases home tuition is used as a temporary measure after exclusion from school and during the search for a placement in an institutional setting – such as another mainstream school, special school, PRU or local college. Overall, home tuition has not been found to be beneficial to excluded children and the revised guidance says that it is 'not usually appropriate for permanently excluded pupils, although it may sometimes be the only short-term option' (DFEE 1999b: para. 5.23). One of the reasons home tuition has rarely been adequate is that it is often part-time (OFSTED 1993), irregular and provided by people with no experience of pupils with behavioural and learning difficulties (Parsons et al. 1994). Moreover, although it is the duty of the LEA to carry out inspections of home tuition, the law does not state specifically what form the tuition should take and leaves LEAs to define what 'suitable' provision might be. The national curriculum is not a statutory requirement for those children being educated at home (Petrie 1993). Petrie (1992) found that although most LEAs monitored home education, this could comprise just two visits a year, and some LEAs did not conduct any visits.

The revised DFEE guidance contemplates the child will be set work at home by the school immediately following the exclusion, in order to preserve the continuity of his or her education. In practice, even when work is set it will probably not be marked. Hamilton (1997: 228) comments that 'the lack of feedback and interaction does little to sustain the child's interest in learning'.

Pupil Referral Units (PRUs)

PRUs were placed on a statutory footing by the Education Act 1993 (section 298),[6] as an alternative provision by LEAs for excluded pupils and others unable to attend school. It was estimated in January 1998 that there were 344 PRUs England and Wales with 8,267 sole and 4,019 dually registered pupils; they had a pupil-(qualified) teacher ratio of 6.9 (CIPFA 1998: 10). (OFSTED (1999) para 10.1 reports that there are 320 PRUs in England.) The majority of the pupils at

PRUs are aged 14–16 years and most of the units have between 10–30 pupils (ibid.). A 1995 survey by the DFE found that 23 out of 101 LEAs who responded did not have PRUs and 45 did not provide PRUs for primary school aged children, while one LEA had 18 PRUs. In 13 LEAs less than 10 hours' tuition a week was provided. Overall, 36 per cent of the PRUs surveyed provided only part-time education. During 1995, a quarter of primary aged pupils excluded from school were in attendance at PRUs compared to over one-third of excluded secondary school pupils (Parsons 1996). PRUs commonly have waiting lists; Hamilton (1997: 229) notes that it is 'not unusual for an excluded child to wait anywhere between 8 and 16 weeks for a place at the unit'.

The OFSTED report *Education for Disaffected Pupils* (1993a) reported on the inspection of 39 PRUs within 10 LEAs between 1990–1992. There were alarming findings concerning the poor quality of teaching and the curriculum and the lack of clear aims, objectives and resources within the units. Among the units, 23 did not have a committed ethos of returning the child to mainstream schooling; rather, the centres worked as a permanent alternative, with the majority of pupils attending on a part-time basis. Only 16 of the units offered the hope of reintegration and even when it occurred it was rarely successful. Although some units did offer a flexible curriculum and were organized and consistent in their approach, most lacked clear objectives and failed to offer a stimulating learning environment. Learning was often below the children's academic ability. Despite a good rapport between pupils and staff, the educational environment in the majority of the units was not flexible enough to be tailored to individual needs. The report went on to conclude that within some units the teaching hours were lower than those recommended by the DFEE and that inter-agency co-operation and links were inadequate. It is fair to conclude from the report that many of the units surveyed were being used as 'sin bins' with little attention being paid to the young person's individual educational development and little hope of their reintegration into mainstream schooling. Overall, 15 units were described as having major deficiencies.

No doubt to encourage improvement and greater coherence the aims of PRUs were outlined within DFE Circular 11/94 (but are not in the recently revised guidance): PRUs should (DFE 1994a: 12)

- Promote a disciplined, intellectually challenging environment with high expectations.
- Offer a flexible and broad curriculum, promoting moral, physical and mental development. The full curriculum does not have to be covered, but mathematics, English and Science must be, as well as physical and social education. (The revised circular refers only to sex education, careers education and guidance and a balanced and broadly based curriculum (as per section 351(1) of the Education Act 1996).)
- Prepare the child for adult life, through participation in work experience and career guidance.

- Be run by qualified teachers and training should be provided to enable teachers to deal with difficult children.
- Take into consideration the ages of pupils and the reason(s) for their exclusion when placing the children into work groups.
- Establish links between schools and welfare services.
- Be used on a part-time basis along with mainstream schooling where necessary for children attending school.
- Aim to reintegrate the child back into mainstream education: 'PRU cannot be regarded as an acceptable long-term alternative to placement in a mainstream school.'

According to Garner (1996), however, PRUs are merely the same units as those which existed in the 1970s, providing the same level of resources under the same circumstances as the 'off-site units' under which name they were previously known. Garner conducted a comparative analysis of the units (PRUs and off-site) and concluded that little had changed other than the name. There was scant evidence to suggest that PRUs were any better at promoting the reintegration of excluded pupils. Garner concluded that the PRUs had inadequate accommodation, were situated in poor areas of town, had old and often out-dated equipment (which was viewed as a serious concern by the children), and experienced constant vandalism. Although there was a broader range of subjects offered in the PRUs than in the previous off-site units, there were fewer courses than were available in mainstream settings.

A recently published OFSTED survey of half of the PRUs reveals a continuation of some of these problems – notably in relation to accommodation and resources – but on the whole has presented a more positive picture (OFSTED 1999). Although provision was still often part-time, a particular problem for pupils with statements of special educational needs, a majority of pupils were found to be making satisfactory progress and, in an increasing number of units, many pupils were successful in gaining GCSEs. OFSTED regards this as representing 'a considerable achievement' (ibid., para. 10.2). Teaching was for the most part good (two-thirds was satisfactory or better) and staff numbers were generally sufficient. Pupil attitudes were at least satisfactory in the majority of PRUs, and 'often good', but attendance was unsatisfactory or poor. Resources were barely adequate, however, and while the accommodation was generally satisfactory or better, there were 'a small number of PRUs where accommodation was seriously inadequate, with consequent implications for health, safety and hygiene as well as for teaching and learning' (ibid., para. 10.7).

Some parents have viewed PRUs in a positive light. Those who feel that their child could not cope with mainstream schooling often regard a PRU as a place where individual attention can be provided (CRE 1996). Moreover, if PRUs were run more effectively they could help excluded children by giving them more time to assess their situation, receive individual attention which might help to find the root of their problem and put into effect a possible remedy

(Normington, in Blyth and Miller 1996). Indeed, despite their problems there are many examples of good practice within some PRUs. Normington (ibid.) describes a PRU panel consisting of educationalists, teachers and persons with experience of dealing with children with behavioural and emotional problems, meeting on a regular basis to discuss newly referred pupils. The primary goal of the particular unit is for pupils to return to mainstream schooling within six weeks. For children nearing school leaving age, a flexible approach to the curriculum is taken, one that will help to equip the young person with the necessary skills to secure future employment. One aim is to increase the pupil's self-esteem through careers advice, work experience and outdoor activities. It is not only excluded pupils who are accommodated by the PRU, but also students that are at *risk* of exclusion – thus the aim is to prevent the exclusion taking place. The PRU collates data on each pupil's educational and behavioural needs, and on the basis of this information forms a plan of action which will help the child with any problems, forming the groundwork for reintegration. Before the pupil is reintegrated a case conference is held involving the school, the PRU, educationalists and the parent. The PRU believes that older children who will not be reintegrated into a school should be kept separate from the younger children, as reintegration is the primary aim. In this unit, of the 39 students (surveyed in the year of the research) one received another exclusion from school, one other began a college course, but the rest were successfully reintegrated into mainstream schooling (Normington in Blyth and Miller 1996).

Section 48 of the Education Act 1997 (amending Schedule 1 to the 1996 Act) has made it possible for LEAs to establish management committees for PRUs.[7] In cases where an LEA has more than one PRU, it is possible that joint management committees be set up for these units, with approval from the Secretary of State. Hopefully, through the establishment of such committees, a higher level of commitment to individual needs and a wider curriculum and multi-agency approach will be established. Currently the government suggests that a broad approach to the curriculum should be undertaken in which the national curriculum does not have to be followed. This suggests, however, that there is no hope for the children and young people to gain some of the forms of qualification that have already eluded them. Moreover, there is, therefore, still a risk that PRUs will be seen as a dumping ground where children who are a problem within their school are sent. Here the children will not be able to 'contaminate' the other children and thus upset the social order of the classroom and school. The procedures of PRUs have in the past often been more concerned with providing a place where the children can be watched and a disciplinary control exerted on them than a place of rehabilitation. It is clear that the government wants this to change, as part of its overall strategy to try to get excluded children back into mainstream schools as quickly as possible.

Colleges of Further Education

In many cases excluded children are close to the compulsory school leaving age and it is not always feasible for them to re-enter mainstream schooling. Instead, their LEA may, in order to fulfil the requirements of section 19 of the Education Act 1996 by ensuring suitable alternative education, enrol the child at a local college.[8] Excluded pupils normally enter courses that are vocational in nature, such as NVQs, which aim to equip young persons with skills suitable to enter specific occupations.

Approximately 50 per cent of secondary school children permanently excluded from school come from years 10 and 11. A survey by the DFE (1995) of such children in 11 LEAs found that some were placed within further education (FE) colleges; however, most were placed within PRUs. The survey found one exception where an authority placed 140 pupils within FE colleges on a part-time basis. FE colleges are often used in association with PRUs, with a pupil spending perhaps two days per week at a college and three days at the PRU. In general, FE placements are less popular with LEAs than using a PRU.

A Positive from a Negative?

Excluding a child from school is not always regarded as a wholly negative prospect. For many parents, their child's permanent exclusion can result in the child receiving the provision and help they may desperately need. Permanent exclusion may have the benefit of providing a child with the opportunity to enter a new mainstream school with a clean slate and continue with their education after a short stay in a PRU or in attendance at a college of FE. The authors found that although most parents disagreed with the exclusion of their child, some did find it beneficial in the long-run:

> He is now at a special school and under the small class regime is showing marked improvement.
>
> My son is now receiving better education and more help ... where he now attends. He is now [a] much happier and contented child ... I feel that this is the best thing to happen.
>
> She is now in a centre for teenagers with a behavioural problem, she is very happy there and has excellent reports from the centre.
>
> He is doing subjects he would never have done in mainstream school, it was the best thing to happen to him.
>
> We have now got him into another school after going to a unit and we feel a good thing has come out of a bad as he is now getting help.

It is, however, unfortunate that the child often has to undergo exclusion to find a place in a more appropriate learning environment.

Policy Challenges to School Exclusion

Policies to tackle exclusion are being developed at various levels. It is clear that reductions in school exclusion are part of a broader drive to improve educational standards across society and to raise levels of social inclusion. It would clearly be impossible here to discuss all of the measures introduced or planned by the Labour government to secure the improvements that are deemed necessary in the field of education, several of which are now coming into operation under the SSFA 1998 (see Harris 1998). There is only scope here for a relatively brief discussion of developments.

At the national level, the most obvious place to start with is the Social Exclusion Unit. The unit, launched on 8 December 1997, views social exclusion as: 'A shorthand label for what can happen when individuals or areas suffer from a combination of linked problems such as unemployment, poor skills, low incomes, poor housing, high crime environments, bad health and family breakdown' (SEU web page). The unit focuses particularly on issues where solutions have been hard to find and where governmental agencies need to work together. The unit draws on experience from the public, private and voluntary domains, and encourages the ideal of self-regulation through people taking responsibility to help themselves. The unit raises issues for consultation. The ultimate aim of the unit is to prevent social exclusion rather than solely trying to deal with the consequences. So far the unit has compiled reports on truancy and school exclusion, sleeping rough, teenage parents and, most recently, support for young people not in education, training or employment.

The first report published by the Social Exclusion Unit, *Truancy and School Exclusion* (1998), examines the causes of school exclusion and the groups most at risk of exclusion. It also proposes a strategy for lowering rates of permanent exclusion, which is now being implemented. It includes performance data on exclusions, broken down by ethnic group (reflecting the seriousness of the exclusion problem among some such groups), and recommends the targeting of OFSTED inspections on schools with high exclusion rates. The report also highlights the fact that local strategies for minimizing exclusion and assisting children at risk of exclusion will feature in the arrangements for education action zones, now introduced (on a pilot basis) under the SSFA 1998. Education action zones were one of the initiatives referred to in the government's White Paper *Excellence in Schools* (DFEE 1997a), which offers 'policies designed to benefit the many, not just the few' (at p. 11). Curriculum reform, such as the development of citizenship education (QCA 1998), is also aiming to make the education system more inclusive. There is also a new drive to tackle school exclusion specifically, under the SSFA 1998 and the revised DFEE guidance, both of which are referred to extensively throughout this book, and in targeted grants to LEAs, such as those aimed at assisting children most at risk of exclusion ('social inclusion grant') (DFEE press release 512/98). Overall £500 million is being invested from 1999–2002 to reduce exclusion and truancy, and from April 2000 a new Youth Support Service, aimed at supporting schools in tackling these problems, is being piloted (Secretary of State for Social Security 1999: 52).

The problems of ethnic minorities were addressed by the CRE (1997) in a good practice guide to counteract the over-representation of ethnic minorities in the exclusion statistics. The recommendations included a school behaviour policy which advocates that exclusion is only to be used as a last resort; better pastoral care for children at risk of exclusion; active participation of pupils in decision-making processes; wider parent and community involvement; and the introduction of a multi-cultural curriculum with opportunities for children to draw on their own cultural experiences. It also recommended:

- implementation of an equal opportunities policy stating the school's commitment to abolish racism
- teachers to be trained in equal opportunities
- recruitment of ethnic minority staff
- staff support and training in management of racism
- monitoring of exclusions in terms of ethnic origin of excluded pupils and of those teachers involved in incidents of exclusion.

These suggestions, a few of which mirror those made by the Social Exclusion Unit's report (above), have now received some financial backing. The government recently announced a drive to increase the educational achievements of ethnic minority pupils with £430 million being allocated over the next three years. The majority of the money will allow head teachers to focus on improvements within their own schools, with an emphasis upon establishing links with the local community, as well as recruitment of more teachers and assistants, to help raise levels of attainment (DFEE press release 527/98; Secretary of State for Social Security 1999: 53). The government says it will also be examining ways in which the teaching profession can best meet the needs of ethnic minority pupils and to ensure that the national curriculum addresses the needs of a multicultural and diverse society (DFEE press release 10/99).

The revised DFEE guidance (DFEE 1999d) contains recommendations on specific strategies in relation to exclusion among ethnic minorities. It calls on schools to 'monitor the use of sanctions against pupils of ethnic minority background and reassure themselves that the school's behaviour policy against racial prejudice and harassment is being fully enforced' (para. 3.6). More broadly, it emphasizes the need to address under-achievement, for example through the development of a black perspective in the school curriculum (para. 3.7). The government says it is also instituting a proper reporting system in respect of racist incidents in schools, in the light of the Macpherson (1999) report (Secretary of State for Social Security 1999: 53).

Policies in the field of special educational needs are also aimed partly at reducing school exclusion. *Excellence in Schools* (DFEE 1997a) advocated better links between schools and outside welfare agencies, such as social services, and the need to take into consideration the socio-economic factors which may be linked to a child's problems. Established through the recommendations of the White Paper was a National Advisory Group on Special Educational Needs, which produced a consultation paper (*Meeting Special Educational Needs* (1998)). This was followed by an action report by the DFEE, which highlights the need to involve children with special educational needs in inclusive education. The DFEE believes that by including more children with SEN in mainstream schooling social exclusion will be reduced, although it recognizes that support will be needed and that placement in a mainstream setting will not be possible in every case. A revised code of practice on SEN is currently in preparation and is expected to address the issue of behaviour and exclusion.

Turning to the issue of gender, the educational under-attainment of boys has become a subject of concern and, as we have also seen, over 80 per cent of children permanently excluded from school are males. The possible reasons for the over-representation of males in the exclusion statistics were referred to in Chapter 1. While there have been a number of initiatives designed to improve the educational opportunities of girls (for example, the introduction of a national curriculum, with compulsory science and mathematics to age 16, which was expected to help to overcome gender stereotyping), today it is the alienation of young males that is now regarded, by some, as perhaps the most serious problem (see Delamont 1999). *Excellence in Schools* (DFEE 1997a: Chapter 6) suggested that boys aged between 14 and 16 years of age should be encouraged to become involved in work-related learning. The idea that lies behind this is that by the age of 14 boys who have become disaffected with regard to school need a new form of motivation towards the learning environment; one way of achieving this is through involvement of FE colleges and via links between education providers and with local businesses and community organizations. The aim is to bridge the gap between boys' and girls' attainments by the age of 16. The SSFA 1998[9] makes provision for work experience for pupils at Key Stage 4 (ages 14–16), which could be on an extended basis. The DFEE's revised guidance on exclusions does not, however, adopt a gendered perspective. Males *per se* are not included in the groups identified as being at particular risk of exclusion and requiring a specific strategy.

The revised guidance does, however, note the particular problem of 'looked after children' (basically, those in local authority care), who, as we have seen, are also over-represented in the exclusion statistics. It calls for better liaison between social services and schools, so that the latter can be fully aware of the child's domestic and other social circumstances. The government has announced targets for improved educational attainment among children in care (DFEE 1999d: para. 3.4).

Conclusion

School exclusion is a major problem affecting not only particular social groups in which it is common but also society as a whole. It has become closely associated with the wider problem of social exclusion and, not surprisingly therefore, solutions are sought through a holistic strategy aimed at a range of social problems, involving voluntary and private sectors as well as the public sector. The education system cannot solve all the problems associated with the social exclusion of young people; but it can play a pivotal role. Various educational strategies, some of which are specific to particular social groups, are now being implemented with a view to achieving a reduction in school exclusion, which is linked to under-achievement and a range of social problems. Furthermore, the involvement of parents and the family in helping to ensure better school attendance and behaviour is a recurrent theme throughout almost all of the educational policy initiatives in recent years and is stressed in the revised DFEE guidance on school exclusion (DFEE 1999a: para. 2.1).

These various strategies may or may not be successful, but even if they are, no-one expects exclusion from school to be eliminated. There was only a very slight fall in the permanent exclusion rate in 1997/98 and at the present rate of decline it would take many years to get back to the levels of the early 1990s. In 1999 the government believed, however, that a reduction in exclusions by one-third by 2002 was a realistic target (as noted in Chapter 3). Either way, provision will continue to be needed for children who have been excluded and here there is room for considerable improvement, as we have seen. The emphasis now being placed on a multi-agency approach to supporting children who have been excluded from school, and on early reintegration, at least gives some limited cause for optimism.

5 School Exclusion

The Legal Framework

Introduction

In Chapter 3 we saw that the power of exclusion from school is part of the disciplinary framework under statute and the Secretary of State's guidance. The overall emphasis within this framework is on the maintenance of good standards of behaviour and indeed on the prevention of misbehaviour and disruption likely to necessitate the most serious sanction of all – permanent exclusion from school. In this chapter we examine the present law on school exclusion, under the School Standards and Framework Act 1998, and its evolution. The chapter focuses on the decision to exclude and the procedural steps which must be followed immediately after the decision has been taken. We explain the current legal limits to the power of exclusion, charting their development and considering their rationale. We also consider the DFEE's revised guidance, issued in July 1999, on the circumstances in which a head teacher should or should not exclude a child. We also look at the process of investigation leading up an exclusion, or the making permanent a fixed-term period of exclusion. Throughout, the discussion is informed by developments in the courts, from which has come important judicial guidance. What is so significant about this area of the law is how new so much of it is – the power of exclusion was more or less completely unregulated prior to 1986 but there is now an elaborate and continually evolving legal framework – and how rarely it was the subject of litigation prior to the 1990s, when the exclusion rate was much lower.

There is often a legal adviser to the appeal panel at an exclusion appeal hearing. Moreover, the revised DFEE guidance (DFEE 1999a: Annex D, paras 20 and 31) recommends that ideally the clerk should have 'some legal training' and that where possible the chair should have 'a legal background'. Even so, it is important that all members of appeal panels have some understanding of the law on exclusion. Indeed, in our survey of panel members, 62 per cent regarded knowledge of the law as important or fairly important to their role, and a further 19 per cent thought it was extremely important. Only 19 per cent considered such knowledge to be unimportant. Unfortunately, the law has become increasingly complex, particularly in view of the case law that must also be considered.

The Power to Exclude

The discussion here is confined to state sector schools. Independent schools are not covered by the statutory power of exclusion. Although the common law basis to the teacher's disciplinary authority is equally applicable to both sectors, there is a contractual basis to the power of exclusion in the independent sector. As noted in Chapter 2, a parent could bring an action for breach of contract against the proprietor of an independent school where he or she alleges that a child's exclusion is unjustifiable.

Evolution of the Law on Exclusion

Prior to the Education (No. 2) Act 1986 the power of exclusion in the state sector derived from the disciplinary authority of teachers at common law, based on the *in loco parentis* principle – the teacher was 'in the place of a parent' and could therefore exert discipline over the child by implied or express delegation of parental authority.[1] The teacher's disciplinary authority was held to extend to acts occurring outside school, for example where a pupil fought or misbehaved on the way to or from school;[2] it continues to do so, as was underlined in a recent case arising from a child's exclusion following his alleged brandishing of a knife at a bus stop after school,[3] and by Brooke J's comment in a 1994 judgment that 'it would be a very sad thing if head teachers did not have authority, in an appropriate case, to use disciplinary action in relation to the behaviour of pupils of the school towards each other off the school premises'.[4]

The Elton Committee (1989) recommended that the teacher's disciplinary authority should be put into statutory form to remove any doubt about whether it was of sufficient legal force to prevent a teacher from being liable in respect of particular forms of action. Detention was specifically mentioned, but exclusion was not. Unjustifiable exclusion had already been held, over half a century earlier, not to give rise to liability under the law of tort:

> the question for me is what is an appropriate judgment, having regard to the jury's finding that the defendant did not act upon reasonable grounds in expelling the plaintiff, bearing in mind that they awarded a farthing damages. … It was said that the mere fact that the defendants in the circumstances refused to continue the girl's education involved a tort giving rise to a claim for damages on her part, but I do not think that any such claim is sustainable in law.[5]

Nevertheless, if an exclusion decision was unlawful for the purposes of public law the decision could, and still can, be overturned by an appeal panel or quashed by a court (see Chapter 2). The question of what would make an exclusion unlawful in this way is discussed below.

In the same year as the Elton Report came the Children Act 1989, the relevant provisions of which were implemented in 1991. The Act authorizes those with 'parental responsibility' for a child to arrange for others to carry it out on their behalf.[6] As it is accepted that parental authority includes disciplinary authority, within the limits imposed by the criminal law[7] or international human rights law,[8] it is arguable that merely by sending a child to school the parent is arranging for teachers to exercise such authority on their behalf. But in any event anyone who is caring for a child may, under that Act, 'do what is reasonable in all the circumstances of the case for the purpose of safeguarding or promoting the child's welfare'.[9] As one of us has argued elsewhere, the sum total of this is that teachers would have disciplinary authority *per se* by virtue of the 1989 Act (Harris 1995: 313). Leaving aside this statutory basis for disciplinary authority, the Elton Committee in any event thought that teachers continued to enjoy their traditional authority at common law simply by virtue of their professional status. The position in the United States is very similar: teachers are said to have 'inherent authority' over pupils in their role as educators (Lawrence 1998: 144).

The Education (No. 2) Act 1986 (Section 22(f)) was the first to confer a statutory authority to exclude. The power extended to all forms of exclusion and seemed to reside exclusively with the head teacher:

> The articles of government for every county, voluntary and maintained special school shall provide …
>
> for the power to exclude a pupil from the school (whether by suspension, expulsion or otherwise) to be exercisable only by the head teacher.

This power was subsequently incorporated into the Education Act 1996 (section 156) and is now found (without the references to articles of government, which have been abolished) in section 64 of the SSFA 1998, although it is now expressed somewhat differently (see below).

Until the Education Act 1993 three types of exclusion were used by schools: indefinite, fixed term and permanent. The Education (No. 2) Act 1986 acknowledged their use by specifying distinct procedural requirements in respect of each of them.[10] The first two types were commonly referred to as 'suspension' although this term was not used in the legislation. The most commonly imposed form of exclusion in practice was fixed term. In a survey by HMI conducted in 10 LEA areas between 1990 and 1992 it was found that 75 per cent of school exclusions were fixed term and were usually for two to three days (OFSTED 1993a: para. 6). The survey did not report on the use made of the power to exclude for an indefinite period – indeed there was no requirement for the school to notify the LEA of an indefinite exclusion unless it would mean that the child would be excluded for more than five days in aggregate in a school term or would miss an opportunity to take a public examination.[11] Nevertheless, there was evidence that this power was widely used and there was some concern about the uncertainty this form of exclusion caused for the child and his or her family, particularly as LEAs were often slow to make provision for the child when a return to school was likely. Back in the 1970s the Taylor report on school government had recommended that no suspensions from school should be for an indefinite period (it proposed that they should be for a fixed term of no more than three days) (Taylor 1977). A survey undertaken by Manchester LEA in 1982 showed that in one year 32 pupils in its schools had been on prolonged suspension, meaning suspension that lasted for longer than 80 days (Bayliss 1982). In 1993 OFSTED also recommended the abolition of the power of indefinite exclusion (OFSTED 1993b: 1) and this change was effected by the Education Act 1993, from 1 September 1994, subject to transitional arrangements which enabled those indefinitely excluded at that date to remain excluded until the end of September 1994 at the latest.[12] The minister referred in the House of Lords to the concerns which had been expressed 'about the scope for abuse that the category offers and the uncertain position in which it leaves both the child and the parents. In some cases, children of compulsory school age were ending up in what might best be described as an educational limbo.'[13]

The 1993 Act also restricted the power of fixed-term exclusion by providing that a pupil could not be excluded for one or more fixed periods if in aggregate exclusion totalled more 15 school days in any school term.[14] It has since been estimated by OFSTED that annually there were 100,000 fixed-term exclusions of between 5 and 15 days in aggregate per term (Social Exclusion Unit 1998: para. 2.2). As a further disincentive to exclude from school the 1993 Act provided that where a pupil was permanently excluded the funding the school received in respect of that pupil (as the appropriately weighted proportion of the school's budget share under local management of schools or in other cases the appropriate amount under regulations) should be transferred away from the school as from the exclusion date[15]. The school receiving the child following his or her exclusion would also receive the funding for that child. Thus arrangements had been made 'for the money to follow the child'.

There was increasing evidence that some schools had been over-willing to use the power of exclusion. The total number of exclusions rose from 2,910 in 1990–91 to 3,833 in 1991–92 (DFE 1992; Parsons 1996a), well below the levels of the past few years (see Chapter 1) but a sufficiently steep rise to intensify concern. Moreover, it was also clear that rates of exclusion from individual schools varied widely and that (as we have noted in earlier chapters) black children were significantly over-represented in the exclusion statistics (OFSTED 1993a). The government introduced guidance on exclusions in Circular 10/94 (DFE 1994b), part of a series of guidance on 'pupils with problems',[16] to reinforce the message from the legislation that while schools needed to have the ultimate sanction of exclusion for cases where there was no alternative to its use, there was a need to encourage restraint in exercising this power and for schools to reflect carefully on the kinds of circumstances in which exclusion was justified. The circular said (para. 5):

> There is evidence that exclusion rates differ considerably between schools, even where the pupil population is of a similar socio-economic background.[17] Some broad guidance might help to produce consistency in this difficult area. The Secretary of State believes that it should be clear in each case of permanent exclusion that:
>
> - it is a last resort: the school has take all reasonable steps to avoid excluding the child; and
> - allowing the child to remain in school would be seriously detrimental to the education or welfare of the pupil, or to that of others at the school.

The circular advised on the 'reasonable steps' that schools should take before excluding a child – such as interviewing pupils and parents and in some cases negotiating agreements with them (such as behaviour 'contracts'); identifying any special educational needs the child may have; and issuing formal warnings. It also outlined the factors that should be considered in any decision to exclude a child. These included the child's age and state of health; his or her record at the school; any unique or special circumstances, such as domestic problems; the extent to which parental, peer or other pressure might have contributed to the child's behaviour; the severity of the child's misbehaviour and the likelihood of it recurring; the extent to which the behaviour would affect the normal functioning of the pupil or other pupils; and whether the pupil was the perpetrator or part of group, because there was a need to avoid 'using one pupil as a scapegoat' (para. 21). The Circular also drew attention to the need to be sensitive to children whose problems might be the result of a special educational need and, in the case of pupils from ethnic minority groups, to 'take particular care to ensure that they apply disciplinary procedures objectively and consistently across all cultural groups' (para. 32). The Circular reminded head teachers that a failure to do so could constitute a breach of the Race Relations Act 1976.[18] In *Mandla v Dowell Lee*[19] the House of Lords held that a refusal to admit a Sikh child wearing a turban to school constituted unjustifiable and unlawful race discrimination contrary to the Act. The Circular warned that exclusion was 'not an appropriate response to pupils who cannot comply with uniform or dress regulations for cultural or religious reasons' (para. 26). It advised schools to adopt a flexible response to the needs of some minority groups as regards school uniform (e.g. girls wearing modest dress for cultural/religious reasons).

Before Circular 10/94 there had been very little to guide schools on the use of the power of exclusion. There was a general legal principle that the punishment of pupils had to be 'reasonable' in the circumstances, moderate in its severity and not intemperate in its administration, laid down by the Chief Justice Cockburn in *R v Hopley* (1860).[20] Furthermore, the Schools Regulations 1959 provided that a pupil should not be refused admission to or excluded from school on 'other than reasonable grounds'. In many ways the 1994 Circular was placing and elaborating these principles in a modern context. While circulars of this kind are not legally binding – and until the SSFA 1998 there was no statutory obligation to have regard to the guidance on exclusions – it was clear that a head teacher, governing body or appeal panel failing to follow the guidance in Circular 10/94 could find it more difficult to justify the reasonableness of their action if it was called into question before a court. In *R v London Borough of Camden and the Governors of Hampstead School ex parte H*[21] the Court of Appeal gave considerable attention to Circular 10/94 in reviewing the lawfulness of a decision by a committee of the governing body to reinstate two pupils responsible for firing an air pistol, which was discharged and inadvertently injured another pupil. In several places the guidance referred to the need to consider the interests of the misbehaving pupil and those of others at the school (as in the extract from para. 5 cited above). The court agreed that the legislation and the guidance indicated that the situation of the victim was not the main concern of the disciplinary procedures, but considered that 'where, as here, there was a child victim the overall case did require some serious investigation of the effect that the proposed setting aside of the head's decision would have on the injured boy'.[22] The court held that the committee had not properly considered the impact of the reinstatement of the two pupils on the victim and thus on the school as a whole.

In the *Northamptonshire* case, decided in 1997,[23] the court was reviewing the decision of an appeal panel not to reinstate a permanently excluded pupil aged 7. It was argued that the panel had failed to have regard to the guidance in Circular 10/94 and that accordingly the decision was unlawful. The court rejected the argument by counsel for the LEA that the panel had not been obliged as a matter of law to have regard to the guidance. The court proceeded on the same basis as Kennedy L.J. in the *Camden* case (above), that the guidance was a 'highly material consideration in the decision-making process'.[24] The question for the court was therefore whether, on the facts of the case, 'the decision was taken without having regard to any relevant part of Circular 10/94. It is in my judgment plain that it was not so taken.'[25]

Unfortunately, the 1994 guidance did not have the desired effect in restraining the use made of the power of exclusion, especially permanent exclusion which, as we saw in Chapter 1, continued its steady rise. As shown in Table 1.1, the annual total of those permanently excluded from schools in England rose by 1,500 between 1994/95 and 1996/97. It was clear that the various forces (which have been discussed elsewhere in this book), such as market pressures, that were driving up this number were having a continuing effect and were not being checked by the guidance or legislative measures. It is in fact possible that the Education Act 1993 (above) had actually contributed to the increased use made of the power of permanent exclusion by taking away or reducing powers in relation to some of the less severe forms of exclusion: as we saw above, indefinite exclusion was prohibited and fixed-term exclusion limited to 15 school days in aggregate per term. Indeed, this was recognized by the government when it introduced an amendment to the limit on fixed-term exclusion via the Education Act 1997. The new limit became '45 school days in any one school year'.[26] There was no termly limit as such. The minister explained that the purpose behind this change, which took effect from 1 September 1998,[27] was to help to provide more scope 'to set in motion effective action to tackle a pupil's problems before he or she returns to school' but at the same time to 'help to avoid the need for permanent exclusion in some cases'.[28] A further reform designed in part to reduce the number of exclusions (and the periods for which excluded pupils were out of school) was the introduction of a duty on LEAs to prepare behaviour support plans. From 1 April 1998 LEAs were required to prepare, review and publish a statement of the arrangements they had made in connection with the education of children with behavioural difficulties. These arrangements included assistance for schools in dealing with behavioural problems of individual pupils.[29]

The 1997 Act also imposed a specific duty on exclusion appeal panels to having regard 'to both the interests of [the excluded] pupil and the interests of other pupils at his school and members of its staff'.[30] This reflected the guidance given by the court in the *Camden* case above. Appeal panels would also have to take account of the disciplinary measures (school rules etc.) publicized by the head teacher as specifically required under the 1996 Act, as amended.[31] This change reflected another judgment,[32] when the court in effect confirmed that the reasonableness of an exclusion could be judged partly with reference to the strictness of the disciplinary regime within the school: in this case, it justified the failure to reinstate a pupil whose permenent exclusion was based on a failure to apologize after he swore in school in the presence of, but not directly at, a teacher. Although neither of these new criteria were expressly imposed on head teachers or governors considering reinstatement, those who did not follow them ran the risk of having their decision overturned on appeal. This duty did not apply if the appeal panel decided that the pupil in question was 'not guilty of the conduct which the head teacher relied on as grounds for his permanent exclusion'.[33] Leaving aside the use of the word 'guilty', which no doubt reinforced the perception of some panel members as well as some parents and children that the proceedings are quasi-criminal in nature (see Chapter 9), this exception in effect meant that the appeal panel would have to engage in a two-stage process in determining the appeal. They would first have to determine whether the child was responsible for the behaviour which resulted in the exclusion; and, second, they would have to consider the reasonableness of the decision in the light of the circumstances (on which the circular provided guidance). The two-stage process reflected the guidance in the Code of Practice on appeals (Association of County Councils 1994: para. 13(e)).

The Power to Exclude Under the School Standards and Framework Act 1998

The law on exclusions is now contained in the SSFA 1998. There has been no change of substance to the power of exclusion, in terms of the power being restricted to permanent exclusion or to exclusion for no more than 45 school days in any one school year. However, as noted above there has been a change in the way that the restriction of the power of exclusion to the head teacher has been expressed. The power is now expressed thus (in section 64):

> (1) The head teacher of a maintained school may exclude a pupil from the school for a fixed period or permanently …
> (3) A pupil may not be excluded from a maintained school (whether by suspension, expulsion or otherwise) except by the head teacher in accordance with this section.

It remains a moot point whether the power to exclude may be expressly or implicitly delegated to a deputy head teacher or other teacher. In a recent case the judge, Mr Nigel Pleming QC, referring to the role of the head teacher in the exclusion process, said 'it is his [the head teacher's] decision and only his decision which can result in exclusion'.[34] Nevertheless, the power of exclusion is, arguably, delegable. The standard terms of employment of deputy head teachers, as laid down for many years in the various editions of the *School Teachers' Pay and Conditions Document*, include the undertaking of 'any professional duties of the head teacher delegated to him by the head teacher'. Moreover, the *Document* also provides that a deputy can be authorized to carry out any of the head teacher's duties 'in the event of the head's absence from school'. On the face of it, this would seem to enable the head teacher to delegate disciplinary functions – including the powers needed for their effective performance. On that basis, if a head teacher was going to be away from school for a couple of days and the deputy head would be *de facto* in charge, one would expect the deputy to be able to exclude a pupil in an emergency situation. He or she might be able to do so in any event as agent for the governing body where a pupil, by his behaviour, has revoked his or her implied licence to be on the premises. But the apparent restriction laid down in section 64 of the 1998 Act raises a question mark over such a view. McManus (1998: 107) argues that the School Teacher's Pay and Conditions Act 1991, under which the regulations imposing the *Document* are made, could not have been intended by Parliament to authorize the delegation of a power which the 1996 Act (now replicated in the 1998 Act) expressly restricted to the head teacher. In our view, however, the general purpose and tenor of the provisions on delegation included in the *Document*, and the subtle shift in emphasis resulting from the change in the wording of the statutory power of exclusion itself (which no longer uses the word 'only'), all point to the deputy head teacher having the power to exclude in the absence of the head teacher. In our view the advice in DFE Circular 10/94 that the power to exclude could be exercised by the deputy head teacher 'exceptionally … in the head teacher's absence' (DFE 1994b: para. 14) would certainly be sound if still in force. However, the recently published replacement circular (DFEE 1999a: para. 6.2) goes further by providing that in the absence of the head teacher the power may be exercised by 'the most senior teacher who should make it clear that they are acting in the head's absence'. No authority is stated in support of that contention. However, the 1998 Act lays down a requirement that 'any person or body' exercising the 'functions of the head teacher' is, in discharging those functions, to have regard to the guidance given by the Secretary of State.[35] Provided the *Document* authorizes the senior teacher concerned to exercise functions of the head teacher the advice would appear to be accurate.

What is also new is a definition of 'exclude'. The Act states that it means 'in relation to the exclusion of a child from a school … exclude on disciplinary grounds (and "exclusion" shall be construed accordingly)'.[36] The most important change, however, is the requirement (under section 68) noted above for head teachers and governing bodies (and appeal bodies) to have regard to the guidance issued from time to time by the Secretary of State when exercising any of the disciplinary functions specified under the Act, including the power of exclusion. The Social Exclusion Unit had proposed that the guidance on school exclusions should have statutory force (Social Exclusion Unit 1998: 29). Among other things, the new guidance incorporates (DFEE 1999a: Annex D, para. 35) the two-stage test for appeal panels referred to above. We discuss this test further in Chapter 9.

The guidance also covers in some detail measures that can be taken to handle signs of disaffection at school. In the case of pupils who do not respond to these measures, a 'pastoral support programme' would be necessary, with external agency involvement. A decision to exclude, the guidance advises, should only be taken (para. 6.2.):

- 'in response to serious breaches of the school's discipline policy'
- 'once a range of alternative strategies have been tried and have failed'
- and 'if allowing the pupil to remain in school would seriously harm the education or welfare of the pupil or other pupils'.

The first of these reinforces the principle of proportionality – that the punishment should be proportionate to the wrong committed. The second criterion continues the principle expressed in the previous circular that exclusion should be a matter of 'last resort'. The idea that the school has tried a range of strategies (of which the guidance itself offers numerous examples) before deciding to exclude could well come into consideration when the matter comes before the appeal panel. In *R v Solihull Borough Council ex parte W* one of the contentions of the applicant was that neither the head teacher nor the appeal panel who upheld the exclusion examined sufficiently the methods short of exclusion that could have been adopted by the school to deal with the applicant in the particular circumstances. Latham J rejected this argument: both had 'had well in mind that exclusion was a measure of last resort' and the court felt that decision to exclude was a rational one.[37] Latham J also concluded that it was not necessary for a head teacher or appeal panel, when required to demonstrate that exclusion was ordered as a last resort, 'to set out each and every option that could have been open to them, short of the exclusion, to reject it and give reasons for such a rejection'.[38]

Turning to the third of the above criteria, the requirement for appeal panels to have regard to these matters has been dropped from the legislation itself but by virtue of the guidance they are still factors which must be taken into account.[39] Nevertheless, there is no mention here (despite a reference in the previous version of the statute, as amended by the 1997 Act) to the need to have regard to the interests of the staff at the school.

The guidance is fairly dogmatic that exclusion should not be used as a response to particular problems, namely (para. 6.4.):

- 'minor incidents such as failure to do homework or to bring dinner money'
- 'poor academic performance'
- 'lateness or truancy'
- 'pregnancy'
- 'breaching school uniform policy including hairstyle or wearing jewellery'
- 'the behaviour of parents, for example, by extending a fixed period exclusion until the parents agree to attend a meeting ...'

The last of these seems to negate the effect of a court ruling in 1995[40] when the court held that the mother's defiant behaviour at the school, refusing to sign an agreement with the school following her child's suspension from school the previous term and, when visiting the school, helping physically to thrust her child into the classroom, were relevant matters in determining whether a fixed-term exclusion should be made permanent.

The guidance establishes a number of other principles. These can be summarized as follows:

- 'Permanent exclusion is not normally to be administered for a one-off or first offence'.
- Specific steps must be taken by a head teacher who is considering excluding a pupil for a single block of more than 15 school days in a term, including a plan to enable the pupil to continue his or her education and to assist the LEA in planning appropriate educational arrangements for the reintegration of the pupil following his or her exclusion.
- Fixed-period exclusion might in some cases be more appropriate than permanent exclusion in relation to drugs-related problems.
- Pupils with statements of special educational needs should only be excluded permanently in exceptional circumstances.
- Heads should avoid excluding a pupil with special educational needs part way through the assessment process, as sometimes happens at present.

Overall, the guidance on exclusions (part 6 of the circular as a whole) is perhaps less prescriptive or detailed than might have been expected. For example, it omits a reference to the pupil's previous record at the school or the severity of the behaviour *per se* as factors to be considered. Instead, these matters are subsumed within more general considerations, namely, that alternative strategies have been tried but have failed or the risk of serious harm to pupils if the child is permitted to remain at the school. Much of the guidance in the case law on such issues will nevertheless continue to be relevant. For example Turner J noted in one case, in which a boy was excluded permanently after being involved in deflating a member of staff's car tyre after previous periods of fixed-term exclusion for other acts of misbehaviour, that even without the guidance (in Circular 10/94, from which the judge quoted extensively in his judgment),

> common sense would suggest that if a pupil misbehaves frequently, was often guilty of disruptive behaviour in respect of which he had been frequently disciplined, if the head teacher, the rules of the school and general ethos of the school … were to retain any credibility, although any given incident might not on its own have justified the ultimate sanction, that was the sanction which it was necessary to impose.[41]

This judgment highlights the important principle of proportionality as regards the level of punishment to be imposed. It should be stressed, however, that the courts are in general reluctant to rule specifically on the reasonableness of the degree of punishment in any individual case, provided the decision-taker in question has had regard for the relevant considerations in coming to his or her conclusion. As Brooke J said in a case where a pupil in his GCSE year was excluded for an incident off school premises (in response to insults, the boy had removed another pupil's trousers and possibly his underpants and socks), there was 'a prima facie case that the penalty is disproportionate to the offence, although that must, essentially, be a matter for the school authorities'.[42]

Returning to the revised DFEE guidance, some issues, such as the exclusion of ethnic minority pupils or pregnant schoolgirls, are not dealt with under the specific section on exclusion but are to be found elsewhere (see especially part 3). Particularly important is a reference within the section on the appeal hearing (in Annex D) to the factors that the appeal panel should take into account in assessing whether exclusion was a reasonable response to the pupil's conduct. They include those matters towards which the head teacher's attention is directed (above) but also the matter of proportionality where a number of pupils were involved: 'relevant factors must include … where other pupils were involved in the same incident and were also disciplined, the fairness of the permanent exclusion in relation to the sanctions imposed on the other pupils involved' (para. 35). This reflects a statement by Collins J in a 1998 case in which a 12-year-old pupil (D) at a city technology college was involved in a series of incidents on a bus returning a number of pupils from a school founder's day service. Several pupils were involved in spitting, bad language, insulting behaviour and coin throwing. Collins J gave a clear indication that to be reasonable a decision to exclude must at least take account of what other pupils may have done:

> The problem arises because others involved had not been expelled. Thus, the only basis for expelling D must have been either that his part in it was very much greater than the others (and at the moment I see no real evidence to support that) or that his record was worse than the others. So far as his record is concerned, that is a matter very much in issue. I know nothing of the record of the others who were involved and who were not excluded permanently. All I can say is that if it comes to a rehearing, it seems to me that the governors will have to consider very carefully whether it is appropriate to exclude D permanently having regard to his involvement because one cannot look at punishment in isolation, one must look at it in the context of the others involved. *Otherwise there may be unfairness if one is picked out and others are not.* But subject to that, I do not think there is a basis for a disproportionality argument.[43]

Given the government's apparent determination to reduce the incidence of school exclusion it is perhaps surprising that it did not take the opportunity to restrict the power of exclusion further. It is true that, if acted upon properly, the new guidance could reduce the rate of exclusion, even though previous guidance with this aim does not appear to have been particularly successful. The government clearly felt that other planned changes would, together with the revised guidance, have a dampening or deterrent effect in relation to the power of exclusion. These changes include those being made to the method of calculating performance data in school league tables so that schools will no longer benefit from excluding under-achieving pupils, and the targeting for early inspection under the new LEA inspection regime (introduced under the 1997 Act) those LEAs with a high rate of exclusion (including those whose schools exclude disproportionate numbers of ethnic minority pupils). Those who felt that the government should have amended the legislation and restricted the power of exclusion further included Baroness David. She proposed an amendment to the School Standards and Framework Bill which would have prohibited the exclusion of a child unless 'all reasonable steps have been taken by the school to avoid excluding the pupil' and unless the head teacher was satisfied that allowing the pupil to stay would be 'seriously detrimental to the education or welfare of the pupil, or to that of others at the school'. These criteria, while not accepted for inclusion in the legislation, are, of course, now within the official guidance (above), albeit worded differently. Another amendment she proposed would have restored the previous limit of 15 school days per term for fixed-term exclusion. A further, interesting, proposal was for a power to make regulations requiring head teachers to minimize periods of fixed-term exclusion and to set up meetings with the pupil, the parents and the pupil's teacher, the purpose of which would be to identify the cause of the child's misbehaviour and agree steps to prevent its recurrence. Given the way that permanent exclusion is often preceded by a period or periods of fixed-term exclusion, such a meeting could well help to prevent a worsening of the child's problems.

Investigation of the Circumstances

The guidance is clear that a head teacher must not issue a decision to exclude 'in the heat of the moment' but only after taking various steps (DFEE 1999a: para. 6.3) The head teacher should check whether the incident appeared to be provoked by racist or sexual harassment. He or she is further advised to consult with appropriate persons where relevant, avoiding anyone who might play a part in the review process later on, such as a member of the governors' discipline committee. It is also important that the head teacher considers all the relevant facts and firm evidence relating to the incident or behaviour, taking into account the school's policy on equal opportunities. If there is doubt about whether the pupil was responsible for the alleged conduct, the head teacher should not exclude. This does not, however, lay down a clear standard of proof in terms of the degree of doubt that the head teacher would need to have before he should decide not to exclude the child. The guidance advises that the pupil should be permitted to give his or her version of the events, although it is not explained how and in whose presence the questioning should take place. It was suggested by the judge in one recent case[44] that the principles of criminal investigation in the Police and Criminal Evidence Act 1984 do not apply here and that there is no reason why an alleged culprit should not be interviewed on his or her own by the head teacher. However, the judge also emphasized the importance of the pupil concerned being given a proper opportunity to give his or her version of events – to have a chance to 'exculpate himself'.

In a case in Northern Ireland[45] where this did not happen, the court quashed the decision to exclude from school for five days a 13-year-old girl who had been found to have deliberately kicked at a door, breaking a glass panel. The application for judicial review had alleged that it had been unlawful for the head teacher not to have given her an opportunity to express her version of events. The court found the failure to consult the pupil had constituted a breach of natural justice. This issue has also been considered in the United States courts. In *Goss v Lopez*[46] the Supreme Court held that a failure by the school authorities to give a suspended student an opportunity to present his version of events amounted to a denial of due process of law contrary to the Fourteenth Amendment to the US Constitution, which provides that a state may not deprive a person of life, liberty or property without such due process. The court commented that it would be a 'strange disciplinary system in an educational institution if no communication was sought by the disciplinarian with the student in an effort to inform him of his dereliction and to let him tell his side of the story in order to make sure that an injustice is not done'.[47]

If the matter came to appeal, therefore, the appeal panel would need to consider whether the head teacher had taken the advised steps in determining whether the excluded pupil was responsible for the behaviour alleged. The importance of a proper investigation was emphasized by a recent case[48] in which a pupil was injured after an attack at school by a large group of pupils and required hospital treatment. The head teacher conducted an investigation that afternoon and found that a teacher, a lunchtime supervisor and a head of year had each recognized both of the alleged main protagonists. The two teachers had accompanied the supervisor to the school office where she had identified the two attackers from school photographs. The deputy head interviewed one pupil (S) and, following a pupil witness statement, the matter was reported to the police. Meanwhile S was kept at home by her mother. Matters were investigated further by the school. The supervisor confirmed her identification of the two attackers and several pupils identified S and another pupil as culprits. After half term there was further questioning of pupils after which the head teacher decided to exclude S permanently from school. When the matter came before the governing body there were conflicting statements but the governors nevertheless upheld the exclusion. The appeal panel met but adjourned to enable it to see the photographs in question. It was unable to see them, however, as they were still with the police at the time it was decided that there could be no further delay and the appeal should be heard. The appeal panel upheld the decision not to reinstate, placing particular weight on the evidence of the supervisor. S then applied for judicial review, alleging that the procedure leading to the decision to exclude had been flawed and that the head teacher had failed to consider less serious penalties.

The court held that: there should be a proper decision by those conducting the inquiry as to what were the crucial issues of fact to be resolved and how they could be resolved; careful and even-handed consideration must be given to all the evidence; and searching enquiries involving the calling of bodies of oral evidence was not necessary in every case.[49] The court accepted that the governors or appeal panel (and thus the head teacher also) would have to deal with hearsay evidence. But it was not satisfied that there had been a proper investigation of the circumstances in which the identification of the culprits took place. The appeal panel should have taken oral evidence from, and asked questions of, witnesses involved. The court felt that although the head teacher had not spoken to the alleged suspect, this was condonable given the child's absence from school. (As noted above, normally those investigating would need to hear from the alleged culprit, as the guidance advises, and so should the appeal panel.[50] Finally, the court concluded that in view of the gravity of the offence and the previous record of S it was clear that the school and appeal panel did appreciate that permanent exclusion was a matter of last resort and that in the circumstances there was no alternative to permanent exclusion.

Although the current guidance is silent on the point, the courts have recently advised that the head teacher should keep notes of interviews with pupils conducted as part of the investigation of an incident.[51] Indeed, it is advisable that the head teacher keeps a detailed record of the investigation he or she has carried out. Not only will this provide prime facie proof of the evidence on which the decision was based, it will also help him or her to prepare a report on the matter which may assist the governing body's discipline committee or the appeal panel. In one case[52] the court stated a principle that the appeal panel is entitled to rely on the head teacher's report of his or her investigation rather than hearing from the witnesses direct, particularly when, as in the case itself, the hearing was some six months after the alleged incident (although such a delay is somewhat unusual for exclusion appeals). However, this does not relieve the panel of hearing from the child him/herself, as this is a matter of fairness[53] (see further Chapter 9).

Procedural Steps Following the Decision to Exclude

The head teacher is required to take various steps following the decision to exclude. These are now specified in section 65 of the SSFA 1998. There is guidance in Annex D to the DFEE guidance (DFEE 1999a), to which the head teacher must have regard.

'Reasonable steps' must be taken by the head teacher to inform the relevant person (namely the parent or, if aged at least 18, the pupil) of: the period of exclusion or the fact that exclusion is permanent; the reasons for the exclusion; the fact that he or she is entitled to make representations about the exclusion to the governing body (discipline committee); and the means by which such representations may be made (s. 65(1); see Chapter 6). These steps must also be taken if the head teacher has decided that a period of fixed-term exclusion should be made permanent (s. 65(2)). The section requires this information to be communicated 'without delay'. The guidance advises that the parent should be notified 'immediately, ideally by telephone' followed by a letter within one school day. Normally, the exclusion should begin on the next school day (DFEE 1999a: Annex D, para 1). The guidance suggests (ibid. para 2) that the letter informing about exclusion should explain not only why the head teacher decided to exclude but also the steps which were taken to avoid exclusion. It should also inform the parent who to contact about stating their case to the governing body's discipline committee, and the date by which representations should be made, and should contain information on the parent's right (under the Education (School Records) Regulations 1989)[54] to see the child's school record (see Harris 1995: 162–165). Research has shown that parents will need to see their child's school record to avoid being at a disadvantage at hearings, but that they often face a difficulty in gaining access (Cohen et al. 1994: 19).

The guidance recommends that in the case of both permanent and fixed-term exclusions the letter should also explain 'the arrangements for enabling the pupil to continue their education, including setting and marking the pupil's work' (op cit. para 2). This has been a neglected area in the past (as noted in Chapter 4) and this is therefore a welcome piece of advice. In relation to cases of permanent exclusion the guidance seeks to put an onus on the excluding school to continue the child's education. This does not, however, reflect traditional thinking on this matter and is in some ways inconsistent with the onus placed on LEAs to make suitable provision for children excluded from school (see Chapter 4; and see below). Nevertheless, as we saw in Chapter 4 the child should remain on the excluding school's register until the permanent exclusion is confirmed on review by the governors or following the appeal.

Where the exclusion is permanent or made permanent, or the circumstances are such that as a result of the exclusion the pupil would be excluded from the school for a total of more than five school days in any one term or would lose an opportunity to take a public examination, the head teacher must inform the LEA and the governing body (or its discipline committee) of the exclusion, the reasons for it and the length or permanency of the exclusion (SSFA 1998, section 65(3)–(4)). The guidance says that the information should include the child's gender, ethnicity and special educational needs status and should indicate whether the child is in the care of the local authority. This is clearly aimed at facilitating the monitoring process but it also perhaps puts the LEA on notice of possible support needs. The guidance further advises that fixed-term periods of exclusion of between one to five days should normally be reported on a termly basis.

As noted above, once the child is excluded from school the LEA has a duty under section 19 of the Education Act 1996 to make arrangements for provision of suitable full-time or part-time education. As we saw in Chapter 4, LEAs have not always complied fully with this requirement. The guidance (DFEE 1999a: Chapter 7) stresses the importance of ensuring that wherever possible the child is reintegrated into mainstream schooling at the earliest opportunity. Separate guidance directed at LEAs (DFEE 1999b: Chapter 5) specifies steps that should be taken following a permanent exclusion for the child's needs to be assessed, initially on an interim basis if necessary. In particular, it states (as noted in Chapter 4) that LEAs should bring the matter before a 're-integration' panel,[55] although the matter could be dealt with by an officer instead. An individual 're-integration plan' should be drawn up, taking into account the 'context and culture of the pupil'. LEAs should involve parents in the process of reintegration, including the selection of a particular school for the child. Ultimately, as noted in Chapter 4, LEAs have a power to direct a school (but not a school from which the child has been excluded) to admit a child who has been excluded from school.[56]

The guidance implies that the duty on the LEA to make arrangements for the child's education only applies once the child has been excluded for 15 days (DFEE 1999b: para. 5.1). The assumption seems to be that until this point the child would be the responsibility of the excluding school. The logic for this is that the governing body or its discipline committee has between 6 and 15 days from the date of receiving notice of exclusion from the head teacher in which to convene the meeting to consider the exclusion, if it is an exclusion of over 15 school days (DFEE 1999a: Annex D, para. 9). More time (up to 30 days) is permitted for exclusions of between 6 and 15 days in a school term (ibid.). The meeting is discussed more fully in Chapter 6.

Conclusion

The power of exclusion from school has been subjected to increasing regulation since 1986 and the law has thus become considerably more complex. As we have seen, the courts have paid close regard to the DFEE's guidance on exclusion and have held that it should be taken into account, and there is now in any event a specific statutory duty on head teachers, governors and appeal panels to have regard to it. The revised guidance itself has incorporated many of the principles established in the courts over the past five years, but those exercising the power of exclusion will have to be aware of further case law developments, some of which will doubtless turn on human rights issues under the Human Rights Act 1998 (as noted in Chapter 1).

As a matter of general principle the courts are reluctant to interfere with essentially educational matters, such as the merits of decisions to exclude. As Coghlin J said in a 1997 exclusion case: 'I remain extremely sceptical of any suggestion that the day to day exercise of disciplinary powers by a professional teacher should be subject to the unwieldy and time consuming supervision of the law.'[57] Nevertheless, in practice there are important legal constraints and the courts will continue to be asked for guidance as to their application. Head teachers, governors and LEAs will need to be particularly careful to follow the various procedural requirements. Even if the exclusion itself was on the face of it a reasonable response to the misbehaviour, a failure to follow the correct procedure can result in an unfairness which would justify intervention by a court.

From the perspective of an appeal panel, it can readily be seen that the task of applying the law correctly in judgeing the fairness of a head teacher's decision to exclude, on the evidence, is now a far more difficult matter than it was when the appeal system was first established under the Education (No. 2) Act 1986. It is noted in Chapter 7 that the revised guidance recommends that persons with legal qualifications should be sought by LEAs to chair appeal panels and that the clerk to the panel should ideally have some legal training. Given that there is no strict requirement for there to be lawyer chairs for these panels, this advice is clearly highly appropriate. It must, however, be borne in mind that nearly 90 per cent of cases of permanent exclusion do not come before appeal panels. Moreover, fixed-term exclusions are not within panels' jurisdiction. Very many exclusion decisions, based on complex legal requirements, will therefore be taken by laypersons and without expert legal scrutiny.

6 The Governing Body's (Discipline Committee's) Reinstatement Meeting

Introduction

This chapter examines the role of governing bodies in considering whether an excluded child should be reinstated at school. The SSFA 1998 requires the governing body to consider the circumstances in which the child was permanently excluded (including where a fixed-term exclusion is made permanent), or excluded for a fixed term of more than five days in any one term or for a fixed term which would mean that he or she loses the opportunity to take a public examination.[1] Various parties, including the parents, may attend a meeting and/or make representations to the governing body (see below). The revised guidance (DFEE 1999a) recommends, and the legislation now requires there to be a pupil discipline committee comprising three or five governors (excluding the head teacher), with a clerk.[2] References to the governors or governing body in this chapter may be taken to refer also to the discipline committee, unless the context suggests otherwise. The governors must also consider representations concerning exclusion for a fixed term of five days or less, but there is no duty for a meeting with parents in such cases.

This is a crucial stage in the process of review of exclusion decisions, not only because the outcome of the governors' deliberations will determine the necessity for an appeal to an appeal panel, in a case of permanent exclusion, but also, as we shall see, because the experience of the reinstatement meeting of the governing body may influence parents' perceptions about the value of making an appeal. It would appear, from our evidence, that the majority of parents *do not* exercise their right to make representations to the governing body and that, despite the statement in the previous guidance (DFE 1994b: para. 58) that the governors' role is 'by no means a "rubber-stamping" exercise', those parents who do are highly unlikely to be successful in having the head teacher's decision overturned. Inevitably, this raises questions about whether the governors' lack of independence in the matter prejudices their fair disposal of a case.

In this chapter the results of the Liverpool John Moores University (JMU) research are supplemented by the findings of a separate study conducted at the University of Leeds. Both pieces of research included an investigation of perceptions surrounding the reinstatement process at governing body level. The JMU research data for this chapter have been collated from responses to postal questionnaires from head teachers, governors and parents of permanently excluded children. The Leeds research questioned (via questionnaire) head teachers and LEAs about their perceptions of governing body meetings to review exclusion decisions.[3]

Background

The meeting convened by the governing body to consider reinstatement is open to the parent (or the pupil if aged 18 or over) and the LEA. Each may make oral representations to the governors, but the governors must also consider any written representations.[4] If the governors, after consideration of the evidence, believe the head teacher to be unjustified in his or her decision to exclude, they must direct the school to reinstate the child where practical and determine whether the reinstatement should occur immediately or by a particular date. The parent and LEA must also be informed of the decision, and the 1998 Act now requires that in cases of permanent exclusion the governors must provide in writing reasons for their decision and information about the right of appeal, including the fact that the notice of appeal should state the grounds of appeal and an indication of the last date on which an appeal may be brought.[5]

The Education (Exclusion from School) (Prescribed Periods) Regulations 1999 (SI 1999 No. 1868) require the meeting to be convened:

- within 6 to 30 school days, if the exclusion is fixed term for less than 15 school days in a term; or
- within 6 to 15 school days, if the exclusion is permanent or for more than 15 days;
- if practicable, sooner, where the pupil would miss a public examination while excluded.

The guidance says that the minimum period is necessary as a 'cooling off period' and to allow the parent and LEA time to prepare their case. It also says that the parent may be accompanied by a 'friend or legal representative' at the meeting. Curiously, there is no reference to *lay* representation. The child may attend the meeting and present their case if this is what the parent and child want: 'But the parent remains the appellant unless the pupil is over 18'. The use of the word 'appellant' is also slightly odd, given that the right to make representations to the governors at this stage is not generally thought of as an appeal as such.

The guidance says that in deciding whether to reinstate the pupil the governors should consider the parent's and the LEA's statements. They will also, of course, have a statement from the head teacher of the reasons for the exclusion. The governors are also directed towards the question whether: the head teacher followed the guidance itself on the appropriateness of exclusion; attempts were made to improve the child's behaviour; and alternative strategies to exclusion, such as the 'pastoral support programme', outlined in the guidance (see DFEE 1999a: parts 4 and 5), were attempted but have not succeeded. They are also advised to consider whether any other strategies might even now be used. There is very little guidance about the conduct of the meeting itself.

In theory, the governors should be able to provide a relatively speedy and effective review of the merits of an exclusion decision. However, the effectiveness of this review hinges on the governing body's ability to act independently of the head teacher and not slavishly follow his or her view of the case. Here public law questions step into the frame, in particular that of acting fairly and taking proper account of all relevant considerations. Indeed, it is critically important that the principles of natural justice should be applied, and in particular that each side has an adequate opportunity to present their case and to have it properly taken into consideration by the governors. In one case where there was a failure to give a parent an opportunity to attend a meeting with the governing body in respect of a fixed-term exclusion of 15 days, thus denying her a chance to present her side of the case, there was held to be a breach of the legislation and guidance and a clear unfairness.[6] Natural justice was also denied in another case where the governing body had an 'exclusion panel' to consider reinstatement. Potts J held that there had been potential bias, in that membership of the panel included a teacher governor who was also the head of year of the pupil excluded and therefore had too close a connection with the child. Potts J also emphasized that 'The exclusion panel was not performing an administrative function. It was performing a quasi-judicial function.'[7] This reinforces the need for the governors to act fairly in their review function and possibly brings into play the requirements of Article 6(1) of the European Convention on Human Rights (shortly to be, in effect, incorporated into English law via the Human Rights Act 1998): 'In the determination of his civil rights ... everyone is entitled to a fair ... hearing'. The research studies assessed conformity to these principles and also examined the question whether the governors' review was tending to uphold the rights of the child and his or her parent.

This quasi-judicial role might be compromised if school governors reviewing an exclusion are unduly influenced in their decision by a perceived need to avoid possible friction between the governing body and head teacher or not to be seen as undermining the head teacher's authority. If rubber-stamping the head teacher's decision is a common occurrence the integrity of the decision-making process is called into question. It would suggest that reform is needed and, in any event, make it all the more important that the exclusion appeal panel, to which the parent could refer the case if the governors have decided against him or her, operates effectively.

The Two Research Studies

The Leeds Study

The Leeds sample comprised 10 LEAs (to which questionnaires were sent) and 50 schools (in aggregate) from within their areas (via questionnaires sent to head teachers). The questionnaires were divided into two parts, with one seeking quantitative data with regard to rates of exclusion, types and numbers of schools, numbers of pupils on the school roll, and gender and ethnicity of pupils, and the other aiming for qualitative data based on respondents' perceptions of various issues surrounding the reinstatement meetings of the governing body. Four LEAs responded to the questionnaire, including one London borough, one metropolitan borough and two county councils. The number of reinstatement meetings attended by the officer of the LEA (where this information was available) ranged between 75 and 315.[8]

A total of 15 replies were received from head teachers. Their schools varied in size from 410 pupils to 1,800 pupils on roll. The schools were predominantly mixed gender, comprehensive and county, although the sample did include three single-sex schools, two selective schools and one bi-lateral school. There were schools from each of the four responding LEAs' areas and the rest were from five LEAs which had not responded to the LEA questionnaire. Geographically, the respondent schools were situated in a range of urban and rural areas. The rates of exclusion varied from, at one extreme, one school having only one permanent exclusion – the first in the history of the school – among other schools having only low numbers of fixed-term exclusions (of four days or fewer), and at the other end, an inner city school which reported numerous fixed-term exclusions and 33 permanent exclusions over the three-year period. Only one relatively small school in a rural area had experience of the LEA exercising its power to reinstate, and only the inner city school with the highest rates of exclusion had experience of the governors exercising the equivalent power. Across the sample as a whole rates of exclusion were relatively low and reinstatement meetings were quite rare. Although some respondents' experience was broad, having been gained over a number of years, some head teachers had little direct experience of these procedures in practice, and it seems that they were therefore offering a more hypothetical view of them.

The JMU Study

Although the JMU project was primarily concerned with the operation of the independent appeal panel, it did explore some issues relating to the governing body's reinstatement meeting, and some respondents in any event gave unsolicited comments about it. The JMU survey was framed more widely than the Leeds study, eliciting responses from parents and school governors, in addition to head teachers, from county, voluntary and grant-maintained schools across LEA areas.[9] The sample comprised one largely rural county, one mixed urban/rural authority, and three metropolitan boroughs. A total of 67 replies were received from school governors (94 per cent of whom were the chair of the governing body), 106 from head teachers and 289 from parents of excluded children (267 from parents who had not appealed to the independent appeal panel and 22 from those who had). The replies generated statistical data concerning the make-up of the governing body panels, such as age, gender, ethnicity and occupation, as well as quantitative and qualitative data concerning the involvement of the parents and excluded child in the meeting and on the fairness of the hearing in relation to particular parties. The survey also looked at the effect of the governing body reinstatement meetings (in terms of the way hearings were conducted and their outcome) on the parents' decision whether or not to appeal to the independent appeal panel (discussed in Chapter 8).

Despite the fact that the Leeds and JMU studies were conceived entirely independently, publication in a joint form was viewed to be beneficial because the studies had common aims. The following sections of this chapter report the findings of the two studies.

The Governing Body

Make-up of the Governing Body

When the JMU and Leeds research was conducted the school governors could delegate the responsibility of hearing exclusion cases to a sub-committee. Normally known as the disciplinary panel, it would be constituted from the governing body. Only grant-maintained schools were required (by their articles of government) to have a 'discipline committee', but, as noted above, new legislation requires that all schools should appoint such a committee, comprising three or five governors and served by a clerk appointed by the governing body.

The JMU sample was not restricted to persons who served on disciplinary panels. In practice, however, most governors performed this role at one time or another, although some schools did not have disciplinary panels or committees at the time of the study. As noted above, most of the respondents were chairs of governors, who frequently participate in exclusion reinstatement meetings. Among the respondents (67 in total), the largest category (43 per cent) were LEA appointed governors. Within the remainder, 37 per cent were co-opted governors, 12 per cent were foundation governors and 8 per cent (5) were elected parent governors. A breakdown of the occupations of co-opted governors revealed that they were all from middle-class backgrounds, as predominantly were the other categories. However, the Leeds study found a broader social mix.

Only 20 per cent of the governors in the JMU study had a background in education; and of the remaining sample, 20 per cent were from managerial positions within business or industry, 12 per cent had a legal background, 8 per cent were from the police service, 8 per cent were from the voluntary sector, 20 per cent were other professionals and the remaining 16 per cent came from a variety of other occupations.

Turning to ethnicity and gender, the JMU survey found that white males were over-represented among chairs of exclusion panels. Two out of every three respondents were male, and only 3 per cent of all respondents were non-white.

Perhaps the most pressing concern is the under-representation of ethnic minorities here, especially in light of the over-representation of African-Caribbean pupils in the exclusions statistics and evidence that cultural differences between teachers and black pupils may be a factor in it (see Chapter 4).

Experience and Training of the Governing Body

It is the responsibility of the LEA to secure that governors receive (free of charge) such training as is 'necessary for the effective discharge of [their] functions'.[10] The training will be at no cost to the school. The Act in effect leaves the content and format of the training to be decided upon by individual LEAs. In the Leeds study the LEA and head teacher responses were unanimous in stressing the importance of governors receiving appropriate training on exclusion issues.

We were unable, within the scope of each study, to conduct an evaluation of governors' training on exclusion, including the conduct of reinstatement meetings. It seems to us that one issue that needs to be addressed is the importance of acting impartially, as well as following the statutory requirements and the guidance (as outlined in Chapter 5). We uncovered some evidence of bias, which we discuss in more detail below, and this is an issue that needs urgently to be tackled in training on exclusion meetings. One LEA in the Leeds study noted that some governors seemed to be predisposed towards reinstatement whilst others tended to be biased in favour of the head teacher; and one LEA noted that some governors seemed to feel that they had blindly to support the school at all costs. Many of these responses lend support to the conclusion that many governors seem to be incapable of using their powers impartially to uphold parental or children's rights where appropriate, or to promote child welfare or rein-in the head teacher's wide discretion (an issue discussed in more detail within the sections on the effectiveness and fairness of governing body meetings below). We believe that more effective and extensive training to address these issues is needed.

In the light of our findings (see further below), we were surprised that the majority of head teachers within the Leeds study believed that their school's governing body possessed the requisite training and experience to carry out their functions in the area of exclusion and that others felt that although there had been no formal training there was sufficient experience in exclusion matters. Only a small minority believed the training and experience of governors was insufficient.

The Governing Body's Meeting

Attendance at the Meeting

As noted above, the parent and the LEA are entitled to attend the meeting, and the guidance also advises that the excluded pupil should be allowed to attend if the pupil and parent agree to this. The guidance further states that the parent may bring a friend or legal representative. Often the head teacher or other members of the teaching staff at the school and any other person who may be a witness to the incident(s) in question will be invited to attend, either for part or all of the meeting. Regardless of the fact that the parent can take a friend for support, the JMU study found evidence that less than half of parents attend the reinstatement meeting, with 48 per cent of governors stating that the parent rarely attends, and 22 per cent of governors stating that the parents are always absent. Only 22 per cent of governors stated that the parents are always or generally present, and a further 6 per cent stated they are present in approximately half of the cases.

The JMU study also confirmed that it was not particularly common for the excluded child to attend the meetings. Of those governors who responded to this question, 33 per cent said that the child never attends the meeting and 52 per cent that the child sometimes attends. Only 14 per cent reported that the child was always present. The governors were also asked whether they would grant an excluded child who attended an opportunity to present their views: 62 per cent stated they would always do so and 16 per cent stated they would do so in some cases, whereas 22 per cent stated they never would. The guidance now recommends that the child should be permitted to give their views if they and their parents want this. The JMU survey also confirmed that the child generally has the opportunity to state their views in writing: 67 per cent of governors said the child always has this opportunity, 12 per cent said sometimes and 22 per cent stated never. Overall, the results show that, even before the revised guidance, in a majority of cases the child would not have been denied the opportunity to present their views. However, it was certainly not standard practice for the child's participation to be encouraged or permitted. The study also found that although in the majority of cases the child has the opportunity to attend the meeting, they rarely take it. This raises questions about whether the governing body makes it sufficiently clear to the parent that the child's presence might be helpful and that the governors' view is that the child has a right to attend. Without such encouragement, the child's right of participation under Article 12 of the UN Convention on the Rights of the Child (see Chapter 1) is undermined.

At the time of the research it was left to the governing body's discretion whether an LEA representative could attend the reinstatement meeting. Within the Leeds survey, an overwhelming majority of LEAs stated that they had a representative present at all reinstatement meetings. (One respondent commented on their lack of input into the equivalent process in grant maintained (GM) schools, which lay outside the LEA sector.) According to DFE

Circular 10/94, which was in force at the time of both research studies, the LEA's role at the reinstatement meeting is to gain information on the case, thus facilitating the authority's own subsequent decision-making on the matter if the governing body upholds the exclusion. Although most of the LEAs within the Leeds study confirmed that this was indeed the objective behind their attendance, the study also discovered that some see their presence at the meeting as involving more than mere information gathering. All of the LEAs also stated that their role was to ensure that the meeting was carried out according to proper procedures. In addition, one LEA believed that part of their purpose in being there was to support the parents.

The 1998 Act has now conferred a right on the LEA to make representations at the meeting, and the revised guidance contemplates that LEAs will play a more active role than in the past by giving 'their view on the appropriateness of the exclusion', with reference to, for example, 'how other schools in the Authority have responded to similar incidents' (DFEE 1999a: Annex D, para. 17). The LEA's view could be communicated in a written statement also.

Perceptions of the Meeting

Turning our attention to perceptions of the reinstatement meeting, the majority of the head teachers, LEAs and governing bodies within the JMU and Leeds studies viewed the meeting's role and procedures positively. However, these views contrasted strongly with those of the parents, an overwhelming majority of whom described the meeting in negative terms.

Head teachers within the Leeds study saw the meetings as essential rather than simply useful. Moreover, some were keen to confirm that they viewed the governors' panel as integral to the role of the governors in relation to the management of pupil behaviour in the school. One noted the value of the careful consideration that the governors give to the issues and another valued the experience of the governors that underpinned it. Various positive features and advantages of the meetings were noted by head teachers: they provided reassurance for parents that the incident had been investigated; they acted as a check on the head teacher's power; and they provided scope for a broader perspective on the issue, rather than just a decision based on one person's (the head teacher's) opinion. The governors' experience and knowledge of the school and their understanding of the effects of pupil misbehaviour there were also seen as strengths and contrasted with what the respondents perceived to be the limited appreciation of these factors shown by the LEA and independent appeal panel. A further strength which was noted was that the meetings helped to ensure a consistency of approach in exclusion cases. They were even felt by one head teacher to 'support the best traditions of justice before the law'.

Among the governing bodies and head teachers in the JMU study the overwhelming majority believed that the procedures at the reinstatement meetings were fair to all parties – the head teacher, the governing body, the parent, the classroom teacher and the child. The highest difference in opinion concerned the perceived fairness to the parents and the child: 94 per cent of head teachers believed the procedures were fair to the parent compared to 86 per cent of the governing body sample; with regards to fairness to the child, 93 per cent of head teachers thought that the procedures were fair compared to 83 per cent of governing body respondents.

Qualitative responses were also collated, revealing the reasons behind these opinions. Within the head teacher sample of the JMU study, the commonly cited example of fairness was the correct following of recommended procedures. Other perceptions included the appropriate balancing of interests and the application of the principle that exclusion should be a last resort. Four head teachers even mentioned that parents had praised the meetings. Within the governing body sample the greatest number of governors referred to an informed balance of interests in which all parties had the opportunity to state their case, followed by a correct application of a generally fair procedure. Finally, the breadth of experience of the governing body and, as with the head teacher responses, the fact that exclusion was used only as a last resort were widely cited. Thus very similar reasons were cited within the head teacher and governing body surveys, but with differences in the weight attached to them. A few parents within the JMU study made statements which supported the positive picture presented by the head teacher and governor surveys, saying that the governors were helpful and implying confidence in the governors' ability and effectiveness:

> The governors agreed that all reasons the school gave were trivial and petty.

> I was advised by the school governors to seek help from my MP which I did and this helped my son quicker by getting him into a pre-assessment centre to get him statemented, which he has now had done.

All the surveys nevertheless found a degree of negativity. Of those head teachers and governors within the JMU study who believed the procedures were unfair to the classroom teacher, most stated this was because the governing body panel could only get a 'flavour' of the amount of time spent on the child by the teachers and its impact on the school. A few head teachers commented that if the governors are only brought in at a late stage, when exclusion is imminent, they may not know the full history of the child's case. Some head teachers believed the procedures were unfair to the staff, because governors do not always consider the school's situation when deciding to reinstate. One respondent stated that a head teacher might feel that he or she is on trial for making the decision to exclude. One governor commented that the head teacher can only present his/her case with regard to the specific incident whereas the 'parent can give full rein to any comment they wish to make!'

Whilst the majority of the governors and head teachers within the JMU study believed the procedures to be fair to the parents and children, some did raise concerns about the way that inarticulate parents were disadvantaged and the fact that due to the parents' lack of information to support their case the school's case often seemed so much stronger. One LEA within the Leeds study felt that parents needed a truly independent advocate in these proceedings, noting that where the parents were represented by the LEA or an educational welfare officer (EWO) there would be a conflict of interest. Some of the governors suggested ways in which the procedure could be made more fair, such as by supplying the parent with a list of names (and roles) of those present at the meeting or by having 'agreed rules of evidence and procedure'.

A minority of the head teachers in the Leeds study were quite critical of the review process as a whole, particularly the existence of a 'cosy' relationship between the head teacher and governing body which might lead to bias against the parent. (An LEA also stated that on occasions it seemed as though individual governors had made up their minds in advance.) Some heads also complained that the meetings were either unnecessary, because the real issue was that the child was in the wrong school (for instance, the child might be felt to require placement in a special school), or took up too much staff time, although in each case they still felt the proceedings might have some value.

Although, as noted above, some parents found the governors helpful, most parents in the JMU study were generally far less positive about the reinstatement meeting than the majority of the head teachers and governors. Comments included:

> The governing body undertook to implement the school's policy and did their job – but there was no compassion, no sense of caring and certainly no love or care shown.
>
> It is a farce! The meeting with the governors was very threatening to a child – ten men in suits! They said nothing, I asked very little …
>
> When I went to see the governing body they were all snobs and made me feel low. They talked to me like I was the pupil again, it was a waste of time.
>
> Very formal and quite frightening which made me unable to say all I really wanted to say.
>
> The governing body are not for real, they are not made up of real people i.e. working class … they treat you like a sub-human.

The second of the above comments mentions the formality of the proceedings and the intimidation the parents and child felt due to the number of governors present and even their dress. DFE Circular 10/94 recommended that the procedure should not be over formal, but the revised guidance does not repeat this, although it recommends (and the legislation now requires) that these meetings should be run by a small (three or five member) discipline committee, as noted above, which might make it less intimidating than when (as has sometimes been happening) there are more governors present.

Parents within the JMU study were also troubled by the apparent lack of independence of the governors' panel. In particular, some parents believed that the panel acted merely as a rubber-stamp to the head teacher's decision (an issue which is a central concern of both studies):

> The governors already made up their minds and said they do not want my son in their school.

> In our case the panel had already made their minds up, nothing I could have said or done could ever have changed that.

> The board of governors are also on the side of the school [and] my son's problems were not really considered.

> I felt the governing body had to agree with the head otherwise the head teacher would have felt undermined.

One way in which this lack of independence appeared to manifest itself was in the relationship between the head teacher and the governing body:

> To me it is a complete waste of time … the board of governors in our case were all friends of the head master so they sided with him.

> I put a very good case to the governors and I believe they were tempted – but I know the head teacher persuaded them … he was brought back into the room with the governors, privately after the main meeting … I have since been told that was out of order.

Indeed, some parents perceived the governors to have been unquestioning of the head teacher's version of events or of his/her conclusions as regards the justification for exclusion, whilst being dismissive of, or not interested in, any points the parents put forward. As one parent said: 'I do feel the governing body who I sat in front didn't listen to me but took full notice of the head mistress as she sat and distinctly told lies.' Several parents commented that they felt that their views or those of their children were simply ignored. In one case the parent was not informed in advance that he could bring his daughter (the excluded child) with him to the meeting. He commented: 'On the night of the governors' meeting we were informed that my daughter could have come with us which would have mattered to us, she could have defended herself, the whole thing in our opinion is one sided.'

The worrying aspect of all this is that it may well result in individual parents having little confidence in the review process. As is revealed in Chapter 8, this is one of the reasons why many parents do not take their case beyond the governing body to the independent appeal stage, or why they or their child do not attend the appeal hearing. As one parent said: 'My son attended meetings with the governing body and felt unimportant and humiliated which put him off attending the appeal hearing.'

The Governing Body and the Power to Reinstate

As noted in Chapter 5, the governing body (via the pupil discipline committee) has the power under section 66 of the SSFA 1998 to direct the head teacher to reinstate an excluded child if the facts which emerge in the meeting suggest that the head teacher's decision was unjustified, judged partly with reference to the question whether other strategies have first been tried but have failed, or if the procedural guidance was not followed correctly. Overall, the head teachers within the Leeds study did not regard the possibility of the governors exercising their power of reinstatement as affecting (for example, by inhibiting) their own decision to exclude. Nevertheless, one head teacher stated that the thought of reinstatement might cause him to hesitate and some of the other heads noted the possibility that it could affect their decisions, because the governors' power emphasizes the seriousness of the step being taken and because heads would be under pressure to show that they had got all of the administrative procedures right so that the panel would be satisfied that they had taken all possible steps to prevent exclusion. The LEAs were also asked if they thought that the possibility of reinstatement of a pupil would affect the head teacher's decision to exclude; this produced similar responses to those given by the head teachers, with many stating that it did not make a difference in every case, but all implied that it could sometimes have an effect, for example by making heads more cautious.

As to whether there was a possibility of friction being caused between the governors and the head, one head teacher in the Leeds study commented that 'the trust that exists between the head teacher and the governors ensures acceptance'. Of course, the fact that reinstatement is a relatively unusual event means that the head teacher's authority is rarely threatened by the governing body in this context. One head teacher commented that in practice the governors seemed ready to back the school's authority. Overall, most of the Leeds head teachers did not regard the power of reinstatement as a potential cause of friction. A minority, however, did notice a strain in relations at times. One of these explained that this had occurred where the governors had been critical of the head's and staff's role.

Several head teachers said that they felt that the main difficulty in the reinstatement process arose not from governor involvement but rather from the involvement of the LEA. Two also noted that where solicitors had been involved this was unhelpful: these head teachers were concerned about procedures becoming too legalistic. Nevertheless, as noted above, the guidance makes it clear that the parent may be accompanied by a legal representative.

The Reinstatement Decision

Both studies investigated the frequency of reinstatement by the governors and LEA, and found that reinstatement is rare. The JMU study found that reinstatement by the governing body is more common than reinstatement by the LEA. In the survey of head teachers, 76 per cent (79 out of the 104 who replied) stated that none of their exclusion decisions are overturned. Among the rest, 18 per cent stated that not more than one in ten of their decisions is overturned and only 6 per cent stated that their decisions have been overturned more frequently. Within the Leeds study the largest number of reinstatements reported by any LEA in any one year was four; in many of the years in question individual LEAs reported no reinstatements. Within the head teachers' sample, only an inner city school with the highest rates of exclusion had experience of the governors exercising their power to reinstate. These results show that the parents' concerns that governing bodies merely rubber-stamp head teachers' decisions could be justified.

The Leeds study also asked both the LEA and head teacher samples what they believed to be the main considerations that the governing body committees used in deciding whether or not to reinstate. A few of the LEAs referred to the balancing act between the needs of the child and the needs of the school and to the support that might (or might not) be available to the school if the pupil were to be reinstated. Another response, whilst acknowledging these factors, also focused on the degree of blame that might be attached to the child and whether the behaviour was likely to recur. Head teachers reported that the principal factors that influenced the governors in their reinstatement decision included, in particular, the need to weigh the welfare of the excluded child against the impact of reinstatement on other pupils' education. Other factors mentioned included: the support that the school had given; the past record of the child and the efforts the school had made in responding to the child's behaviour; the impact on the school, especially the staff, of overturning the head's decision; the impact on the school of the child returning; the seriousness of the offence; and finally whether the school had the resources to meet the child's needs. Most responses indicate that relevant considerations do predominate (see further Chapter 5).

Reference was also made to the context in which these decisions are made, such as local management of schools (LMS), open admission, the danger of race discrimination, the lack of resources available to address problems, and schools which bypass parental rights. There was a suggestion that some schools pressurize parents into withdrawing their child and seeking a place at another school rather than suffering the stigma of exclusion.

The Leeds study found that there was a variation in practice as to whether the LEA representative remained in the meeting or not during the governors' deliberations and decision-making. This issue gave rise to the greatest divergence in views about the role of the LEA in the process and possibly of LEA perceptions of the requirements of public law. It suggests that it is not only the school and its governors who may misunderstand the requirements of procedural justice. The decision must be seen to be that of the governors and the governors alone and the presence of an officer of the LEA would prejudice this.

Within the Leeds study clear differences of opinion emerged amongst the LEAs as to whether the governors' power to reinstate made it easier or more difficult for them to exercise their own power to reinstate, with a few feeling that it made no difference, although one LEA noted that it might be easier to support an exclusion where it was appreciated that the parents had had a fair hearing by the governors. Another noted that it was always difficult for the LEA to direct reinstatement against the wishes of the school. Indeed, there was also a feeling among a few respondents that it was difficult to reverse a decision by the governors when a school had the option (which the SSFA 1998 has now ended) of seeking grant-maintained status, taking the school out of the LEA sector.

The divergence of views among LEAs on this question may be in part explained by the difference of approach. One of the LEAs that felt that the existence of the governors' power of reinstatement had no effect on the difficulty of exercising their own power to reinstate noted that in most cases where reinstatement was achieved it was through a process of dialogue and co-operation. This was one of the LEAs where the representative was present for the final decision. It seems likely that here the process has been somewhat subverted from a rights model with winners and losers and replaced by a model where reinstatement can be seen as a joint decision made in the knowledge of what support the LEA can offer.

If the governing body (via the discipline committee) decides not to use its powers to direct reinstatement the parent may appeal to the independent appeal panel.[11] This is the subject of later chapters.

Conclusion

The information gained in the Leeds and JMU studies indicates that while the governors, or their discipline committee, are not completely incapable of defending parental rights or protecting children's welfare or the public interest in keeping pupils in school, there are reasons for concern. Specifically, the research studies have established that there is a tendency for governing bodies not to act wholly impartially and for them to rubber-stamp head teachers' decisions. It was disturbing to find that a number of LEAs, head teachers and parents viewed the governors as often seeming to have made up their minds in advance. There is a need for better training for governors and for more socially representative discipline committees, although the Leeds study found panels with a reasonable representation of persons from 'working-class' backgrounds and confirmed that these members do not hesitate in making their views clear, even where those views conflict with the views of the chairs.

Although the evidence suggests that some governors may be too concerned to support the head teacher in this context, it is necessary to bear in mind the commitment to act fairly evinced by some governors in the survey. Furthermore, it is important to remember that without having been privy to the circumstances which have led to the making of comments about a lack of independence of action it is impossible to know for certain whether the exercise of powers has in fact been influenced by bias.

A charge of disloyalty made by some head teachers about the governors who reinstate seems to suggest that a head might have a distorted view of the functions of the governors in this context. But while a comment such as this suggests that governors may have incurred unjustifiable displeasure simply for carrying out their duties with appropriate seriousness and fairness, equally it might reflect the frustration of a head whose authority has been gratuitously undermined.

As regards the meetings themselves, while most head teachers, LEAs and governing bodies believed them to be effective and fairly conducted, the parents took a different view. Many of the parents had found the meeting stressful and some parents had felt intimidated and inferior. Fear of such processes is a fact that has been well documented in the context of other areas of law and adjudication and may account for relatively low rates of attendance and representations made (remember that the JMU study found that parents attended reinstatement meetings in less that half of cases and that the presence of the child was even less likely), rather than them being attributable to any apathy on the part of the parents. The research also uncovered a degree of formality in the conduct of the meetings. Formality and legalism are often the price that has to be paid for some measure of procedural fairness, however. Some head teachers were more concerned that a decision might be challenged due to defective procedures than on grounds that the professional judgment of those involved was defective.

The existence of this review stage does not appear generally to influence head teachers' decisions or be a cause of friction between head teachers and the governing body. Overall, there was widespread support for the reinstatement meeting, although one wonders whether this would be the case were the governors to overturn the head teacher's decision more frequently. The LEA involvement in the process seems to have been regarded as a mixed blessing, however. On the positive side, clearly the LEAs themselves and most of the schools feel that it helps to ensure fair play, but beyond this there is confusion over its purpose. The new guidance now makes it clear that the LEA's role is to advise on the appropriateness of the exclusion. The LEA will therefore need to demonstrate independence and so the practice the research uncovered of the LEA's representative being present for the final decision would seem to be inappropriate. Once the decision is taken the LEA and governors can have further dialogue. Indeed, the new guidance says that if the decision is to reinstate, the discipline committee 'should discuss with the LEA whether extra short term support would help to ensure successful re-integration' (DFEE 1999a: Annex D, para. 13).

The Leeds study found that some LEAs seem to operate a welfare-based model rather than a rights-based model for review of decisions to exclude. The former was called for by some governing bodies and parents within the JMU study, who favoured a case conference approach. The advantage of this is that it allows re-entry to be negotiated rather than imposed. It also avoids the likelihood that reversal of an exclusion will be taken as a slight and allows careful consideration of the resources that might be made available to support re-entry, which cannot really happen where it is presented as a *fait accompli.* The difficulty, of course, is that it is not consistent with the legal framework. The rights based model has its own strengths but governors and LEAs rarely enforce these rights. Thus, the legal framework either needs tightening up or abandoning in favour of a welfare based system – a system which stands more chance of being effective in keeping pupils in school wherever possible and in addressing the rights of the child.

The deficiencies of the governors' review stage seem too grave to allow the present system to continue as it is, and even with the now more independent appeal stage and the increased LEA involvement in supporting pupil inclusion under the SSFA 1998, it seems unlikely that many more governing bodies will suddenly gain the confidence to be other than unquestioningly loyal to the school and, in particular, its head teacher, in this context.

7 The Exclusion Appeal Panels

Introduction: Historical Background to the Appeal Panels and their Composition

There is a long tradition in this country of lay participation in judicial decisions, including tribunal adjudication. As Street noted, with reference to the social security tribunal system, 'Not the least of its virtues is that the citizen plays such an important part as ... decision-maker' (Street 1975: 32) (although, ironically, the lay element has recently been eliminated from social security tribunals: Sainsbury 2000). Often the layperson is in fact a person with specialist knowledge or experience in the field of dispute, although detached from the particular case in issue. The standard constitution of tribunals which lie under the supervision of the Council on Tribunals is two lay members sitting with a legally qualified chair who can bring to bear his or her legal skills to the interpretation of relevant legislation, the assessment of evidence (although this is a joint task) and the fair conduct of a hearing. Yet such a constitution is not found in exclusion appeal panels.

The exclusion appeal panels were first introduced in 1987 but their origins lie in the Education Act 1980, which established education appeal committees (EACs) to hear appeals in school admission cases. The Education (No. 2) Act 1986 extended the jurisdiction of EACs to include appeals in cases of permanent exclusion from school. The committees had already become responsible for certain categories of appeal under the Education Act 1981 concerning the education of children with special educational needs, but this jurisdiction ended with the establishment of the Special Educational Needs Tribunal in 1994 (see Harris 1997). Although the two surviving jurisdictional areas (admissions and exclusions) are quite different, there are common issues concerning the selection, make-up and training of the panels. This chapter, therefore, draws on evidence about the committees as a whole. However, it also contains the findings of the research into matters relating specifically to the exclusion appeals panels.

The EACs were introduced to provide a local forum to hear and determine appeals – initially, as noted above, over school admissions. The right of appeal was supplemental, but also integral, to the new rights for parents to express a preference for a school. Although the 1980 Act established a norm of adherence to parental choice, admission could be denied on three specific grounds (see Harris 1993: Chapter 5). The most problematic of these has been that the admission of the child would 'prejudice efficient education or the efficient use of resources' (s.6(3)(a), replicated in later legislation and currently in s. 86(3)(a) of the School Standards and Framework Act 1998). The application of the 'prejudice' ground has presented particular difficulties for the appeal panels. These have resulted in legal challenges in the courts and the consequent emergence of a substantial body of case law.

It had not been envisaged that difficult legal issues would present themselves before EACs. Moreover, there was considered to be an overriding need to maintain informality in hearings. Therefore, it was not considered necessary to have lawyers to chair the committees, despite the fact that there was evidence from studies of other lay appeal panels revealing procedural shortcomings and an inability on the part of panels to distinguish departmental policy from the law and to act independently (Herman 1972; Bell 1975). There was nevertheless considerable parliamentary debate during the passage of the 1980 Act on whether an independent appeal system was needed. There were many calls for such a system, but the Act as enacted provided (in Schedule 2) for the majority of the committee to comprise appointees of the body against whose decision an appeal would lie.

The committees comprised three, five or seven members. In county schools two, three or four of the members respectively were LEA-appointees. It was considered essential that the appeal committee should include members of the LEA because they would have a clear knowledge of the background considerations that had influenced the LEA's admissions decisions.[1] The importance of this local knowledge was regarded as outweighing the problem of lack of independence. However, members of the local education committee could not serve as a chair of an EAC. The non-LEA members were required to be drawn from persons with experience of education or with knowledge of local educational conditions and from parents of school pupils (who were nevertheless barred from sitting on an appeal which concerned their own child's school). In voluntary schools the majority of members had to be governing body appointees and the minority members were appointed by the LEA. When grant-maintained school status was introduced under the Education Reform Act 1988, the appeal committee for these schools comprised governor appointees, and the majority had to be drawn from members of the governing body itself.

When, in 1986, the government's amendment to the Education Bill, to establish exclusion appeals, was being debated, the opposition put forward suggestions for a more independent and more representative appeal body. The government's plan was simply to extend the jurisdiction of the existing EACs. The opposition recommended that an appropriate membership of the committee would be 'a parent, a teacher – obviously not connected with the school – a representative from the local authority and a lawyer on the basis that sometimes the evidence given to such a tribunal will be questioned'.[2] (We shall return to the need for a lawyer chair later.) The government's defence of its position was that EACs' 'record to date clearly demonstrates the committees' determination to act independently' and that the similarly constituted committees hearing exclusion appeals in Scotland had 'dealt perfectly satisfactorily with a significant number of cases that have come before them' and without having 'lawyers or other people unconnected with education' on them.[3]

EACs, including those set up in grant-maintained schools, fell under the jurisdiction of the Council on Tribunals. This reflected their judicial role. The Council has monitored their operation and the training of members (for which no provision has in fact been made in the legislation). The Council was concerned about the lack of independence of the committees; it found their overall composition unbalanced (Council on Tribunals 1988: para. 2.35). The Franks Committee's report (1957) had concluded that impartiality was one of the three hallmarks of a good tribunal (the others being openness and fairness). It seems that in the case of EACs the government expected that the obstacle to impartiality presented by the committees' lack of independence would be overcome through adherence to a code of practice on appeals, which the Council initially developed, and from training of members. We shall return to this issue in Chapter 9, when considering the question of bias.

The Council on Tribunals thought that the constitution of EACs might give rise to 'a suspicion (particularly among parents whose appeals have been unsuccessful) that an Appeal Committee will tend to defend decisions rather than approach them with an open mind', on the basis that 'most of its members have a direct connection with the original decision maker' (Council on Tribunals 1988: para. 2.34). Complaints made to the local government ombudsman (see Chapter 2) also provided evidence of a lack of impartiality in practice (Harris 1993: 156). The Council on Tribunals, which supervises the operation of over 50 different tribunal and appeal panel systems, had commented in 1992 that 'amongst all the tribunals under our supervision none has given greater concern' (Council on Tribunals 1992: para. 1.18). It was troubled not only by the panels' lack of independence and impartiality, as noted above, but also by their failure to adopt a 'judicial approach' to their task (an issue to which we shall return to when discussing the appeal hearing itself, in Chapter 9). The Council was reasonably optimistic that some of the difficulties would be overcome following the adoption of a revised Code of Practice on appeals in 1992. Nevertheless, it also called for structural reforms in the case of exclusion appeals, via new legislation to require legal qualifications for chairs of panels (ibid.: para. 1.28). The Code merely advised that the *clerk* to the panel in the more complex cases should have legal qualifications (Association of County Councils 1992: para. 4(b)).

Initially, the government planned (as was announced in the *Parent's Charter* (1991)) to address the problem of lack of independence by introducing 'lay assessors'. They would sit as members of the committee but would also have the duty of reporting to the local authority on the conduct of EACs. However, the

Council on Tribunals felt that the introduction of these assessors in EACs 'would be incompatible with the integrity of the adjudicative process that, as tribunals under [the Council's] supervision, they should properly exercise' (Council on Tribunals 1993: para. 2.14). The government dropped these proposals and instead made provision in the Education Act 1993 (sections 266 and 267 and schedule 16) for a new 'lay' member for EACs, recruited via advertisement.[4] Originally lay members were to be drawn from a list maintained by the Secretary of State, but this was later felt to present too many administrative difficulties (Council on Tribunals 1993: para. 2.16). There was to be only one 'lay' member on a committee irrespective of its size. The lay member was required to be nominated by the LEA in the case of county and controlled schools and by the governing body in the case of other schools. Eligibility to be a lay member[5] depended upon having no 'personal experience in the management of any school or the provision of education in any school (otherwise than as a governor or in any other voluntary capacity)' and no connection (of a kind which could compromise impartiality) with the relevant person or bodies – the LEA or its employee or member (in the case of county and controlled schools) or the school or its governors or employee (in the case of aided and special agreement schools). Grant-maintained schools' appeal committees were also required to have lay members.

Further changes were also made by the 1993 Act to strengthen the independence of EACs. First, members of the LEA or education committee could no longer form the majority on EACs determining appeals in respect of county or controlled schools. This did not affect the majority held by LEA *appointees* as a whole, but the bar on chairmanship of an EAC was extended to include LEA members in addition to members of the education committee.

The Council on Tribunals concluded that the changes made by the 1993 Act would enhance the committees' independence but felt they did not go far enough in the case of exclusion appeals. In particular, the Council reiterated its view that there should be lawyer chairs or that exclusion appeals jurisdiction should be transferred to the Special Educational Needs Tribunal. However, if neither of these options was feasible the Council wanted all appeal hearings to be chaired by the lay member (ibid., paras 2.15 and 2.17). The Council reported that the government considered that this would present 'substantial difficulties' in that

> in practice it would be difficult to draw up lists of individuals capable of chairing appeal committees and potential lay members might be deterred by the prospect of having to chair; and if they turned out in practice not to be good chairmen the credibility of the appeals system generally would suffer.
>
> (ibid.: para. 2.15)

The changes to the appeal committees in 1993 had set in place a system that was more independent than before but with no additional professional expertise. Indeed, as noted above, the main qualification for lay membership was a *lack of* personal experience of educational management or provision. Moreover, the legal expertise that the Council on Tribunals had felt was needed was absent. There was also no change to the size of the appeal committees. The legislation continued to provide that the panel could comprise three, five or seven members. The 1992 Code recommended that the size of panels should be kept to a minimum because a large panel can be daunting to parents; it also argued, less convincingly, that a smaller panel offers a better prospect of impartiality (Association of County Councils 1992: para. 3). At the same time, it acknowledged that a panel of three could become inquorate if one member became unavailable. The Code said it would be helpful to convene a panel of five for a hearing, to meet this eventuality. This guidance was preserved when the Code was revised in 1994, save that it was noted that if one person dropped out a further member should be stood down to achieve a panel of three members (Association of County Councils 1994: para. 4(c)). The Council on Tribunals expressed disappointment that the changes made via the 1993 Act did not include a reduction in the maximum size of EACs, arguing that they were 'still often too large and thus intimidatory in their effect upon parents and pupils, and the maximum size should be limited to five members, with three sufficient in most circumstances' (Council on Tribunals 1993: para. 2.17). In practice, however, it must be very rare to find seven panel members on an exclusion appeal. In our observations of 48 hearings in seven LEA areas in 1997 and 1998 there were no panels greater in number than five: 41 (85.5 per cent) had three panel members and only seven (14.5 per cent) had five members.

The pre-1996 legislation was consolidated into the Education Act 1996 but no substantive changes were made to the constitution of appeal committees until the School Standards and Framework Act 1998 (below). The revised Code of Practice in 1994 did, however, take on board some of the concerns which had been raised about chairing of panels. The Code recommended there should be separate panels of 'expert and experienced chairs wherever possible' (para. 1(e)). However, what neither the Code nor the government seemed to have taken fully on board was the need to ensure exclusion appeal panels of a more appropriate composition. The Council on Tribunals argued that exclusion appeal committees 'require the possession of high skills and abilities on the part of both chairmen and members' (Council on Tribunals 1992: para. 1.28). Various training initiatives were under way (see below), but there was nothing in legislative terms to guarantee that panels would have the expertise that might be needed.

In any event, very little was known about how appeal panels were selected and about other aspects of their composition, such as gender and race (matters completely ignored by the Code of Practice). African-Caribbean children were considerably over-represented in the exclusion statistics, as noted in Chapter 4, and DFE Circular 10/94 acknowledged the need for schools to 'confer equal value on all cultures and avoid stereotypes' (DFE 1994b: para. 32). It was and remains important for appeal panels to be representative of school communities in terms of race and gender, to maximize the overall objectivity of appeal panels and the perceived fairness of the system as a whole. Yet no guidance on this had been issued and the position in practice was unclear.

Constitution of Appeal Panels under the School Standards and Framework Act 1998

The government was clear that it wanted a more independent appeal system. In opposition the Labour Party had promised it would introduce appeal bodies 'independent of the LEA' for admissions appeals (The Labour Party 1995: 11). Once elected to government it gave a commitment to introduce 'independent appeal panels' for admissions and exclusion appeal cases (DFEE 1997a: Chapter 7, para. 32; DFEE 1997b). There was an understanding that the appeal panel would be 'entirely independent of the school and the LEA' and that there would be consistency in their membership regardless of school category.

Our survey started shortly after the publication of the government's proposals and continued during the parliamentary progress of the School Standards and Framework Bill. The observations of appeal hearings supported the case for a more independent system, as the evidence presented in Chapter 9 shows. Nevertheless, the rather more subjective views expressed by LEAs, governors and head teachers demonstrated little support for reform. Across all categories of respondent (although with variations between them) a majority did not consider that a more independent system was needed (see Table 7.1).

A majority of panel members believed that the panels were already independent. Those who took the opposite view were mostly concerned about the presence of local councillors on panels. LEAs who supported greater independence also felt that no one connected with the authority should serve on the appeal panel, to ensure fair decisions and improve public perceptions as to the impartiality of the system. LEAs against did not want to change a system that they considered to be working well or felt that independence would be achieved at the expense of knowledge of and insight into school life and disci-

Table 7.1 *Pre-SSFA 1998 views of panel members, governors, head teachers and LEAs on whether a more independent appeal system was needed*

	Whether more independence needed (%)		
	Yes	*No*	*Don't know*
Appeal panel members	25%	66%	9%
Governors	27%	53%	20%
Head teachers	13%	77%	10%
LEAs	20%	69%	11%

plinary problems. Comments included: 'Increased independence is likely to bring with it increased ignorance of educational implications'; and 'Current balance (with local authority members) reflects the need in all exclusions to consider the whole school effect of an exclusion or reinstatement'. LEAs could also point to the fact that the administration of exclusion appeals was generally carried out by the Chief Executive's Office, either the committee services or legal services sections, rather than by the education department. Like LEAs, the head teachers and governors who were opposed to reform were concerned that educational perspectives should be brought to bear on the adjudicative process. If panel members' own assessment of their knowledge is anything to go by, most have a good awareness of school discipline problems: 29 per cent in the survey rated their knowledge as 'exceptionally good,' while 41 per cent regarded it as 'good' and 27 per cent as 'adequate'; only 2 per cent confessed it was poor.

The government was already committed to reform, as noted above. The School Standards and Framework Bill proposed that panels should not include governors of the school in question, or members of the LEA, or persons whose connection with the school or LEA might raise doubts about their ability to act impartially. It also adopted the Council on Tribunals' recommendation that the maximum size of the committee should be five members. The Council was, however, disappointed that there would be no requirement for exclusion appeal hearings to be chaired by a lawyer. The Council's chair, Lord Archer of Sandwell, proposed an amendment to the Bill during the Committee Stage in the House of Lords which would, in effect, have required a lawyer of five years' standing for exclusion appeal panels. Essentially, Lord Archer was arguing that the seriousness of the issue to be addressed ('the nearest analogy to penal proceedings among statutory hearings') and the need for procedures to be fair and in accordance with the law were such that the skills of a lawyer chair were essential.[6] The government opposed the amendment, arguing that it would make it 'difficult to convene a hearing within the strict time limit which applies in exclusion cases' and would increase costs.[7] It nevertheless indicated that guidance which would be issued would emphasize that legal qualifications can be an advantage for chairing an appeal panel; accordingly, the revised guidance issued in July 1999 (DFEE 1999a: Annex D, para. 20) includes this advice. We discuss the need for lawyer chairs below and in Chapters 9 and 10.

The constitution of exclusion appeal panels is set out in Schedule 18 (para 2) to the 1998 Act. All members of panels are appointed by LEAs, irrespective of the category of school involved. Panels must comprise three or five persons and *at least* one must be a lay member (previously they had to include just one such member, but no more than that) and at least one must be drawn from persons 'who have experience in education, are acquainted with educational conditions in the area of the authority or are parents of registered pupils at a school'. The second category is thus defined in exactly the same broad way as non-LEA members appointed by LEAs for county and controlled schools under the 1986

Act (above). Eligibility to be a lay member is unchanged from the 1993 Act (as incorporated in the 1996 Act).

All persons are disqualified from membership (under para. 2(7)) if they are:

(a) members of the appointing authority or of the governing body of the school in question; or
(b) employed by the authority or governing body, otherwise than as a teacher; or
(c) if they have had, at any time, any connection with the authority or the school or with persons in (b) above, or with the pupil who has been excluded, if it is a connection that 'might reasonably be taken to raise doubts about his ability to act impartially in relation to the authority, the school or the pupil in question'.[8]

At the Council on Tribunals' suggestion, the Act makes provision with regard to the situation where a panel of five has commenced its consideration of an appeal and one of the members dies or becomes too ill to continue. Provided there are sufficient of the members to comprise a panel of three (with at least one lay and one other member) it may continue its consideration and determination of the appeal (para. 2(9)).

As the decision appealed against is made by the governing body, the new system has achieved independence for the panels by ensuring that all appointments are made by LEAs. Moreover, as the outcome of the appeal may have particular consequences for the LEA, it ensures that, while the appointment is made by the authority, members have no connection with the authority that could influence their decision. Our research supported the Council on Tribunals' view that the appeal panels had certainly needed to become more independent and the reform is clearly to be welcomed.

The Act maintains the wide discretion as regards the recruitment of persons to serve on the panels and the selection of chairs (there is no restriction on the eligibility of panel members as regards chairing a panel), although it preserves the system of advertising for lay members. Many of the existing members will continue to be eligible, but some new appointments will obviously have to be made. The Act is silent about training of appeal panel members, which has been left with individual LEAs. The new guidance states merely that LEAs should ensure that members receive 'appropriate' training and that 'Apart from formal training courses this might include attendance at an appeal hearing as an observer' (DFEE 1999a: Annex D, para. 23). This is discussed further below.

As regards new appointments, our research suggests that recruitment practices need to aim towards securing that more persons from ethnic minority backgrounds are recruited and that younger panellists should be sought to complement the current blend in which older age and experience predominate. We now turn to the results of our surveys of recruitment practices and the social make-up of panels.

Recruitment and Selection of Exclusion Appeal Panel Members by LEAs

In the case of lay members, recruitment is required by law to be by advertisement (in a local newspaper), as noted above. In our survey of panel members (111 replies), 43 per cent of members replied to an advertisement. However, lay members comprised 53 per cent of the sample who responded, which suggests that some of the lay members were recruited before advertising became mandatory (with effect from 1 September 1994). Note that there is no retirement age or prescribed minimum or maximum period of service for either category of appeal panel member. Authorities are required to advertise for lay members of appeal bodies once every three years,[9] and some authorities tie the length of appointment to this period (Rawlings 1998).

There is no prescribed manner of recruitment of other members of panels. When our research was conducted, the arrangements were that aided, special agreement and grant-maintained schools appointed non-lay members of appeal panels in relation to their own schools' decisions and LEAs did likewise in relation to county and controlled schools. In our survey, 48 per cent of the members were recruited by direct approach from the LEA and 13.5 per cent were nominated, including 6.3 per cent who were recommended by other members. As noted above, almost all of the rest responded to an advertisement.

Information on recruitment provided to us by LEAs indicates that a more rigorous selection process operates in relation to lay members compared with others. This might be expected, given the fact that the principal qualification for lay membership is a lack of personal experience of the education system. A number of LEAs indicated that they conduct interviews to select lay members from those who respond to their advertisement. On the other hand, appointment of 'education' members almost always seems to occur without interview. For example, governors or ex-teachers simply volunteer or their names are submitted by schools or professional associations, and provided they meet the basic eligibility criteria they are normally appointed. One authority told us that most of the education members are 'retired head teachers who are recruited within the education department'. However, in another authority selection of both categories of members is based on a comprehensive questionnaire completed by the applicant/nominee.

The practices adopted by many LEAs for the recruitment of the 'education' member seem to result in a preponderance of members whose experience of education has been gained at school level and in a professional capacity. Indeed, in our survey of panel members, 30 per cent cited education as their current or most recent occupation. This excludes members whose experience of education has been as a school governor only. The advantages of education members' knowledge of disciplinary issues within schools has to be set against the disadvantage of their narrower perspective on the matter under consideration, in the sense that they are more likely to empathize with the head teacher's disciplinary action than see the matter from the pupil's perspective. This helps to emphasize how important the introduction of the lay member has been, in terms of reducing the dominance of educators on the appeal panel, even though the educators' perspective tends to prevail.

The make-up of a panel obviously depends as much on the selection of panel members for the particular day's hearing as on the pool of persons recruited. Under the 1998 Act the selection of members is a matter for the LEA exclusively. The DFEE's guidance advises LEAs to 'establish a clear procedure for selecting potential panel members and for appointing the chair' (DFEE 1999a: Annex D, para. 20). Many LEAs admitted to us that the principal criterion adopted was the availability of particular persons on the day. A significant number of the LEAs selected members in rotation, generally in alphabetical order. Approximately 10 per cent of the 99 LEAs who responded said that they made a positive effort to ensure a mixed gender panel but only 6 per cent mentioned mixed ethnicity. One authority informed us that it was its policy to have a panel comprising both genders and white and ethnic minority members, but several others explained that the small numbers of panel members recruited from ethnic minorities made it difficult to ensure their representation on panels: 'Sadly this authority has only one black panel member.' For a number of authorities the presence of ethnic minority members on a panel was in any event dependent upon their availability. One LEA told us: 'We are limited in that we only have three ethnic panel members. If we know in advance that the child being excluded is from an ethnic minority, we try to have one panel member from an ethnic minority group, but this is not always possible'. Our survey of panel members and observations of hearings has confirmed the small number of ethnic minority exclusion appeal panel members overall. As we comment below, there is clearly a need to recruit more panel members from ethnic minorities.

Some LEAs made specific reference to the level of experience as a factor behind selection of members for a hearing. This is particularly important where the chair is concerned. A number of authorities make a deliberate attempt to include an experienced member on a panel when there are others who are less experienced. While experience is clearly an important factor in selection, the record of performance seems to play a much less significant part. Only a couple of authorities said that account is taken of previous performance, either as a chair or panel member. One told us that the clerk keeps a list of members 'and will have identified those members who demonstrated the necessary qualities'. The small number of LEAs making reference to this criterion suggests that most LEAs fail to undertake systematic monitoring of members' performance in appeal hearings. Similarly, there is a lack of emphasis on prior training. Only one LEA mentioned that training was a pre-requisite for selection for a hearing. In our survey of panel members we found that over one-third had been selected for their first hearing without prior training (see below, p.128).

Age, Gender, Ethnicity and Social Class of Appeal Panel Members

Age

The age profiles of members in the survey is shown in Table 7.2. The table shows a preponderance of persons above the age of 50 and that more than half of panel members were aged over 60. Clearly those aged 60-plus have the benefit of availability and experience because many, perhaps most, will be retired. These qualities would clearly apply to the retired head teachers who often serve on these panels. On the other hand, it is surprising to find among the membership persons above the retirement age (70) for membership of many other tribunals, including all those concerned with social security and child support, and for the lay magistracy. Both of the two oldest serving members were aged 78 and there was another aged 77 and two aged 75. The youngest member was aged 32, one of only two aged under 40. There was a much older age profile across the exclusion appeal panel membership in our survey than is evident among the lay members of the Special Educational Needs Tribunal (SENT). In a survey of the SENT, 32 per cent of the lay members were aged under 50 (Harris 1997: 47). By comparison, only 19 per cent of exclusion appeal panel members were aged 50 or under.

Gender

It was noted above that many LEAs make a conscious effort to ensure that both males and females are represented among the panel members. A mixed panel ensures that at least one member of the panel will be of the same sex as the parent and the child (if in attendance). Given the preponderance of boys among permanently excluded children (83 per cent in 1996/97 and 84 per cent in 1997/98 according to DFEE statistics: DFEE 1998b and 1999b) and among those whose parents have appealed (94 per cent in the 48 cases we observed), it is perhaps not too problematic (apart from in the few cases involving girls) that

Table 7.2 *Age profiles of appeal panel members in survey (n = 111)*

Age band	*Nos*	*Percentage of total membership*
Under 30	0	0
30–40	2	2
41–50	19	17
51–60	34	30
61–70	43	39
71–80	13	12

males also predominate among the membership of panels. In our survey of panel members 69 per cent were men and 31 per cent women. However, of the total number of panel members involved in the 48 hearings that we observed women were not greatly in the minority: there were 88 males and 70 females. Correlation of these two sets of figures suggests that, even allowing for the possibility that a higher proportion of men than women completed a questionnaire, women panel members are likely to be selected for a hearing more frequently than their male counterparts. The reason for this is not clear.

Ethnicity

We commented above that there was a need to recruit more panel members from ethnic minority backgrounds, particularly given the over-representation of black children among those permanently excluded from school (6.2 per cent of permanently excluded children in 1997/98 were black Caribbean but this ethnic group constituted only 0.76 per cent of the school population: DFEE 1999d: table 4). In our survey of parents and children, 73 per cent of those who appealed were white, 9 per cent were black (African/Caribbean), 9 per cent were Asian and there were 9 per cent others. We found that ethnic minorities were more likely than white people to appeal (see Chapter 8).

In a previous study of the SENT, 92 per cent of lay members were white (Harris 1997: 48). However, in exclusion appeal panels the proportion of white members is even greater. Among the panel members in our survey 96 per cent were white, 2 per cent black (African/Caribbean), 1 per cent Asian and 1 per cent described themselves as 'mixed race'. In the observed cases 96 per cent of panel members were white, 3.5 per cent were black and 0.5 per cent were Asian. Black people are therefore under-represented among panel members in comparison with their representation among appellants. Note that 97 per cent of the governors who conducted the review of the head teacher's decision (i.e. the stage prior to an appeal) were white. The under-representation of black people is a serious problem, particularly given the strong message of the Lawrence inquiry report that school exclusion among ethnic minorities is one of the areas of the education system that needs to be looked at in the quest to tackle 'institutional racism' and racism in society as a whole (Macpherson 1999: Recommendation 68).

Many LEAs in our survey said they wanted to recruit more persons from ethnic minorities but had not been successful in doing so. Comments included:

> Despite our advertisements for lay members referring to a shortfall of members of ethnic minorities … response to [them] has not resulted in any significant solution to this.

> In general not enough black candidates respond to become panellists.

> Had difficulties in recruiting from ethnic minority groups.

In Brent (which was *not* one of the six LEAs in which we carried out detailed work) an approach was made by the LEA to the local Racial Equality Council and this resulted in interest from some community groups. That authority also holds open evenings for potential recruits (Rawlings 1998). There are clearly social and perhaps cultural barriers to be overcome, but these kinds of initiatives might help to improve recruitment from ethnic minorities.

Social Class / Occupational Background

Most of the panel members in our survey were drawn from middle-class professional/managerial backgrounds. While 10 (10 per cent) described their current or most recent occupation as a local councillor, which is clearly not determinative of social class, the other 93 respondents were either drawn from education professions (30 per cent), the legal profession (6 per cent), management positions (16 per cent), the police (2 per cent), other professions (12.5 per cent), voluntary workers (5 per cent) and other occupations (18 per cent). This suggests that at most only around 20 per cent would *not* have been from a middle-class social background. A number of the comments from LEAs confirmed this picture, also indicating that the disparity between panel members' backgrounds and that of the parents hinders panels' ability to understand the social context to children's misbehaviour:

> Panel members tend to be retired and middle class, therefore have little in common with most of the parents.
>
> Some panels are still middle-aged, middle-class white men.
>
> Panels come from comfortable middle class families without problems and have little understanding of social problems and pressures affecting single parents, low income families and families with problems and easily judge parents and the way they bring up their children.

On this basis, it is easy to see how criticism could be levelled at the panels for adopting middle-class professional perspectives on what is in many ways a social problem among mostly disadvantaged sections of local communities. It is a familiar argument heard in relation to the magistracy. However, it does not fully take account of the current statutory role of the exclusion appeal panels. It would nevertheless assume greater importance if our recommendation that the appeal system be given, or encouraged to adopt, a more welfare-orientated approach were adopted.

Legal Qualifications and Experience of Panel Members

It was noted above that an attempt was made during the passage of the School Standards and Framework Act 1998 to introduce an amendment requiring legally qualified chairs of exclusion appeal panels. At present only a small minority of panel members have legal qualifications (6 per cent in our survey). The principal arguments for having a lawyer chair are that it would ensure greater adherence to the judicial approach that appears often to be lacking, better attention to detail, a more effective weighing-up of evidence, a fairer procedure in that the governors' case for not reinstating would be properly tested by the panel, and that reasons for decisions would be more likely to be adequate and properly worded. It would also help to ensure a more appropriate and skilful handling of child witnesses than, as we shall see in Chapter 9, happens at present. Finally, it would also make it more likely that the law is correctly applied. While the Council on Tribunals has consistently argued that exclusion appeal cases should be transferred to the lawyer-chaired Special Educational Needs Tribunal, noting the fact that many excluded children have special educational needs, it considers that the seriousness of exclusion cases and the need to ensure greater fairness are such that the introduction of lawyer chairs for exclusion appeal panels would be a suitable alternative (Council on Tribunals 1992: para. 1.28; 1993: para. 2.15; 1998: para. 1.27).

As noted above, the government rejected a requirement for lawyer chairs on the grounds of cost and the practical difficulty in ensuring that panels can be convened quickly. The other principal argument traditionally presented against lawyer chairs of tribunals is that they make the proceedings more formal and thereby make the system as a whole more intimidating and thus less accessible to ordinary members of the public. It was largely on that basis that few panel members, governors, head teachers and LEAs in the survey believed there should be lawyer chairs (see Table 7.3).

LEAs were the most vehemently opposed to lawyer chairs. In addition to concern about formality, many argued that a lawyer was not needed because the panel had access to legal advice from the clerk or the council's legal representative. Some argued that lawyers' chairing skills were no better than those of

Table 7.3 *Views on whether exclusion appeal panels should have lawyer chairs*

	Heads (%)	*Panels (%)*	*LEAs (%)*	*Governors (%)*
Should have lawyer chair	8	8	4	16
Should not have lawyer chair	83	88	90	68
Don't know	9	4	6	16

others. Many head teachers thought that the process would become too legalistic and believed that common sense was if anything more valuable than legal skills:

> The last thing parents and schools need is the application of a pedantic legal mind.
>
> Lawyers manipulate law not seek justice.
>
> Keep lawyers out. The process is about common sense and good sense, lawyers are about neither.

Few heads appreciated the role lawyers could play in ensuring that the proceedings themselves were conducted fairly. Those who supported lawyer chairs spoke mostly of the greater independence they would bring to panels.

Panel members voiced similar arguments against lawyer chairs to those articulated by other groups. However, a particular concern that they alone raised was that a lawyer chair might dominate the other members of the panel; indeed a few argued that other panel members would be redundant. There was also a rather jaundiced view of lawyers, similar to that expressed by some of the head teachers (above):

> Lawyers are only interested in the law.
>
> Lawyers are concerned with the law and not people.
>
> Too nit-picking and tend to be more concerned about law and not the child.

The general opposition to lawyer chairs from those within the system seems to be borne out of a perception that the appeal system is working well as it stands and that the only benefits lawyers would bring would be knowledge of legal points, which legal clerks are capable of assisting with. Rather than seeing lawyers as ensuring a well-ordered and fair process, they see them as making the system formal and court-like. They either fail to see the current procedural problems (discussed in Chapter 9) that lawyer chairs could help to prevent or are ignorant of the way lawyer chairs conduct other appeal hearings. Other research suggests that their fears are justified only in relation to some and by no means all lawyer chairs (e.g. Baldwin et al. 1992; Harris 1997). The experience of the Special Educational Needs Tribunal has shown that a blend of legal and educational experience on a panel contributes most positively to an effective forum for resolving education disputes (see Harris 1997).

Training

Whether or not exclusion appeal panel members fully recognize it, their role is judicial. As such, training is essential to ensure that principles of justice are properly applied, the legal framework (including the DFEE's guidance to which panels are statutorily obliged to have regard) becomes familiar, and the independent judicial role is fully understood, particularly as most members of the panel are non-lawyers. Considerable emphasis on judicial training at tribunal level has been placed by the Lord Chancellor's Department. In the case of education appeal panels in general there have been a number of local training initiatives (Council on Tribunals 1997b) and others by the Association of County Councils, with the Tribunals Committee of the Judicial Studies Board (JSB) becoming involved; but standards of local training have been variable (Council on Tribunals 1993: para. 2.59) as has the level of administrative and financial support for training.

What has also varied, as noted above, is the practice of requiring training as a pre-requisite to sitting as a panel member. It was surprising to find that quite a number of panel members in the LEA areas covered by our research had not received any training prior to their first sitting. Despite the importance of their role, approximately 38 per cent of the panel members in the survey had not received prior training and 53 per cent of panel members had had initial training but no further training. Overall, at the time of the survey 32 per cent of the panel members had not at any time had any training. Of those who had had training, less than half received any training in the previous twelve months. These findings mirror the broad picture presented in the Council on Tribunals' report ('Digest') of training of education appeal panels across England and Wales (Council on Tribunals 1997b). In our view, LEAs ought to be placed under a statutory duty to train exclusion appeal panel members, as the Council on Tribunals has suggested (Council on Tribunals 1998: para. 1.30). Moreover, although the DFEE's guidance now stresses that it is important for LEAs to make arrangements for training of panel members (including attendance at a hearing as an observer) (DFEE 1999a: Annex D, para. 23), it ought also to advise that no member should sit unless or until he or she has had initial training for the role and observed a couple of hearings, as is the practice in many other tribunals. On behalf of the Council on Tribunals, Lord Archer of Sandwell moved an amendment to the School Standards and Framework Bill to that effect in the House of Lords; it was withdrawn on government assurances that the guidance would state that members must have had such training before they can serve.[10] However, the revised guidance on exclusion appeals contains no such advice.

Across the LEAs in our survey the kind of training provided varied widely – from the provision of an information pack and guidance notes through to intensive training meetings with role play exercises, video and other presentations followed by discussion, and lectures on the legal framework and procedural issues. There is an annual training day in many other authorities. The training provided is not always specific to exclusion appeal panel work. A number of authorities were in the process of revising their training and the replies indicated that LEAs in general were beginning to take it far more seriously. It was therefore disturbing to find that some authorities still had to admit that they did not provide any training for members of exclusion appeal panels. It should also be noted that only a minority of LEAs were providing administrative staff handling exclusion appeals with specific training. Approximately 50 per cent did not provide any training to these staff and of the other authorities only about half (i.e. 25 per cent of LEAs who responded) provided training specifically on exclusion appeals work. Most of the panel members in our survey who had received training were positive about it: two-thirds of them regarded it as having been good or excellent. Only a small number were dissatisfied.

Commission on Racial Equality guidance recommends that members of exclusion appeal panels should be trained on equal opportunities issues (CRE 1997: 11). Only a small number of LEAs in our survey said that they provide such training for panel members and little mention of it is made in the Council on Tribunals' survey report on training of education appeal panels (Council on Tribunals 1997b). Even if these two surveys under-represent the amount of equal opportunities training that is undertaken, it is very likely that considerably more is needed.

It seems that, on the whole, not enough emphasis is being placed by LEAs on training of appeal panel members. We noted earlier that there is no statutory obligation on LEAs to arrange training. The Council on Tribunals urged the government to include in the School Standards and Framework Bill a requirement for LEAs to provide the necessary resources to support such training. This did not occur, but the DFEE has reportedly offered to support LEAs who were found by the Council not to be providing training by offering places on 'Training the Trainer' courses (Council on Tribunals 1998: para. 1.29). Despite this support, and additional funding promised by the minister during the debates on the Bill (although only admission appeals were mentioned specifically),[11] there remains an unjustifiable disparity in provision that can probably only be removed or significantly reduced by putting these appeal panels under the supervision and direction of a national body, or at least regional bodies.

Conclusion

The reforms under the 1998 Act have set in place a framework for independent decision-making. However, whether that will result in greater impartiality in practice depends upon the way the membership of the appeal panels go about their task and how they perceive their role, which the Act has not changed. As already noted, the absence of a judicial approach has in the past been criticized by the Council on Tribunals. Our research finds further, disturbing evidence to reinforce the Council's observations. In our view, this evidence, which is presented in Chapter 9, strengthens the case not only for better training of panel members but also for a further change to the constitution of exclusion appeal panels – the introduction of lawyer chairs.

Having said this, the present system is generally successful in recruiting people with wide-ranging and mostly relevant experience. Often they are people who have additional adjudicative experience: 60 per cent of appeal panel members in our survey had experience of serving on other appeal bodies (in many cases school admissions appeal panels) or as magistrates. A majority of LEAs in our survey (64 per cent) considered that the panels contain an appropriate balance of expertise (as opposed to 24 per cent who did not and 12 per cent who were unsure). Nevertheless, there is clearly a need for more guidance on the recruitment of members, particularly with a view to ensuring greater representation of ethnic minorities. Indeed, a number of LEAs admitted that one of the major flaws with the current appeal panels is the under-representation of ethnic minorities among the membership. Consideration should also be given to an upper age limit, in order to ensure consistency with other tribunals exercising judicial functions and thereby reinforce the judicial role of the panel which members often fail to appreciate fully.

If exclusion appeals were brought within the jurisdiction of the SENT, as the Council on Tribunals has repeatedly recommended, one of the advantages would be that they would be part of a national system. The SENT has a national President and a secretariat based in two offices serving the whole country. Transfer of this work to the SENT would help to ensure consistency in relation to training matters in addition to quality control. As the Council on Tribunals has commented, exclusion appeals 'are part of the workload of what is essentially a very busy tribunal system, with no central organization to guide and monitor the standard of the tribunals' work or decision-making' (Council on Tribunals 1995: para. 2.32). When recommending a judicial head for individual tribunal systems the Council has, however, excluded 'the locally-based tribunal systems such as the Education Appeal Committees' (Council on Tribunals 1997c: para. 2.26). A judicial head would be desirable, however, as he or she could also monitor appointments to panels, which does not happen centrally at present. On this basis, there may well be a case for putting the exclusion appeal system on a national footing, although this would involve an (albeit relatively small) additional financial cost (see further Chapter 10).

8 Bringing Appeals

Access to the Arrangements

Introduction

The effectiveness of any redress mechanism depends greatly on its accessibility. This has been increasingly recognized in relation to court procedures in recent years, culminating in the reforms to civil justice in 1999 initiated by Lord Woolf MR. One of the great advantages of tribunals, compared with the courts, has been the relative ease with which ordinary members of the public can take their grievance before what is today widely recognized to be a *judicial* forum: the increasing judicialization of tribunals over the past twenty years has effectively ended the debate about whether tribunals operate as 'administrative' as opposed to 'judicial' bodies.

The accessibility of tribunals has traditionally been considered to derive from the ease with which the procedure can be initiated, the speed with which the matter will proceed, a relative lack of legalism which minimizes the need for legal representation, and the informality of both the procedure and the hearing itself. On the face of it, bringing an exclusion appeal is a very straightforward matter: all the parent has to do is to give written notice of appeal, setting out the grounds on which the appeal is made.[1] No form is prescribed, although some LEAs use them. However, research has shown that in practice there are barriers to bringing an appeal and that many of those who do appeal need advice and representation to be able to mount an effective challenge. The increasing judicialization of tribunals has been accompanied by stricter procedures, with better prospects of legally correct decisions and the fair conduct of hearings. But it has nevertheless had some negative effects on the accessibility of appeal procedures and has tended to hinder the ability of unaided appellants to participate fully in the appeal process. The problems for appellants have been compounded by the growing legalism that has been an inevitable consequence of the more intense regulation of most of the fields of activity over which tribunals hold jurisdiction. In particular, in many of the tribunals operating in welfare-related fields such as education and social security, there has been a fundamental shift from discretion-based to ruled-based decision-making which reflects the increasingly complex and prescriptive legal framework within which these service areas operate (see, for example, Baldwin et al. 1992).

It cannot therefore be assumed that, while it is important to provide citizens with information about their remedial rights, doing so will guarantee the accessibility of redress mechanisms. It is now widely acknowledged that access to justice often hinges on access to effective advice and representation services (e.g. Genn and Genn 1989; Genn 1999) – an area that has hitherto been neglected by government in relation to welfare law areas but is now beginning to receive official recognition (although only in relation to advice and assistance and not specifically representation) through the proposals for community legal advice services presented by the government in early 1999 (Lord Chancellor's Department 1999). When tribunals are described as providing an 'informal' appeal process it often fails to be recognized that informality is a relative concept and that while appeal procedures such as those which are the subject of this book are not as complex as those found in most courts, bringing an appeal can still be a daunting and at times confusing process for many people. In particular, socially and economically disadvantaged groups and some ethnic minorities (including recent immigrants) can face enormous cultural and other barriers when contemplating recourse to what more advantaged groups would find a straightforward appeal process and one that is reasonably accessible. Indeed, there is evidence from another study concerning education appeals (appeals to the Special Educational Needs Tribunal) that shows that middle-class parents are far more likely than less advantaged groups to make use of the appeal system; moreover, ethnic minority parents are likely to be under-represented among those appellants (Harris 1997: 76).

This chapter examines access to the appeal arrangements by considering the legal requirements concerning the bringing of an appeal and the evidence from our research into the reasons why, as we saw in Chapter 1 (see Table 1.1), nearly 90 per cent of parents whose children are permanently excluded from school do not appeal. The chapter also assesses the availability, sources and quality of advice.

Bringing an Appeal: The Legal Requirements

Parents[2] of children who have been permanently excluded from school must be informed of their right of appeal, and of the last day on which an appeal may be made, by the discipline committee of the governing body when it informs them of its decision (and the reasons for it) not to reinstate the child.[3] The requirement is that the discipline committee should provide all the required information 'forthwith' following its decision. The DFEE's guidance (set out in full in the Appendix) interprets this as meaning that the discipline committee should write to the parent within one school day of its decision (DFEE 1999a: Annex D, para. 14). Under the previous legislation,[4] if the school was a county, controlled or maintained special school the LEA had this duty. Now it rests with the governing body (itself or its discipline committee, if one has been set up as required by the guidance) in every case. However, the guidance recommends (at para. 25) that the LEA should also write, within three working days of the discipline committee meeting, giving details of how to appeal and the last date on which an appeal may be made. The letter should also give the name and the contact details of the clerk to the appeal panel.

As noted above, the appeal must be in writing stating the grounds on which it is made.[5] As under the previous legislation, the parent must bring his or her appeal within 15 school days of the date on which they were given notice of the discipline committee's decision.[6] This is (unless the appeal period spans an end of term or half-term break, during which there are no school days) a very short time limit compared with many other appeal systems, where a more typical limit would normally be not less than four weeks.[7] Moreover, there is no provision for late appeals: the guidance states bluntly (at para. 26) that 'no appeal may be accepted if it is made after the time for lodging notice of appeal has expired'. This contrasts with appeals to the Special Educational Needs Tribunal (SENT), which must be brought within two months[8] (although in relation to those appeals there is a duty to inform the parents only of their appeal right and not the time limit for appealing – see Harris 1997: 72–83), and the regulations enable an extension of time for an appeal to be granted by the President of the SENT in exceptional circumstances.[9]

Reasons for Current Rate of Appealing

A low appeal rate might suggest that an appeal procedure is less accessible than it could be. We saw in Chapter 1 official national statistics for England showing that only about one in ten parents brings an exclusion appeal. In our survey of parents only one in twelve brought an appeal. Both rates are significantly higher than when exclusion appeals were first monitored in the early 1990s but still show that the appeal right is considerably under-utilized. A majority (70 per cent) of the parents in our survey who did not appeal nevertheless felt that the exclusion of their child had been unnecessary. This prompts the question why, if they clearly disagreed with the school's decision, did they not appeal. Our research has found that there are a number of reasons why parents do not bring an appeal. For many of the parents, what limited the accessibility of the appeal system was not a lack of knowledge but rather a lack of confidence that the appeal system had anything positive to offer them.

Parents' Reasons for not Bringing an Appeal

Overall, the parents who had not appealed divided into those who lacked confidence in the outcome of an appeal and those who believed the child would be better off making a fresh start in another school. In the first group were the parents who simply believed that there was no point in bringing an appeal because they were unlikely to succeed. This is obviously a standard reason for not bringing an appeal in any kind of situation and in relation to any right of redress. It only appears problematic when a potential appellant's low expectations are engendered by such factors as misinformation or bad or inappropriately given advice. The parents in our survey had in some cases been deterred by advice proffered by the school. Comments included:

> Told not to. Told it would be a waste of time. They did not want him back at the school.

> The school told me I could appeal but they did not think it was worth it because they said I had no chance of winning.

> I was told by the headmaster who rang me at home and told me he was expelling my son and don't bother appealing as the governorship is always on his side and I would be wasting my time.

In our view head teachers should normally refrain from giving advice about the likely outcome of a particular appeal. They are not in a position to give independent advice and they are at risk of abusing their position by dissuading parents from exercising a legal right. It would be far better if they simply advised parents to seek advice from the LEA or from an independent agency.

A further factor in parents' low expectations was the way the reinstatement meeting with the governing body was conducted. This meeting represents a gateway into the appeal system – all parents must pass through it and receive the governing body's (or, more probably now, the discipline committee's) decision before being able to exercise the right of appeal. Unfortunately, quite a number of parents fail to distinguish between the independent appeal body and the first tier internal review conducted by the governing body (or its committee). They consider the two forums to be so closely linked that if one proves unhelpful to them they have little reason to doubt that the other one will also be against them. It was because they found meeting with the governing body such a negative experience – not just in terms of the outcome but more particularly the hostile, insensitive or uninterested approach towards their case in the meeting (as noted in Chapter 6) – that a number of parents in our survey considered that there was little point in bringing an appeal. Some doubted they would receive a fair hearing before the appeal body.

What also affected the judgement of a number of parents about the virtues or otherwise of bringing an appeal was not so much the likely outcome but the thought that the exclusion could be a blessing in disguise. Many of the parents told us that they had not appealed because they had felt that their child would be better off in another school. In some cases this was because the child had special educational needs which the parents did not consider had been adequately met in the school which had excluded him/her. In other cases the parents felt that the child had been victimized by the school and that to return there would not therefore be in the child's best interests. Several parents also commented that they had decided not to appeal in order to avoid any delay in the child's admission to another school; they had felt that no attempt would be made by the LEA to find a place for the child at an alternative school until the appeal had been decided. For example, one parent told us: 'I had to think about my child's education – he would not have been able to be educated until the appeal was concluded so it would be another three months out of school.' Indeed it was surprising how frequently parents mentioned the time an appeal would take to be resolved. Some claimed to have been advised that an appeal would take several months to be heard. Yet the statute requires the appeal to be heard within 15 school days (see Chapter 9). Comments from parents included:

> Advised against it as it could be lengthy and L was 15 years old, ready to take exams.
>
> I was told it would take up to 18 months, in the meantime my child would not get any education.
>
> Our son had already lost 7 weeks schooling – we understood that an appeal may take three months to come about.

It is clear that many parents were ignorant about the timetable to which the appeal procedure was required to operate. Other evidence suggests that some parents' perceptions might have been correct: by no means all appeals are heard within the statutory time limit (see Chapter 9).

Most parents were not ignorant of the right of appeal. However, a minority claimed they had not been informed that they could appeal by the school or LEA. One asked the rhetorical question: 'Do you think I would have had my son away from school for nineteen months if I would have known anything about appeals?' The Commission for Local Administration has in the past upheld complaints that parents were not informed of their right of appeal.[10]

The head teachers' views on why parents did not appeal were in general different from those expressed by the parents. Many of them felt that parents had understood that the school had been left with little alternative but to exclude and that in most cases the permanent exclusion was only imposed after a long period of repeated misbehaviour and lesser sanctions. The following are typical comments:

> The vast majority of parents appreciate that by the time permanent exclusion is activated then the school has done its utmost.
>
> Understand reasons for exclusion – no basis for appeal – exclusion being the end of a very long process.
>
> Usually they know their kids are beyond control.

Knowledge that we exclude as a last resort with justification.

However, a few of the head teachers suggested other reasons. One told us that the school could not give the child adequate support : 'Parents realize that our school is not the best place for their child to be, normally we do not have the resources to give the child the best deal'. Another explained that 'the vast majority of parents of permanently excluded children lack the knowledge or confidence to … appeal'.

We also found evidence that the intervention methods adopted by some LEAs were successful in resolving exclusion disputes. It seems fairly clear to us that LEAs which provide a high level of support to excluded children and work with the parents in trying to find solutions that would meet the child's needs can expect fewer appeals than others. This was undoubtedly a factor in one of the LEAs in our survey, which had a relatively large number of exclusions but disproportionately few appeals.

Parents' Reasons for Bringing an Appeal

Not surprisingly, the vast majority of parents who do bring an appeal disagree with the decision to exclude their child. In our survey 91 per cent of the 22 parents who appealed did not consider the exclusion of their child to have been necessary. Only one parent acknowledged that the school had had a good reason for the exclusion. It became evident to us both from the written responses from parents and the way they presented their case at the appeal hearing (see Chapter 9) that clearing the child's name was the principal motive behind the appeals that were brought, particularly as some parents felt that their child had been branded a 'criminal' by the school (whether or not the incident in fact concerned a potential breach of the criminal law). Some parents felt that the period of exclusion that had been endured prior to the appeal hearing had acted as a sufficient punishment and that their child had accepted that he or she should behave properly on a return to the school. For those parents the appeal presented an opportunity to attempt to convince an independent tribunal that might be more sympathetic to their child's situation than the governors or head had been that the child would behave in future.

It is interesting that very few appeals were concerned with disputes over the facts leading to the exclusion (the comment by one parent that 'P was innocent of the crime he was accused of; he did not do anything wrong' being very atypical). Most parents simply wanted to put forward mitigating circumstances, such as family difficulties or alleged bullying of their child at school, that had contributed to the serious misbehaviour but which they felt the school had simply ignored. Some parents also felt a strong sense of injustice that other protagonists had been treated more leniently than their child over the particular incident. Others were motivated by the threat that exclusion posed to their child's long-term prospects. Comments included:

> There are still children in the school causing damage and being violent to other pupils and teachers and still remaining there whereas my daughter was excluded for trivial reasons which could affect the rest of her working life.

> The school knew J had other problems but ignored them. I didn't know why they were so much against J, he is only a child.

> I was appalled that the boy who brought the [weapon] into school was excluded for only two days. My son had spent 10 years with this school and in my opinion when he had only six months of disruptive behaviour they turned their back on him.

> My son's exclusion was disproportionate in comparison to punishment given to others involved in the same incident. Therefore we believe he suffered an inequality of treatment.

In some cases the sense of injustice felt by the parent resulted from alleged racial discrimination against the child who was excluded:

> My son aged 14 at the time had a fight with a 17-year-old pupil who was not excluded despite the fact that the 17-year-old instigated the fight. My son is black the other boy is white.

> The incident … involved two white girls and two black girls (my daughter being black) – it was disgraceful, the white girls were told to tell lies.

These examples also illustrate the strength of feeling within some parents as a result of their child's exclusion from school. Many parents who enter the appeal process do not expect to receive a fair hearing: for example, only just over one-third of parents in our survey were confident the hearing would be fair (see further Chapter 9). Therefore the fact that they nevertheless pursue an appeal shows just what a strong sense of injustice over the exclusion many of them have experienced.

Social Class, Ethnicity and Age Divisions and Decisions to Appeal

As noted above, a previous study found that middle-class parents were more likely than those from poorer backgrounds to bring an appeal to the SENT and that ethnic minorities were under-represented among appellants (Harris 1997: 76–77). In our present survey we were able to compare the social class and ethnicity of parents who appealed and those who did not. Note that approximately 5 per cent (15) of those referred to as 'parents' were in fact carers (e.g. guardians or grandparents). None of them were among those who appealed. This therefore suggests that children who are living with carers (and who might therefore be under local authority care) are less likely to be the subject of an appeal if permanently excluded from school.

Table 8.1 shows the social class backgrounds of our two groups of parents. It confirms that the more privileged the occupational group the more likely it is that a parent will bring an appeal. Table 8.1 shows that there was a significantly higher proportion of parents from professional/managerial and skilled non-manual occupational backgrounds among appellants than among non-appellants. Conversely, parents from partly skilled, unskilled or economically inactive backgrounds are less likely than others to appeal. This evidence suggests that there may be educational or cultural barriers to utilizing the appeal process among those from less privileged backgrounds, whose access to the system is thus hindered.

Table 8.2 shows the ethnicity of the children whose parents did or did not appeal. Unlike the social class findings, the results here do not mirror those of the SENT study. On the basis that the child's ethnicity will normally reflect that of the parent or carer, it is clear from Table 8.2 that ethnic minorities are slightly more likely to appeal than white people. It is possible that the differential is partly attributable to social class differences, but it could also reflect the particular sense of social injustice felt by some ethnic minorities (especially black parents) over the exclusion itself.

We also looked at age divisions. Among the parents who *did not* appeal, 59 per cent were aged between 31 and 40, 26 per cent were aged 41 to 50 and 9 per cent (21 parents) were aged 51 or older. However, among the parents who *did* appeal, there was a generally similar pattern, save that none were aged over 50. It would be tempting to suggest that the comparative statistics relating to the over 50s show that age might be a barrier to bringing an appeal. However, this seems unlikely given the fact that older people are more likely than others to bring

Table 8.1 *Social class of parents: appellants and non-appellants*

	Appellants (%) (n = 22)	*Non-appellants (%) (n = 261)*
Professional	19	5
Intermediate/managerial	9	7
Skilled non-manual	14	10
Skilled manual	5	7
Partly skilled or unskilled	24	38
Economically inactive	29	33

Table 8.2 *Ethnicity of children whose parents were appellants and non-appellants*

	Parent appellants (%) (n = 22)	*Parent non-appellants (%) (n = 264)*
Ethnicity of child		
White	73	80
Black	9	6
Asian	9	7
Others	9	4

complaints in general (Williams and Goriely 1999: 103). It might possibly reflect a more disciplinarian attitude among older people, so that the child's exclusion from school is more likely to be accepted and less likely to be challenged. Otherwise, it is not clear why the oldest parents are less likely to appeal.

We also looked at the ages of the children who were excluded, in order to determine age groups which were most likely to be the subject of an appeal. Almost exactly two-thirds (66.5 per cent) of the children excluded from school in England and Wales in 1997–98 were aged 13–15 (DFEE 1999d: table 3); in our sample the proportion was slightly higher, at 75 per cent. We found that 64 per cent of the children whose parents did not appeal were aged 13–15 compared with 76 per cent of those whose parents did. Children aged 16 and 17 constituted nearly 15 per cent of non-appeal cases but 19 per cent of appeal cases. In the case of the under-13s the figures were 21 per cent (non-appeal) and 5 per cent (appeal). The figures show that parents of older children are more likely to appeal – probably because they might view more seriously the almost certain adverse effects of a continuing disruption to the child's education (especially GCSE studies).

Information and Advice

As noted above, there is now a statutory duty resting with the governing body to inform the parent of the right of appeal if the decision of the discipline committee is that the child should not be reinstated. Previously, if the school was a county, controlled or maintained special school the duty rested with the LEA. A majority of parents in the survey confirmed that they had been informed by the school or LEA of their right of appeal. Only approximately 10 per cent of parents claimed not to have received this information. In the LEAs surveyed it was common for a standard information letter or booklet to be sent out by the LEA or, in the case of a voluntary aided or grant-maintained school, by the head teacher. In some cases both the head teacher and the LEA sent out this information. The information leaflets and letters we examined were generally clear and included translations into ethnic minority languages (or statements in the relevant language that a guide in that language was available). Nevertheless, the fact that the legislation requires the parent to put his or her appeal in writing and to state the grounds of appeal presents a major challenge to some parents. Many will feel that they need advice, particularly as they are likely to be aware that their appeal letter will set in motion a process that could bring them face to face with officialdom, in a situation of conflict. Only a minority of LEAs or schools provide, within the standard information to parents of excluded children, information on independent sources of advice.

The two issues we wanted to explore via our survey of parents were, first, the availability of advice, and, second, the relationship between receipt of advice and propensity to appeal. Table 8.3 shows the proportion of parents who received advice after the exclusion. The table shows that parents who subsequently appealed were more likely to have received advice than the non-appellants. Even allowing for the fact that some parents will seek advice because they have already decided to appeal, these figures would suggest that the receipt of advice does have a positive influence on decisions to appeal. A further factor is the quality of the advice received. Parents' evaluation of the helpfulness of the advice received is shown in Table 8.4.

The figures in Table 8.4 indicate that parents who appealed considered the advice they received when their child was excluded from school to have been more helpful than did the parents who subsequently decided not to appeal. This reveals a correlation between subjective views on the quality of advice (in terms of its perceived helpfulness) and a propensity to appeal. Taken together, these two sets of figures show the importance of (helpful) advice in improving access to the exclusion appeal process.

Advice was obtained from a variety of agencies. Contrasting the sources of advice among appellants and non-appellants, the most striking fact is that parents who appealed were far more likely to have received *independent* advice. Among the parents who appealed, none had sought advice from the school and

Table 8.3 *Parents who obtained advice following their child's exclusion from school*

	Appellants (%) *(n = 22)*	*Non-appellants (%)* *(n = 267)*
Received advice	68	53.5
Did not receive advice	27	44.5
Don't know	5	2

Table 8 4 *Parents' evaluation of the quality of the advice received following their child's exclusion*

	Appellants (%) *(n = 16)*	*Non-appellants (%)* *(n = 142)*
Very helpful	44	32
Moderately helpful	31	36
Not helpful	25	32

only 9 per cent from the LEA. Among the non-appellant parents, however, 9 per cent had been in receipt of advice from the school and 21 per cent from the LEA. Appellant parents were far more likely to have consulted a solicitor (25 per cent, as compared with 7.5 per cent of the parents who did not appeal). An increasing number of firms of solicitors now offer a specialism in education law; many are members of the Education Law Association (ELAS), a national association formed in 1991. In the future, access to legal advice on matters such as education law could be widened if the government's plans for community legal services (currently operating on a pilot basis only) are fully implemented (Lord Chancellor's Department 1999). Under them, private firms and voluntary sector providers viewed as competent to provide legal advice in the welfare law field will be members of 'partnerships' for the provision of publicly funded or sponsored advice.

The fact that the parents who appealed were more likely to have obtained their advice from a lawyer could be a reflection of the fact that, compared with other advisers, lawyers would be more likely to advise the use of a redress mechanism involving a form of judicial process (see Genn 1999: 103 and 154). Equally, it could simply reflect the greater determination of some parents to fight a battle over a contested education decision with as much weaponry as they can muster. Appellant parents were far less likely than non-appellants to have sought the help of local authority social services or education welfare departments (12.5 per cent as against 24 per cent of the non-appellants). Both groups were, more or less, equally as likely to have sought advice from a citizens' advice bureau or other voluntary organization, a friend or an MP.

When it comes to the hearing itself, the chief form of assistance required is representation. This is discussed in Chapter 9.

Conclusion

Access to the exclusion appeal system is dependent upon information to provide knowledge of the appeal right. It is clear that most parents are informed about their right of appeal, as the statute requires. However, effective access may also hinge upon advice. An independent source of advice is particularly important given the evidence that some schools or LEAs appear to abuse their position by seeking to discourage parents from appealing and the fact that some parents' unwillingness to appeal stems from their failure to distinguish between the governors' meeting to reconsider the exclusion, which they can find unsympathetic and in some cases hostile, and the independent appeal stage. Advice will be of particular benefit to those from socially and economically disadvantaged backgrounds. We have seen that unskilled workers and those who are economically inactive are far less likely to appeal or to have received advice. It can reasonably be assumed that more would exercise their right of appeal if they received advice.

In the past many parents have not been informed about possible sources of independent advice as part of the exclusion process. The recently revised DFEE guidance on the LEA role in pupil support (Circular 11/99) makes no reference to such advice within its section on supporting parents whose children have been excluded from school (DFEE 1999b). Exclusion is quite reasonably presented as a matter for the LEA to respond to, by making alternative arrangements (initially on a temporary basis) and by seeking to reintegrate the child into school. The guidance simply expects LEAs and schools to leave any challenge mounted by a parent to run its course while in the meantime they begin the process of planning the child's future educational provision at school or otherwise. The LEA is expected to discuss alternative schools with the parents at an early stage, to advise the parents on the child's admission to another school, and to ensure that a reintegration plan is prepared within one month of the decision of the governors' discipline committee to uphold the exclusion. If the plan is agreed by the date of the appeal hearing, the appeal will probably not need to be heard (and the guidance intimates that a hearing is inappropriate if it is simply an attempt to 'clear the child's name': DFEE 1999a: Annex D, para. 34). If it is still the subject of discussion or is disputed by the parents, there is a danger that the LEA's intervention will distract parents from, and/or in effect disrupt, the appeal process. It is therefore all the more important that parents who need it receive effective advice, preferably from an independent source, to guide them through these events.

Fortunately, however, there is an explicit reference to an independent source of advice, in addition to advice from the LEA, in the separate guidance on appeals. This requires the head teacher, when informing the parent by letter about either a fixed period or permanent exclusion from school, to include 'the name and telephone number of a contact at the LEA who can provide advice on the exclusions process and the telephone number for the Advisory Centre for Education (ACE) helpline (020 7704 9822)' (DFEE 1999a: Annex D, para. 2). This represents a significant improvement on the previous guidance (DFE 1994b), which was silent on the subject of advice. ACE can advise parents or put them in touch with a solicitor or other local advice agency.

Of course, not all parents want to exercise their right of appeal. The government clearly seems to hope that in the future even fewer parents will appeal and, given a more considered exercise of the power of exclusion by head teachers, will accept the decision and co-operate in alternative arrangements proposed for their child's education. The evidence at present shows that a minority of parents, amongst whom middle-class parents are over-represented, are sufficiently aggrieved and determined to pursue an appeal and in many cases to obtain advice on their rights. Although very little if anything is being done to improve access to the appeal arrangements, such parents will continue to see them as important and to use them.

9 Exclusion Appeal Hearings

Introduction

The appeal panel's task is to determine whether the permanently excluded pupil should be reinstated at the school. As we have seen, in doing so the panel is required to have regard to the guidance issued by the Secretary of State (currently DFEE 1999a). The panel's task is in two stages. These were previously indicated in the Code of Practice (Association of County Councils 1994) and are now outlined in the DFEE's revised guidance (DFEE 1999b: Annex D, para. 35). All references to the guidance in this chapter are, unless stated otherwise, to this revised guidance (see the Appendix to the book).

In the first stage, the panel has to determine whether the pupil was responsible for the behaviour or act(s) which precipitated the exclusion decision. The guidance suggests that the panel has to be satisfied 'on the balance of probabilities' (the normal standard of proof in civil cases under English law) that the pupil did what he or she was alleged to have done. If, and only if, the panel is so satisfied may it proceed to the second question: whether, considering all relevant factors, permanent exclusion was a reasonable response to the pupil's conduct. The panel's decision is binding on the appellant, the governing body, the head teacher and the LEA.[1] It was noted in Chapter 1 that the pupil is not (unless aged 18 or over) a party to the appeal. As far as the decision is concerned, the pupil is not among those on whom it is expressed to be binding: this is of more symbolic than practical significance.

We did not find evidence of a structured approach to the two stages by appeal panels during the hearings we observed. Moreover, save in a few cases where the clerk guided the panel by reminding it of the issues to be determined, it was not particularly evident during the deliberations either. As we shall see, this was mostly because the panel saw its role as disciplinary rather than judicial and this affected its approach to the adjudication. The two-stage approach was in any event certainly not in the minds of appellants bringing the appeal. We saw in Chapter 8 that most parents who appealed were concerned with presenting mitigating circumstances to the panel. These could relate to the child's domestic circumstances or his or her treatment at school, such as bullying by other pupils or victimization by a teacher who 'had it in for him/her'. As we shall see, in many cases neither the panel nor the appellant fully understood the intended purpose of the hearing as contemplated by the legislation.

This chapter explains how appeal panels perform their task. Drawing on the findings from the observation of 48 appeal hearings, evidence from recent reports by the CLA (local government ombudsmen), the Council on Tribunals and others, and our survey of 22 appellants and some of their children, the chapter examines a range of issues relating to the appeal hearing and its aftermath. We report on the venues, the length of hearings, the degree of formality, the participation of individual panel members and the role of the chair of the panel. However, probably the most important issues we address concern the parents and children. We look at their attendance at the hearing and at the extent and effectiveness of their participation. It will be seen that many parents were dissatisfied with the way the hearing was conducted. The observations revealed quite serious deficiencies in the manner in which children were dealt with in course of the appeal hearings. We also report on the use and effectiveness of legal and other representatives.

Arrangements for the Hearing

It is the duty of the LEA to make the necessary administrative arrangements for exclusion appeal hearings before the independent appeal panel. Under the arrangements in force prior to the SSFA 1998, if the school concerned was grant-maintained, voluntary aided or special agreement the governing body had this responsibility. The responsibility for making the arrangements is generally undertaken by the clerk. The clerk's duties include finding a suitable date, informing the relevant parties of it, organizing a panel, ensuring all the paper work is correct and has been made available to all interested parties, arranging an appeal venue and being present at the appeal to minute the hearing. As noted in Chapter 8, the clerk (on behalf of the LEA) will have 15 school days from when the appeal was lodged to arrange the appeal. The Act allows the LEA to hold an appeal hearing beyond the 15-day period, but only if the appellant requests such a delay.[2] The parent might, for example, want further time to prepare for the hearing (perhaps by briefing a representative). The guidance (DFEE 1999a: Annex D, para. 27) advises that requests for late hearings be considered on their merits by LEAs.

The time-scale for organizing the hearing is relatively short. However, it needs to be, given the potential consequences of the child's prolonged absence from school. Many LEAs commented that sometimes time is tight, particularly given the need to find a suitable date on which all parties will be available. Nevertheless, the normal time limit is generally met. This is not surprising considering that much or all of the paperwork (such as the pupil's curricular and disciplinary records, plus any witness statements and copies of correspondence) ought to have been assembled for the reinstatement meeting before the discipline committee of the governing body. Almost all LEAs (96 per cent of those responding) considered that the 15-day time limit allowed enough time for proper administration of the appeal in all or nearly all cases. The principal reason why in a minority of LEAs the 15-day limit is not always adhered to is that sometimes it proves difficult to find a date on which everyone is available, particularly panel members (a problem which might be eased by having a larger pool of panel members from which to draw).

Since the research was conducted it may have become slightly more difficult to find a suitable date, as a result of a change in the legislation. From 1 September 1998 the LEA has had to take 'reasonable steps' to ascertain any times, within the 15-day period, when the appellant or any other person entitled to appear and wishing to do so would be unable to attend.[3] This puts a stronger onus on the LEA to find a date convenient to all. The fact that the list of persons entitled to be present at the hearing was also extended from September 1998 has added to the difficulty. Before September 1998 the panel had a discretion to allow the appellant to be represented or accompanied by a friend: it now has a duty to allow this.[4] Also since then the head teacher and a representative of the governing body have had a right to attend the hearing.[5] The full list of those entitled to attend[6] comprises:

- the appellant
- the appellant's representative or friend
- the head teacher
- the LEA's officer
- the governing body's pupil discipline committee's nominee
- the governing body's pupil discipline committee's representative.

It is the norm for the head teacher of the excluding school (or a deputy) to attend the hearing. This happened in all but one of the 48 cases observed by the researchers. A representative from the governing body attended in only 40 per cent of cases. The school often has other witnesses – such as teachers who may have been present when the incident took place, a form tutor or a head of year – and in some cases it may be necessary for the education welfare officer or the special educational needs tutor to attend. Normally the panel does not object to their presence. The guidance states that the calling of witnesses is at the discretion of the panel 'but should be allowed unless there is good reason to refuse' (DFEE 1999a: Annex D, para. 49). It also notes that the panel has no power to compel the attendance of a witness. Obviously, if a key witness is expected to attend but has not arrived the panel could adjourn the hearing: but the guidance advises as a general principle that adjournment of any hearing would be 'exceptional' (para. 44), and it would clearly result in a further delay in resolving the question of the child's future schooling.

In addition, the panel may permit a member of the LEA to attend as an observer.[7] A member of the Council on Tribunals may also attend a hearing.

Although, as we pointed out in Chapter 1, the excluded pupil aged under 18 does not have a right to attend the hearing, the guidance advises that if the parent requests that the child should attend, the panel should permit it (DFEE 1999a: Annex D, para 29). The frequency with which children attend and their participation in the hearing are discussed in detail below. We observed a few cases where the child was in care and the social worker attended to explain the child's situation or viewpoint. The guidance also states (at para. 30) that the panel has a discretion to permit the parent to bring with him or her more than one friend or representative. It advises that the clerk should seek the panel's agreement in advance: but there would be a need to have 'regard to a reasonable limit on numbers attending the hearing'. Also in attendance will, of course, be the panel of three or five persons. There will also be the clerk to the appeal panel: and, particularly in cases where the clerk is not legally trained, there will normally be a legal adviser from the local authority's legal department. The appeal is to be heard in private unless the LEA directs otherwise.[8]

The SSFA 1998 permits two or more appeals to be combined in the same proceedings where expedient because the issues raised by the appeals are the same or connected.[9] The guidance advises the panel to ascertain that the appellants have no objection to the combining of appeals. We came across a few appeals which concerned exclusions arising out of the same incident. They were not heard together, probably because they were lodged fairly far apart in time.

We investigated the times of day that hearings were scheduled and the amount of time allocated to them. Exclusion appeal hearings need to be long enough to ensure that each side is able to present their case and that the facts are properly ascertained, with questioning of parties or witnesses, while at the same time short enough to reflect the intended accessibility of hearings to ordinary members of the public who may be unassisted. In one case involving a city technology college, where appeals against exclusion were heard by the governing body, it was the practice for the governors to allow just 30 minutes for such hearings. Collins J was critical of this arrangement on the grounds that there would be some cases where it was necessary to go into more detail than in others. He said: '[A] policy of saying no more than half an hour is a dangerous policy to adopt and it ought to be adapted to the circumstances of any given appeal.'[10]

Within individual LEAs, exclusion appeals in fact occur relatively infrequently and hearings are scheduled on an *ad hoc* basis. Unlike both the Special Educational Needs Tribunal, which sometimes schedules separate cases for a morning and afternoon on the same day in order to minimize costs (hiring of venues, travel costs, etc.), and admission appeal committees, which often have to hear multiple appeals involving the same school, it is not all that common for the local exclusion appeal panel to have more than one appeal hearing on a single day. This is one reason why there is less pressure, in terms of time, to complete the hearing quickly. In our survey the majority of panel members (88 per cent) stated that there was no real pressure upon them to complete a hearing by a particular time; only 11 per cent felt that there was (1 per cent were unsure). A few commented that there was more pressure to complete evening sessions (see below) reasonably speedily, to avoid a late night. However, even though panels feel unrushed in hearing a case, the majority of hearings are quite short. In the cases we observed, 48 per cent of appeals observed lasted an hour or less and 82 per cent were concluded inside one hour and 40 minutes.[11] The longest hearing lasted a very atypical 3 hours and 10 minutes while the shortest ran for just 15 minutes. We look at the time taken for different parts of the hearing in more detail below.

We found that hearings were generally conducted during the morning: 65 per cent of cases were heard before lunch compared with 25 per cent during the afternoon and 10 per cent in the evening. This broadly reflects the position across the country. In our survey of LEAs, the majority (72 per cent) of respondents stated that hearings are either conducted in the morning or afternoon while 19 per cent said that some of their hearings take place in the evening and 4 per cent that hearings are scheduled for evening only. The time of the hearing seemed to be dictated by the wishes of the parents and whether those in work could get time off to attend a day-time hearing.

Location of the Hearing

Other than stating that school exclusion appeals should not be held on school premises, neither DFE Circular 10/94 nor its recent replacement guidance offer advice on the venue to be used for the hearing. Out of 98 LEAs which indicated where their authority's exclusion appeals are heard, none cited school premises. Many LEAs emphasized the importance they attach to finding accommodation which is regarded as neutral territory and which is easily accessible to the parents. One LEA mentioned the need to find premises which would not incur a cost to the authority, and another referred to finding premises with parking facilities. An overwhelming majority of the appeals are heard in council buildings of some kind: 89 per cent of respondents stated council premises were always used or were the first preference, if available. Venues referred to included town halls, libraries, civic centres and council offices (but generally not education office premises). Seven respondents also made use of private/commercial buildings, which included leisure centres, a Quaker meeting house, business premises and hotels. Voluntary organizations' buildings and a local college were also mentioned as venues for appeal hearings. The venues at which hearings were observed during the research were mostly (92 per cent of appeals) council premises of some kind. In 60 per cent of the cases the hearing took place in the building within which the appeal was processed (housing the committee section or legal department). We also attended a few appeals which were held in the LEA's building. Others were conducted in a museum, a local college and a conference centre. Additionally, the researchers observed one appeal against a voluntary aided school which was conducted in the offices of the diocese.

In the majority of observations (71 per cent) the room chosen for the appeal hearing was, in terms of size and formality, suitable for the purpose. In the remainder of cases the room was either too small – making the hearing cramped and uncomfortable for all – or was too large and formal. Hearings where the room was too formal tended to be held in large council chambers, typically with heavy wood panelling and high ceilings which contributed to an air of formality. Generally the acoustics in the room were satisfactory for a hearing of this nature; audibility of speech was mostly good. Only in six of the hearings did we experience significant audibility problems. In these cases the room was either too large or noise intruded from outside (in one case from a meeting taking place in an adjoining room separated from the hearing room only by a sliding door).

In our view LEAs need to give more careful consideration to the selection of appropriate accommodation for hearings. Some of the venues currently in use help to create an intimidating environment, particularly the large oak panelled committee rooms in town halls where two of the LEAs whose appeals we attended convene their appeal hearings.

Before and at the Start of the Hearing

Before the hearing starts the clerk ensures that seating and other arrangements for the room are correct. Within all of the LEAs' hearings which were observed the panel members, appeal panel clerk (usually from the committee section or legal department of the council) and/or legal adviser (see below) met before the start of the hearing to ensure they were all clear on various procedural issues and the main details of the case. This preliminary consideration of the issues can also enable any legal points to be clarified. One issue we observed under consideration was whether, in cases of exclusion in which the police were involved, the results of a court hearing or police investigation should be taken into account during the exclusion hearing. Several panels were unsure of this and in fact so were some of the appeal panel clerks. Often a legal adviser employed by the local authority is on hand to provide advice on such matters. (Generally, he or she will remain with the panel during the hearing and the deliberations afterwards (see below).) This time before the hearing also allows the clerk to double check that all panel members have all the paper work, which in practice was not always the case.

In the hearings we observed there was generally an administrative clerk employed by the LEA in addition to the appeal panel clerk. The administrative clerk handled much of the paperwork connected with the appeal and often welcomed the parties at the hearing. The reception role is particularly important and was often mentioned by the parents of excluded children as making a difference to their feelings of apprehension, by helping to ease their anxiety. Within all the hearings which were observed, the parents and the child if present were asked to sit next to the clerk. The clerks viewed this as an important way to make the parents and child feel more at ease and not isolated. Although their role is neutral, the clerk does tend to give more consideration to the parents, which is understandable as the parents are quite often outnumbered by the school and LEA representatives; and in many cases parents have no previous experience of an exclusion appeal hearing or comparable procedure. If during the proceedings it is discovered that any documentation is missing, it is the clerk who arranges for copies to be made available. The administrative clerk plays no other role during the hearing other than to minute the proceedings. After the appeal has finished the administrative clerk will usher the parents and other parties and witnesses out of the room and deal with any enquiries from them. In principle, there is no reason why the appeal panel clerk should not perform some or all of these roles currently performed by the administrative clerk. Indeed, it could help to emphasize the independence of the appeal panel stage. The current, revised, version of the guidance seems to contemplate that there should be one clerk fulfilling all the required roles. We discuss the role of the appeal panel clerk during the hearing below.

The guidance states that the order of hearing should be notified in advance to the parties (DFEE 1999a: Annex D, para. 37). This seems to contemplate that there will be a standard running order. In the past, the Code of Practice (Association of County Councils 1994: para. 17) has contained a recommended order of hearing. The new guidance leaves the matter open. Many LEAs have a booklet or set of notes which are sent out to appellants explaining the running order, but this has not been uniform practice despite the reference in the Code of Practice to advance notification of the standard procedure being 'preferable'. The Code of Practice, which is now out of date, contemplated that the case for the exclusion would be stated first, with the parents then being entitled to ask questions before setting out their own case. This was common practice in the hearings we observed and will doubtless continue to be operated in the future. We comment on the suitability of this order of proceedings below.

The revised guidance also recommends that at the outset of hearing, following a welcome and introductions, the clerk should explain the order in which the parties present will be heard and that they may ask questions after each presentation. It states that the panel should not vary the order of proceedings notified in advance unless or until they have elicited the views on any such change from all parties who are present and entitled to make representations (DFEE 1999a: Annex D, para. 41). The guidance continues to stress that the clerk or chair should explain that the panel is independent of both the LEA and the governing body and that its decision is binding. We regard the statement concerning the panel's independence to be extremely important in reassuring parents that they can expect a fair hearing and an unbiased assessment of their case. Even if the parent is not present at the hearing, making this statement can serve to remind the panel members themselves that they must be impartial, as well as stressing to the school's representatives that although the parent is not present the panel will not be taking sides. We found that the independence of the panel was referred to at the outset in 69 per cent of the hearings, although in half of these cases there was only a very brief reference to it. In 31 per cent of cases there was no statement of the panel's independence. It is to be hoped that the fact that regard must now be had to the guidance will mean that this statement becomes uniform practice.

The Nature and Conduct of the Hearing

We evaluated hearings through the observations and comments from the panel members and participants. We were particularly interested in the degree of fairness. We considered that the issue of formality and informality was linked to the question of fairness, on the basis that the more formal the proceedings the more difficult it seems to be for appellants to present their case unassisted. At the same time, if the proceedings are *too* informal there is a risk that the head teacher or governors will be able to dominate the discussion at the expense of the parents' or pupils' effective participation, particularly as the contingent supporting the decision to exclude is almost always the larger of the two. We were also interested in whether there was any evidence of bias in the way the hearing was conducted, as this could also feed into the decision-making process. First, we discuss the attendance and participation of parent and child.

Attendance and Participation by Parents and Children, Incorporating the Role of Representation

Parents

Attendance rates at the hearing among appellants in exclusion appeal cases are lower than for special educational needs appeals hearings before the Special Education Needs Tribunal, which almost all parents attend, but higher than for social security appeal hearings, which on average approximately 50 per cent of appellants attend (DSS 1998: table H5.03). In the 48 cases observed, the parent attended in 65 per cent of cases.

Other research reveals a close correlation between attendance and success at an appeal hearing (Genn and Genn 1989; Baldwin et al. 1992). DSS statistics for social security appeals in 1997 show that on average 56 per cent of cases attended were decided (at least partly) in the appellant's favour compared with 12 per cent where neither the appellant nor a representative was present (DSS 1998: table H5.03). In our observations none of the parents who failed to attend won their appeal. Not surprisingly, hearings tend to be longer when the appellant attends. When the parent fails to attend the panel often seems to pay less attention to his/her case, assuming that unless he/she has given a good explanation for it the probable reason for the failure to attend was a belief that the case was not strong.

One of the traditional advantages of tribunals compared with courts is that the more informal and inquisitorial approach makes it possible to pursue one's appeal and present one's case without representation at the hearing. The inquisitorial approach is supposed to involve the panel, especially the chair, playing an active role in eliciting details of the facts and points of argument. This in theory means that the appellant can rely on the panel to test the case presented against him or her. However, the reality can be somewhat different to this. For one thing, the inquisitorial approach itself is something of a myth: often, while there are inquisitorial elements, there is an underlying and often quite palpable adversarial element to tribunal hearings, as was shown in a study of the Special Educational Needs Tribunal (SENT) (Harris 1997). Adversarial hearings will tend to put ordinary members of the public, as appellants acting in person, at a disadvantage compared with the experienced and more expert opponents they face. Representation will often be important in evening up the two sides and in ensuring that the key facts and arguments are presented. In practice, unrepresented appellants fare less well than those who have some form of representation (Genn and Genn 1989) and it would be incorrect to assume that representation is less important for appellants in hearings that are more inquisitorial in nature. As we show below, our research and other findings (Baldwin et al. 1992: 109–124) reveal that appeal tribunals or panels are not always very adept at the inquisitorial approach. In particular, they are sometimes unwilling to subject the case against the appellant to rigorous examination (Harris 1997). Baldwin et al. (1992: 114) concluded that in social security appeal cases it was 'unsatisfactory to assume that the best interests of the unrepresented appellant will invariably be served by members of the tribunal'. They concluded that although representation tends to make the proceedings more formal and thus militates against the inquisitorial approach, this is a 'price worth paying' in terms of ensuring that the appellant's case is properly put at the hearing.

In some types of appeal, such as appeals to the SENT or to tribunals dealing with social security cases, there are established representation providers from the voluntary sector (Harris 1997; Genn and Genn 1989), although even here the majority of appellants are not represented. For school exclusion appeals there are fewer specialist representatives and representation rates are low. Parents were represented in 27 per cent of the 48 hearings which were observed: the representative in one in five of these cases was a lawyer. In the postal survey of parents who appealed, 41 per cent had had representation, including 18 per cent who were represented by a solicitor. A number of parents, when asked about representation, commented that they did not know they were entitled to take a representative to the hearing. In one case a parent was advised by the LEA not to have legal representation, only to find that at the hearing the head teacher was, as he put it, 'represented by an LEA lawyer'. Another referred to the information provided by the school/LEA which offered 'active discouragement of legal representation'. It is significant, however, that nearly 50 per cent of the parents who did not have legal representation at the hearing wished in retrospect that they had had it. One confirmed that with hindsight she wished she had had a lawyer to represent her because 'I feel I did not express my son's case strongly enough and thus failed to impress the panel sufficiently.' Another told us: 'A lawyer could have stated my son's situation more clearly.'

The SSFA 1998 requires the right to appeal to be communicated to parents following the discipline committee's decision – but not specifically the right to bring a representative to the hearing. As noted in Chapter 8, the guidance advises that parents should be informed by the school of sources of advice when it informs them of the exclusion. But the guidance to the discipline committee and the LEA covering the period starting with the former's decision not to reinstate does not mention the parents' right to use a representative as something that should be communicated to them. In our view this information ought to be provided to *all* parents following the discipline committee's decision.

In exclusion appeal hearings representation has two particular potential benefits, aside from the obvious one of helping to focus the minds of the panel on the key issues which support the appellant's case and on the deficiencies with the case presented against reinstatement.The first arises from the fact that the parent is often lined up against several people who will present the case for the exclusion – including a lawyer in some cases (although now that the opponent is always the school and not the LEA this is less likely in the future) – plus one or more witnesses (see below). The presence of a representative will help the parent to feel less intimidated and a little more confident (so that his or her contribution to the discussion is likely to be fuller and potentially more convincing). Second, as noted above, hearings tend to be fairly short. Appellants often feel that the hearing is over very quickly and several commented to us that they did not have an opportunity to say all that they wanted as they were swept along by the rapid tide of discussion (see below). An effective representative can aid a more considered and careful discussion of a case.

Having said this, we did not find any direct correlation between higher success rates and parental representation, apart from where the representative attended but the parent did not. Indeed, attendance by the parent and/or representative seems to be a far more important factor (discussed above). It is not entirely clear why representation was not overly successful in exclusion appeal cases, but a number of reasons can be suggested. First, although many parents thought their representative did a good job, we actually rated the quality of representation in the cases we observed to be generally poor. Although a few of the solicitors were reasonably effective, others seemed at times inexpert as far these kinds of proceedings were concerned. As one panel member told us: 'the lawyer representing the parents had very little knowledge of either the relevant law or procedure'. Several legal representatives were inexperienced and ineffectual: in particular, there was not enough questioning of the school's evidence and of whether exclusion was genuinely a last resort. Instead, there was often much emphasis on pleading mitigating circumstances. Several of the social workers or education welfare officers who represented adopted a similar approach. They often demonstrated sensitivity towards both the child's problems *and* the school's difficulties. In this way they were little different to the friends or relatives who represented some of the parents, and it is not particularly surprising that success rates among the professionals who represented were more or less the same as those among friends and relatives. Solicitors were successful in 25 per cent of cases, compared with 20 per cent when a friend, relative or voluntary worker represented and 23 per cent of cases where there was no representation. A further factor is that the representative can sometimes hinder the parent's participation in the proceedings. (As one of the panel members told us, some parents 'felt they could only speak through their lawyer'.) Incidentally, this is also true of participation by children (discussed below). A further factor in these cases is that some panel members seemed resentful of legal representation, either because it altered the character of the hearing by making it more formal or lengthened the hearing. There is evidence of increasing lawyer involvement in education appeal cases (whether admission or exclusion cases) and some panel members are unhappy with this trend, wanting to keep lawyers away. Comments included:

> I think that lawyers often damage a case for their clients. They can antagonize members in some cases.

> The legal representatives usually have to be reminded that the assembly is not a court of law so that as far as possible proceedings are conducted in an informal atmosphere.

> It made the hearing more formal. You were very guarded in what you said and did.

The main barrier to parental participation in appeal hearings was not representation, however. It was the unfamiliarity of the proceedings, the relatively large numbers present and the overall atmosphere, coupled with the approach adopted by chairs of panels. We found that while most parents who had attended felt that they had had an opportunity to state their case, and 64 per cent said they had been asked questions and had responded to them, there were others whose participation was minimal. In our survey 36 per cent of parents told us that they had not said all they had wanted to during the hearing and the same percentage had hardly spoken at all. In our view chairs of panels need to make more strident efforts to involve the parent more fully in the hearing. Some parents need to be assisted by the chair to put their side of the case, as in the case of the parent who told us that her education social worker 'could not speak very good English and I felt I could not explain myself properly'.

One of the problems for some parents was that it was difficult to marshal their thoughts properly once the hearing was under way; and as the hearing progressed the problem worsened because, for example, they were distracted by comments made by representatives of the school. As one told us: 'I became flustered and emotional as the hearing progressed. … I failed to put several questions that I intended to ask and also to present the statement my son had written'. It was partly for this reason that some parents felt that it was unfair that they had to present their case after, rather than before, the case against reinstatement had been put (see below).

The Child

The importance of the child's participation in the appeal was discussed in Chapter 1. We saw that from a children's rights perspective (especially with reference to Article 12 of the UN Convention on the Rights of the Child) there are compelling arguments why children should participate as fully as possible. This is an issue both for appeal panels and the parent's representative. In *R v Governors of Bacon's City Technology College ex parte W*[12] the excluded child, D, aged 12, attended the appeal hearing. Although the panel had wanted to hear from the child the parents' representative, R, who described himself as a 'human rights lawyer', spoke in a long-winded fashion and in effect prevented the child from speaking to the panel. Collins J was critical not only of the representative but also the chair:

> The committee made it plain that they wanted to hear from D and that they were concerned that instead of hearing from D they heard only from [R]. D was prevented by [R's] loquacity from speaking to them ... [I]t seems to me that a competent chairman, faced with that situation, ought to have made it clear that he wanted to hear from D and made it equally clear that unless the representative allowed that to happen, there would be prejudice to D's case because that is effectively what I am being told.[13]

In another decision, Turner J said that it is 'an act of obvious fairness' to hear the child's version of events in an exclusion case.[14]

The prospects of children's participation would probably be increased if the excluded pupil were a party to the proceedings: as we have seen, he or she is neither a party nor has a formal right to attend. The child will attend as a witness, if this is what the parent wants. This means that, as Save the Children (1996: 12–13) has put it, 'A child facing exclusion has no automatic entitlement to challenge accusations made against him or her.' The child was present at only 40 per cent of the hearings we observed (and in 46 per cent of hearings attended by parents in the postal survey). The excluded pupil has no specific right to representation in his or her own right at the hearing, but the child was represented by a social worker in 12 per cent of cases where no parent attended. We also observed a small number of cases where the appeal was brought by the governing body of the school against the LEA's direction to reinstate (a right of appeal that has now disappeared under the 1998 Act: see Chapter 8) and the LEA in effect supported the child's case for reinstatement. In 89 per cent of all the observed cases where the child was present at the hearing the panel, school or LEA asked the child questions. Where the child did not attend, his or her views were communicated by the school, parent or social worker in roughly half of the cases. But in the other half the child's view was not presented at all to the panel.

Most panel members and LEAs in the survey believed that the excluded pupil should attend the hearing and be heard, because it was fair and would help in the evaluation of the case. Only young children and those who would be unduly distressed by the experience should not be present, most believed. Several referred to the interests of natural justice being served by the child's participation and to the fact that the child could shed new light on the matter at issue by providing further evidence. It was, however, slightly worrying that some panel members wanted to see the child primarily to form some judgement as to his or her character or because the child needed to 'face the consequences of his or her action' (suggesting a degree of pre-judgement of the case!):

> It would tell the panel a great deal about the child's attitude.

> The panel can form an opinion of the child.

> It is important for the child to face what they have done in the presence of the parents and have the opportunity of speaking if only to apologize.

> [T]he personality of the child may be a factor better assessed even if contact is very brief.

A few panel members were, however, aware of the dangers of making value judgements and for this reason one thought it preferable that the child should not attend: 'No [the child should not attend] – may cause decision to be influenced by sympathy or the opposite!'

Parents shared the belief of the majority of panel members that the child should be heard: only 5 per cent of those who appealed were against it, compared with 77 per cent who were in favour and 18 per cent who were unsure. Several felt that because the case was about the child it was only right that the child him/herself should be heard. Others were keen that the panel should hear the child's perspective because it would help the members to understand not only what had happened but also the reasons behind it:

> Children have their own problems and can give reasons why the problem occurred.

> Because they have the opportunity to say what really happened.

> If the [panel] had the opportunity to speak to [N] they would have got a better picture.

Our research found that, overall, excluded pupils had made an oral contribution in less than one-third of appeal hearings. Given the fact that in 1997/98 79.2 per cent of children excluded from schools in England were aged 12–15 (DFEE 1999d: table 3) and would have been well able to express a view, we support strongly the argument that more efforts should be made to encourage the child's attendance and participation. Telling the parents before the hearing that their child's views may be helpful to the panel would be a useful start.

During the passage of the SSFA 1998 the government successfully resisted an attempt to force an amendment which would have permitted the excluded child to appear and be represented at the hearing and to make oral and written communications to the panel. It argued that 'to allow the pupil to attend the appeal hearing will not be appropriate in every case, particularly when a young or immature child is involved' and that implying the child's attendance as the norm would create an expectation of attendance that could lead to inferences being drawn by panels from a child's non-attendance in any particular case.[15] One option (although not an altogether satisfactory one) would have been to add a discretion for the child not to be admitted to a hearing on specific grounds, to be reinforced by guidance, which could also have stated that no inference should be drawn from the child's non-attendance. Despite the right of participation in Article 12 of the UN Convention on the Rights of the Child (above, and see the discussion Chapter 1), the government continues to be resistant to the idea that the excluded child should have a right to attend and be heard, which would need to be accompanied by a right to representation: 'the child shall in particular be provided with the opportunity to be heard in any judicial and administrative proceedings affecting the child, either directly or through a representative or appropriate body' (Article 12.2). In its second report to the UN Committee on the Rights of the Child the government nevertheless reiterated its view that 'it will often be appropriate for the child to address the governors' discipline committee or the appeal panel about his or her exclusion from school' (HM Government 1999: para. 9.25.1). As noted above, the recently revised guidance provides that if they or their parent so request, the pupil should be allowed to attend the hearing and speak on his or her own behalf 'unless there is a good reason to refuse' (DFEE 1999a: Annex D, para. 29). Other pupil witnesses' evidence should normally be presented in writing only, according to the guidance, which also advises that such other pupils may appear in person voluntarily and with their parents' consent (ibid., para. 48); none, however, attended in the cases we observed.

Changes are in any event needed to the way that appeal panels deal with children. We found that in practice some panels were not very skilful in their approach to this matter. Questioning of the child was frequently stern and on a few occasions the panel permitted examination that was quite oppressive and intimidating. On one occasion, there were too few seats in the room when the child was called in to answer questions. The child was required to stand while the chair of the panel questioned him (very sternly as it happens), as though the boy was on trial. No effort was made to bring a chair for him from another room in the building. The panel in another area always took evidence from the child only after hearing from all the other witnesses and after asking the parties to leave the room. This was done to make the child feel less intimidated, but it meant that the child was forced to defend himself/herself against the allegations that had been made earlier in the proceedings, rather than the teacher or head teacher having to justify their actions in response to the child's evidence. Panels tended to ask the children about the facts rather than about their feelings or emotions concerning either the relevant incident(s) or the environment at the school. This implied that the panel was not interested in the child as a person.

Parents also recognized the panels' inability sometimes to deal appropriately with the child:

> I think the hearing was too hard and harsh on my child.
>
> I don't feel any person present was qualified to understand the outlook of the child.
>
> One member of the panel interrogated my daughter – his tone of voice was disgusting, he was trying to make her admit to things she had not done. His tone of voice almost reduced her to tears.
>
> It [the appeal system] stinks because it does not give children the right to say what they think and if they do nobody likes it.
>
> My son … was treated as a criminal or dissident.

The children to whom we spoke were glad they had attended the hearing but did not really feel that the panel was receptive to what they had to say. As one told us: 'They were not really interested. … It was a one sided story, only interested in the school'.

After completing our research and while writing this book we advised the DFEE of these problems. We were pleased to see that the new guidance (then in draft) was amended to advise (in its final published version) that 'Appeal panels should be sensitive to the needs of child witnesses to ensure that the child's view is properly heard' (DFEE 1999a: Annex D, para. 29). However, we feel that the guidance could have gone much further in explaining good practice in the questioning of children and in stressing to panels the need to avoid value judgements based on very limited contact with the children concerned.

The Role of the Chair

The research confirmed the critical role played by the chair of the panel. The chair's role is to order the proceedings and he or she needs to guide the parties efficiently through the presentation of their cases, seeking (with other panel members) clarification of points of evidence and inviting each party to question or respond to the other party at the appropriate time. The guidance explains that the chair should also assist a party who is having difficulty in presenting his or her case by intervening and helping 'to ensure that their case is established' (DFEE 1999a: Annex D, para. 38). The guidance also advises that assistance will be particularly important where parents have English as a second language or have literacy problems; some may not have understood all of the paperwork or points presented in evidence. A chair who was too dominant and controlling could inhibit the presentation of evidence, particularly by parents. Those who exerted too little control were more likely to permit a form of questioning of witnesses, for example the child, that was inappropriate (see above). In the cases observed we found that in one in eight hearings the chair exerted too much control and intervened too frequently whereas the chair was generally rather non-interventionist in one in five hearings. We judged the chairing of the hearing to be effective in approximately 44 per cent of cases and broadly satisfactory in a further 21 per cent of hearings. We commented on the selection and training of chairs in Chapter 7.

The Appeal Panel's Clerk and the Legal Advisor to the Panel

The appeal panel's clerk assists the chair and other members of the panel by acting as an 'independent source of advice on procedure' (DFEE 1999a: Annex D, para. 31). As noted in Chapter 7, the Code of Practice on appeals, which was in operation at the time of the research, merely stated that it would be advisable 'in the more complex cases' for the clerk to have legal qualifications (Association of County Councils 1994: para. 5(b)). The guidance now recommends (para. 31) that ideally they should have legal training and experience in the conduct of appeal hearings. We found a considerable variation in practice in the area of clerking. Some of the clerks had legal training, while others did not. Some played an active role during the hearing, whereas the presence of others was barely noticeable. In some cases the role of adviser to the panel was undertaken by a separate person (below).Generally, however, we found the clerks to perform their role efficiently, particularly those who had had legal training.

The presence of a legal adviser to the panel – often a solicitor from the legal or committee section of the local authority – came as something of a surprise, as no such official was referred to in the Code of Practice on appeals (Association of County Councils 1994). Indeed, the Code seemed to contemplate that the appeal panel clerk would perform this role. It is likely that the increased emphasis now placed by the revised guidance on legal qualifications for clerks and chairs will mean that this legal adviser ceases to play a part. In our observations the adviser provided an effective support role in three-quarters of the hearings, although in approximately one in six hearings there were situations where the adviser could have interjected usefully to correct procedural errors. Examples included cases where: the running order of the appeal was inappropriate; there was evidence missing; and the school was permitted to present additional information without the panel being advised to ensure that the family's solicitor agreed.

Some legal advisers moved beyond a purely advisory role to actively assist the parents in their questioning of the school representatives, in an effort to minimize the parents' disadvantage where they were extremely nervous or not very articulate. Nevertheless, in conversation with us several of the legal advisers mentioned specific aspects of procedure about which they was unsure and particular matters that they were uncertain whether the panel was permitted to take into account – such as the child's record from a previous school. Some of the advisers also appeared not to be abreast of case law developments, although in their defence the pace of these developments has been considerable in recent years.

Fairness of the Hearing

The survey produced clear evidence that, as noted briefly in Chapter 8, only a minority of parents entering the appeal process were confident they would receive a fair hearing: 36 per cent expected that the hearing would be fair, while 32 per cent were unsure and 32 per cent were definitely not confident about getting a fair hearing. The reason for such pessimism seems largely to have been the way the school dealt with their case prior to it reaching the appeal stage coupled with the parents' apparent failure to perceive the appeal stage as independent. Following their hearing, many of these parents would have regarded their pessimism as vindicated: 82 per cent of those who appealed did not regard the appeal hearing as having been fair. However, virtually every parent who lost his or her appeal regarded the hearing as unfair whilst all of those who won their appeal regarded it as having been fair. Parents' judgement would, of course, be expected to be coloured by the outcome of the case. Nevertheless, many made specific comments which were also reflected in the appeal observations.

- A significant number of parents felt out of their depth during the hearing: while 36 per cent found the discussion easy to understand, 27 per cent found it difficult and 32 per cent found the proceedings confusing. We should mention here that in approximately one in six hearings we saw evidence of particular problems being experienced by parents in understanding things being said or in keeping pace with the arguments presented.
- While 36 per cent of parents found the panel members' approach reassuring and helpful, 50 per cent did not.
- Many parents experienced negative emotions during the hearing: 60 per cent were nervous; 55 per cent experienced anger; 55 per cent felt frustrated; 27 per cent were unable to concentrate; and 18 per cent felt embarrassed. Only 14 per cent felt reasonably calm during the hearing and only 23 per cent felt confident. One parent said: 'I feel the whole system needs to be looked into as it is very distressing for the child and the parents

involved.' Panel members' comments reinforced this view: the hearing could be 'a daunting experience' for parents and 'parents may well be overawed by the system'. One panel member admitted that 'on several occasions I have found myself having to console parents who have been so nervous and overwhelmed'. Sometimes both sides have to cope with a degree of friction between the parties or between one party and the panel. We saw evidence of friction – sometimes real animosity – in approximately one-third of the hearings we observed.

- Parents often felt outnumbered and were intimidated by the numbers present. On average, there were nine people present (including the panel but excluding the researcher) at the hearings observed. There were ten or more people present in nearly 30 per cent of the hearings. In cases where parents attended, there were on average two persons supporting the appeal, but in nearly half of these cases the two persons were the parent and child and in 17 per cent of hearings they attended the parent was on their own. In attendance and supporting the school were on average three persons (school and LEA representatives or witnesses). These figures hide the fact that on several occasions the parents were considerably outnumbered by the school/governors/LEA party. On one such occasion the chair insisted that the school's witnesses would have to remain outside the room until they were called as there was insufficient room for them and it would have proved intimidating for the parent to be facing such a large contingent of opposition. Parents' comments reflected their feeling of being outnumbered:

> You against the many.
>
> I was alone against several teachers.
>
> I was told the hearing would be informal, three or four people. I wasn't expecting a very large board room full of governors, solicitors, head of year, teacher etc. I wasn't prepared for it.

Picking up on this last comment, in an appeal forum like this a degree of informality is important to minimize the stress and anxiety of the parties, but particularly the parent and child, so that they can feel more confident in presenting their views. As noted above, on the day, the clerk plays a key role before the hearing in reassuring parents and explaining the arrangements, and this process should be continued by the chair at the start of the hearing. Several parents made favourable comments about the fact that the clerk or chair had attempted to put them at ease. In 40 per cent of hearings observed, tea or coffee was provided to the parties, which again helps to relax the parents and make the situation less formal. (We were surprised to find that in one case the school and LEA representative were served tea but not the parents: this hardly projects to appellants an image of impartiality.) We consider that however short the hearing is expected to be, refreshments should if possible be made available to all present.

Once the hearing is under way the proceedings often become more formal, particularly when viewed from the parents' perspective. Approximately 23 per cent of panel members and 41 per cent of LEAs regarded the hearing as generally formal (rating it 4 or 5 on an ascending scale of formality from 1 to 5). In the survey of panel members, however, a large number stressed the importance they attached to keeping the hearing as informal as possible. The observations revealed a fairly wide variation in the degree of formality of hearings. Mostly the variation was due to the differing approaches adopted by different chairs or by the clerks. The guidance states that 'the appeal panel should do everything possible to establish an atmosphere of informality where the parties can present their cases effectively' (DFEE 1999a: para. 33). In general, we found there to be slightly more formality than was appropriate for hearings of this kind.

Fairness also demands that the hearing is thorough in its review of the case for and against the reinstatement of the child. In the cases observed there was considerable variation in the thoroughness with which panels considered the evidence and the issues. The CLA has also reported on a panel's failure to probe the facts sufficiently.[16] We also found that during the hearing, and often also in the course of the deliberations, the panel gave little attention to the DFEE's guidance on school exclusions, then in Circular 10/94.[17] In particular, it often failed to consider whether exclusion had been a last resort or whether the circumstances of the case matched any of the situations specifically referred to in the guidance. The shortness of many of the hearings was also unexpected. Almost 30 per cent of hearings lasted no more than 40 minutes and 48 per cent of them lasted one hour or less. Most, 82 per cent, were heard inside one hour and 40 minutes. Only 18 per cent of cases lasted longer than this; the longest ran for over three hours. Short hearings generally occur where the facts are not in dispute or where the school's case is unchallenged because the parent does not attend or make a written submission. A long hearing can be more difficult for parents to cope with, but a short hearing sometimes means that the evidence is not properly tested. In the survey of parents 32 per cent found the proceedings too rushed. One commented:

> I felt that much more time was given to hearing the case for the school by the head teacher, deputy head teacher and representative of the [LEA]. Panel members were becoming restless whilst I attempted to put the case for my son – this in turn made me more flustered.

It is entirely appropriate that the revised guidance should now remind panels that 'sufficient time must be allowed for each party to put its case' (DFEE 1999a: Annex D, para. 42). It is interesting to note that in hearings where both parties' case was presented to the panel, the presentation of the case in support of the exclusion (including questions) ran for, on average, 23 per cent longer than the appellant's: 43 minutes as compared with 35 minutes.[18] On one occasion the presentation of the case against exclusion was half the duration of the case in favour. Such an imbalance largely reflects the need for there to be a breakdown of the facts within the school's/LEAs presentation.

Appropriate breaks are important in proceedings of this nature, particularly for parents, who can find the intensity of the hearing fairly draining emotionally. Although breaks were offered in only 25 per cent of the hearings which were observed, we considered that there were only two occasions among the remaining 75 per cent of hearings when a break was needed but was not called. This indicates that the chair is generally aware of the importance of offering appropriate breaks. However, we found that on several occasions when a break was suggested the parents seemed particularly pleased, which implies that they had wanted one earlier but had been unwilling to ask. It is especially important for breaks to be considered when the child is present, because he or she can become restless or inattentive during long hearings.

Some parents felt that there was an unfairness in their having to present their case after the school. One parent appears to have had a particularly difficult time:

> Everybody at the hearing had their say before me, head teacher, head of year, governors, etc. I had to wait to speak until the end. When it was my turn one of the governors jumped up and said he had to put more money in the parking meter. We adjourned for 30 minutes. When we got back it was hard to remember what had been said.

The rationale for the parents going second/last is presumably that it gives them an opportunity to know the case against them and to respond to the points raised by the school. There is, however, a danger that it will force the parents onto a defensive footing. It was noted in the study of the SENT (Harris 1997) that parents who present their case after the LEA, as is the standard procedure in that tribunal, were forced to respond to the LEA's arguments rather than concentrating on their own. This is also true of exclusion appeals. In our view it would be better if the parents, who are after all the appellants, presented their case first. They can later respond to the school's case by asking questions after it has been presented. Furthermore, it is common practice for panels to invite the parties to sum up their case, or add any further comments, at the end of the hearing.

On the basis of our observations we believe that, compared with the school and LEA, parents are at a disadvantage in hearings. A number of LEAs also believed that this was the case: 10 per cent said that the parent was always at a disadvantage, while 76 per cent said that this was the case sometimes. We have shown above the numerous factors behind this disadvantage. However, parents who are inexperienced, anxious or inarticulate, can be assisted in various ways by the panel and clerk. Indeed, fairness demands that attention is paid by appeal panel members and their officials to such problems. It was encouraging to find that within most of the appeal hearings the panel tried at least to some extent to assist parents in the presentation of their case by prompting them to explain the surrounding circumstances and other matters. This helped a number of parents to cope with a relatively formal hearing and enabled them to present their case in a more coherent and complete manner.

Nevertheless, we consider that some aspects of the proceedings (including the treatment of children: above) are clearly operating unfairly at present. Our findings reinforce the relatively disturbing picture hinted at by some of the cases which have reached the courts in recent years, where panels have been found to have acted unlawfully by, for example, not ensuring that the parents had copies of witness statements relied upon by the school and in the panel's possession[19] and by not investigating the facts or probing the evidence with sufficient thoroughness.[20]

Bias

In our research we treated the issue of bias as separate from the question of fairness in the procedure. The question of bias relates to the outcome of the hearing as well as the way the parents' appeal is handled within the system. There were different views on the extent of bias. Only 9 per cent of panel members believed that the appeal system was biased in favour of the parents and only 10 per cent thought that there was bias in favour of the governing body. However, 26 per cent of the head teachers and 21 per cent of LEAs regarded the panels as biased in favour of parents; only 6 per cent of heads and 2 per cent of LEAs thought they were biased in favour of the governing body or LEA. As we shall see, these individual perspectives contrast with the objective assessments of the researchers (see below).

Parents commonly perceived from the way the hearing was conducted that the panel had pre-judged their case and some felt that as a result their view would not therefore count. Some parents believed that the panel must have been biased against them and one hinted at potential racial bias:

> When left alone they treated myself as a criminal and teachers and panel were on first name basis laughing and joking.

> No one from the ethnic minority was on the panel.

However, there were also parents who felt that the panel had taken an unbiased view of their case:

> The independence of the panel was refreshing.

> The panel members were uncowed by the head and evaluated the school's actions impartially.

Appeal panel were very fair and listened to both parties without judgement.

In nearly 50 appeal hearings observed during the research, we found that both in the outcome and the way the panel addressed the evidence and reached its conclusions there was sometimes a degree of unconscious bias against the child and parent. Panels often include former teachers. While it is right that some panel members should have knowledge of discipline in schools, some of these members appear to display bias in favour of those who have to cope with disruption and insolence from pupils. Several were heard during deliberations to make statements about the need for a more authoritarian approach in schools in response to indiscipline; and some, for example, indicated by their remarks that they saw it as part of their role to reinforce the fight against the 'gang culture' or the 'drugs culture' rather than simply acting as independent adjudicators. Lord Archer of Sandwell, the chairman of the Council on Tribunals, has also reported on a visit to an exclusion appeal hearing in which the chair of the panel was heard to say: 'the headmaster is a very caring man, and we should support him' (Archer of Sandwell 1996).

We were also concerned about the degree of familiarity between panel members and representatives of the LEA or head teachers. They meet each other frequently at these hearings, so some familiarity is inevitable. Nevertheless, we were concerned at the way that they displayed it in the presence of the parents, because it gave an impression of potential bias. The guidance advises that 'care must be taken to ensure that no party attending the hearing is present alone with the appeal panel in the presence of the others' (DFEE 1999a: Annex D, para. 42). This was probably included in response to a CLA report on a complaint concerning an exclusion appeal hearing in a grant-maintained school where the school's deputy head, who was its representative, spent time alone with the appeal panel prior to the hearing. Indeed, the hearing took place in his office, and he later participated in the drawing up of the panel's reasons for its decision.[21] We believe that panels should take special care not to create any impression of potential bias by displaying too much familiarity with school representatives or witnesses prior to, during or after the hearing. The guidance ought to have emphasized this more strongly.

The Decision and Reasons

Once the hearing is concluded the parties and witnesses leave the room and the panel deliberates and decides. The panel may, in the event of a disagreement between its members, reach a majority decision.[22] If the panel decides that the pupil should be reinstated it must direct that the reinstatement occurs immediately or by a date specified by the panel.[23] The guidance recommends that the reinstatement date should not be more than five school days from the date of the decision, in the absence of a compelling reason for a greater delay (DFEE 1999a: Annex D, para. 51).

The reasons for the decision are discussed by the panel. The clerk generally takes very brief notes. The panel's decision and the grounds for it must be communicated in writing to the appellant, the LEA, the governing body and the head teacher by the end of the second school day following the day of the hearing.[24] This time limit, under the 1998 Act, is much shorter than under the previous legislation, which allowed up to 17 school days.[25] The new time limit means a much reduced delay in most cases, which is clearly in the child's interests. The guidance recommends that the LEA should in fact be informed 'immediately' if the decision is not to order reinstatement and that the parent should be advised to contact the LEA about arrangements for their child's continued education (op cit., para. 55). As noted above, the panel's decision is binding.[26] If the permanent exclusion has been confirmed, the head should remove the pupil's name from the school roll the day after the appeal panel's decision, according to the guidance.

Some appeal panels have failed to pay adequate attention to the requirement to give reasons for decisions. The call for there to be lawyer chairs of panels and legally trained clerks has been partly based on evidence of this failure. While the requirement to give reasons is mandatory, the courts have shown some latitude in relation to the level of detail that lay committees are expected to provide. In one case where the reasons for decision were criticized as inadequate, Turner J considered that account needed to be taken of the fact that the decision letter 'was not drafted by those having legal qualifications', saying that 'I recognize that legal qualifications are not the only ones that count, for experience within the field of education which these committee members and their secretary [have] may count at least as much'.[27] This issue has also arisen in admissions appeal cases, which of course are heard by identically constituted committees (although the recent recommendation for legally qualified chairs for exclusion appeal cases can be expected to establish a difference in the future). In *W (A Minor) v Education Appeal Committee*, Ralph Gibson LJ, discussing the giving of reasons for decisions, referred to 'the code of practice which should guide appeal committees in handling these matters'.[28] The Code of Practice in question (Association of County Councils 1994) dealt with all appeals to education appeal committees (as they are still collectively known) including exclusion appeal panels. In relation to exclusion appeals it stated that the panel's written reasons should be intelligible to a layperson and should 'state briefly the principal facts and arguments which were accepted by the appeal committee and the conclusions on the basis of those facts and arguments' (para. 30). This was clearly consistent with the guidance offered by the courts, which was well put by J. Popplewell in an admission appeal case in 1994: 'reasons must be given which are intelligible and enable the parties to understand why the court or tribunal has reached the conclusion that it has. It is important for the parties to know why they have won or lost'.[29]

Unfortunately, the new guidance does not replicate the Code's advice on reasons. Nevertheless, there is some recent judicial guidance in relation to exclusion appeals. Referring to the requirement to give reasons under the Education Act 1996 (replaced by the SSFA 1998 since September 1999), Laws J said:

> These committees are manned by lay persons who have a difficult, important, and sensitive task to perform … [T]here must surely be a basic requirement, namely that the decision-maker must explain, with whatever brevity, why the decision in question has been taken. And that, I conceive, is the simple duty imposed by para. 14 [of Schedule 16 to the 1996 Act]: the committee must explain, however briefly, why the child has been excluded from the school.[30]

In this case the appeal panel had, in formulating its reasons, incorporated the phraseology adopted by a guide in use in the particular LEA. The reasons stated:

> After careful deliberations the Committee decided unanimously not to uphold your appeal as they believed the permanent exclusion was, in the circumstances, a reasonable course of action for the school. The Committee accepted that [D] was responsible for the actions which resulted in his permanent exclusion.

Referring to these reasons, Laws J said:[31]

> Did this tell the parents why D was being excluded? I do not think that it did. Something more was required to show why the extreme measure of exclusion was justified. … I think the committee were obliged, however briefly, to make it clear what considerations justified the course they were approving. … If the decision letter in this case were adequate, it might readily be thought that the assertion that permanent exclusion was a reasonable course for the school and that the child was responsible for the actions in question would be a sufficient statement of grounds in every instance where the committee decides to uphold permanent exclusion in this kind of case. That could not be right.

This case sends out a strong warning to appeal panels to provide clear and informative reasons for their decision. They must show the basis for their finding that the exclusion was reasonable in the circumstances of the case. Some panels have not managed to do this in the past; indeed, during our research we saw several examples of decision letters that were little better than those in the above case, although they were probably in the minority.

Conclusion

While the problems are not as bad as some of the cases in the law reports have led us to believe, it is clear that exclusion appeal hearings do not always operate fairly and effectively. Our evidence reinforces the concerns raised on a number of occasions by the Council on Tribunals, which has highlighted the need for 'meticulously applied procedures' and a proper 'judicial approach' (Council on Tribunals 1992: para. 1.28) and continues to report an 'inconsistent level of performance of appeal committees handling exclusion appeals' (Council on Tribunals 1998: para. 1.34). We believe that the evidence of the way hearings are conducted reinforces the case for lawyer chairs of these panels, an issue which we discussed in Chapter 7. Although in 66 per cent of the observed cases the overall management of the hearing by the chair was effective, we believe that if a lawyer were always in the chair it is more likely that there would be proper regard for the rights of the excluded child and a more effective testing of the governing body's case against reinstatement. We also believe there would be improved procedural fairness and a better application of the legislative requirements and the principles derived from the case law (remember that in our survey while 81 per cent of panel members believed that a knowledge of the law was important or fairly important to their role, only 6 per cent of panel members had a legal qualification). We were concerned to see cases where the merits of exclusion were at issue but the chair did not ask the panel members whether exclusion was a reasonable response, and a number of cases where the chairing was weak, such as where no effort was made to stop the inappropriately stern questioning of a child by a representative of the LEA. Indeed, the way that children are dealt with at the hearing is perhaps the matter of most concern revealed by our research findings. This is but one of the issues that need to be addressed in the training of panel members and clerks.

It is often argued that judicialization of appeal panels results in greater formality and hinders the ability of appellants to present their own case (see generally Harris 1983). Nevertheless, as the Council on Tribunals (1993: para. 2.15) has said, exclusion appeal cases are 'often complex and highly sensitive in the issues raised'. Accordingly, some judicialization would appear to be justified. The reforms under the SSFA 1998 to make the appeal panels more independent should alleviate some of the main problems regarding bias, but unless training is improved and the new guidance concerning legal qualifications for chairs and clerks is taken seriously there must still be concerns about the capacity of the panels to deliver a fair and effective system of justice.

10 Conclusion

The exclusion appeal system might continue to be seen by some of the teaching unions as undermining the disciplinary role of the head teacher and other teachers in a school, but in many ways their opposition is misplaced. Only one in ten parents appeal and, as we have seen, with only one in five appeals succeeding, only 200 of the 12,000-plus children permanently excluded from school in England in 1997/98 were reinstated as a result of an appeal panel decision. One should not, however, underestimate the importance of the appeal system. Despite its faults, which have been outlined in this book, it continues to provide a reasonably accessible forum to check at least some of the cases of unreasonable treatment of children under disciplinary powers in schools (including the tendency of some governing bodies or their discipline committees to fail to take an objective view and their propensity to support the head teacher in his or her decision to exclude). Permanent school exclusions have been increasing in number fairly dramatically in recent years, until their recent levelling off and slight decline of late. The rate today remains significantly higher than a decade ago. This has prompted government initiatives to reduce it (including targets for LEAs and guidance on good practice for pupil inclusion). Yet for parents whose children have been permanently excluded from school, the promise of future reductions in permanent exclusions and greater social inclusion cannot alleviate their immediate problems. The appeals system offers the parent at least some hope of reversing a decision which many parents recognize to be potentially damaging to their child's future. From the perspective of the child, school exclusion – especially permanent exclusion – represents one of the most serious threats to the child's interests. The right of appeal can sometimes play a crucial role in safeguarding those interests, even though the continuing denial of an independent right of appeal to the child fundamentally weakens the recognition of children's rights in this context and should be rectified in order to secure proper compliance with the country's obligations under the UN Convention on the Rights of the Child.

The exclusion appeal system has now been in operation for well over a decade. Despite the teaching union opposition referred to above (and in Chapter 1), it is well supported by schools, LEAs and parents. School exclusion is a serious matter for the child and to deny a right to challenge the decision before an independent forum would constitute a most serious inroad in the human rights of the child. It would certainly constitute a breach of Article 6 of the European Convention on Human Rights, which would shortly in effect be justiciable in the English courts as a result of the Human Rights Act 1998. As a result of this, and the recent incorporation of a reformed exclusion appeals system in the SSFA 1998, we do not believe that there is any serious political threat to the continuation of the appeal system alongside the even longer established mechanisms of complaint outlined in Chapter 2.

The reforms made by the SSFA 1998, which have seen the appeal system's independence increased and a much greater guarantee of adherence to the DFEE's guidance by appeal panels, represent a welcome improvement. The guidance itself has been strengthened, although, as we have pointed out, there are areas of weakness – for example in relation to the conduct of hearings and especially in dealing with child witnesses. Nevertheless, we believe that, given the importance of the appeal system, which is clearly well recognized, further improvements are necessary to ensure that there are more accessible and effective appeal arrangements – above all a more professional system – capable of addressing appellate needs in the new century. The unfair disadvantage possessed by the parent and excluded child at present needs to be removed. The case for reform is not in any way undermined by any reductions in permanent exclusions which may occur as a result of, for example, the increased pressure on schools to show greater restraint and the exhortation to discipline committees in schools to ensure that all strategies to improve a pupil's behaviour have been tried and have failed. Children will continue to be excluded permanently and the appeal system must be equipped to offer them and their parents effective access to justice.

An accessible redress mechanism is one where the barriers to its use are minimized. Information is critical to this process, and for some parents advice is needed to reassure them that an appeal is worth bringing and to explain the relatively straightforward manner of taking this step. In our view, parents need to be given better information about the exclusion appeal system. The current statutory requirement is merely that they should be informed of their right of appeal. We believe that at the very least the guidance should emphasize that the information about the right of appeal provided to parents should stress the system's independence and accessibility and make it clear that parents may arrange to be represented at the hearing. Parents need to know that they should be well prepared and that they may need to seek independent legal advice. Our research suggests that access to such advice is likely to be an important factor in decisions to appeal. We were particularly concerned that the advice imparted by less independent sources – head teachers and LEAs – often discouraged parents from bringing an appeal. It was particularly troubling to find that some parents had relied upon the advice of the head teacher that an appeal against his or her decision was unlikely to succeed.

The administration of the appeals arrangements at present is generally satisfactory. Although the time limit for the appeal to be heard is not always adhered to, the system is reasonably speedy and the time limit is not problematic for LEAs. We wonder whether the feasibility of reducing the statutory time limit – for example to 10 school days – has been explored. A reduction would help to minimize the period of uncertainty and lost schooling, although we recognize that the guidance seeks to ameliorate the latter by putting an onus onto the school to develop a programme of education for the child while away from school and before the panel has reached its decision.

The exclusion appeal system nevertheless has inherent weaknesses. The procedural shortcomings and the poor handling of evidence and witnesses, especially children, that we often found (there were of course exceptions) leads us to the conclusion that the panels need to be chaired by appropriately trained lawyers. The recommendation in the guidance that where possible those with a legal background be selected to chair panels is an advance on previous advice, particularly in view of the fact that the statute now makes it plain that regard must be had to the guidance. Nevertheless, if (as this recommendation implies and as we and others, such as the Council on Tribunals and Children's Legal Centre, agree) it is important to have a lawyer in the chair, ought not this to be made a statutory requirement? The cost would not be so great given the relatively small number of appeals each year – fewer than the number heard by the Special Educational Needs Tribunal (SENT), which has a lawyer chair.

It might in fact be beneficial simply to extend the jurisdiction of the SENT to include exclusion appeals. The SENT's annual expenditure is currently £2.3 million. As the Council on Tribunals pointed out when making this same recommendation a couple of years ago (Council on Tribunals 1996: para. 2.42), up to 60 per cent of children who are excluded from school may have special educational needs (broadly in line with our own estimate of 50 per cent, based on our survey); and as we saw in Chapter 1, children with statements are around seven times more likely to be excluded than other children. The SENT's expertise on special educational needs would therefore be useful. Moreover, the importance of the decision to be made in exclusion cases surely justifies increased professionalism and the employment of appropriate legal skills to help to ensure that hearings are conducted fairly, such as happened when special educational needs cases were transferred from education appeal committees to the SENT (Harris 1997).

Another argument in favour of transfer is also based on the degree of commonality between these two types of appeal. Both rely on reports and other documentation, such as school records, and both require inputs from specialist witnesses. There would be a need to alter the constitution of the panel slightly, so that only one of the panel members had special educational needs expertise rather than, as is often the case in the SENT, two. Another advantage of transferring these appeals to the SENT would be that they would be brought within a national, co-ordinated, system. This would help to ensure better monitoring and training of appeal panels and clerks. Even if exclusion appeals remain outside the SENT system, better co-ordination is needed, perhaps through a regional system of appeal panels.

There has been some resistance to the idea of transferring exclusion appeals to the SENT, on the part of its President, who believes that the SENT's lengthier pre-hearing procedure – designed to ensure that there is adequate time to assemble the wide-ranging and often detailed evidence that is often to be considered and to prepare the arguments which will be presented – makes it an unsuitable system for exclusion appeals, which need to be disposed quickly. What might, however, be possible is the development of a special, speedier, procedure in the SENT for exclusion appeals. 'Fast-tracking' is common in certain civil court and other judicial procedures and there is no reason why it could not be developed within the SENT system for exclusion cases.

Our evidence has also revealed that ethnic minorities are under-represented on exclusion appeal panels. This is a matter that needs to be tackled with some urgency, in order to ensure that parents from ethnic minorities have confidence in the fairness and impartiality of the appeal system. This is especially important given the fact that African-Caribbean children in particular are considerably over-represented among those excluded permanently from school. Some parents from ethnic minorities seem to have perceived some racial bias when appearing before an all-white panel.

Training for exclusion panel members needs improvement. The evidence suggests that panels, especially chairs, need more extensive and more effective training in all aspects of conducting a hearing of this nature – particularly in ensuring that the hearing is perceived to be fair and in avoiding the kinds of procedural shortcomings we have reported. Panel members also need better training in the law and in how to deal appropriately with children as witnesses, especially in ensuring that children have better opportunities to be heard. We feel that more LEAs should organize training events in conjunction with other LEAs in order to share experience and identify best practice. The involvement of the local authority associations in training, supported by the Judicial Studies Board, has resulted in some progress but not enough. The system is crying out for a national co-ordinating body for training and standards. This could include within its remit the role of appeal panel clerks. In our view the clerk's role in any event needs to be more carefully defined.

We have noted at various points our considerable concern about the way children are dealt with at the hearing stage. After concluding our research, and before writing it up in detail, we recommended to the DFEE that the new guidance (then in preparation) should pay particular attention to the need for panels to treat children and young people with sensitivity. In particular, we explained that it should give clear guidance on ways of involving and questioning the excluded child in the hearing. Although this general point was accepted by the Department, we were disappointed that so little was included within the guidance about the handling of child witnesses. We appreciate that the Department wanted to ensure that the guidance as a whole was not so lengthy as to be unwieldy, but we feel that this is such an important issue that it warranted more extensive coverage. We also recommended that the guidance should explain how evidence relating to the child's previous record (including exclusion from other schools), the school's treatment of other perpetrators of an incident, and the child's personal and domestic circumstances should be considered by panels. Again, not all of these issues, which we have found to cause panels some difficulty, have been addressed in the guidance.

Panel members told us that in some cases they have wanted to make recommendations to the school or LEA. If the panel has conducted a thorough review of the case and heard from the parent and child it would seem to be particularly appropriate that the panel's informed view of the kind of provision the child's needs and situation warrant should be communicated to the relevant agency. We would argue that this should become a standard part of the procedure after the decision has been taken, although the panel could have a discretion over whether to make any recommendations. The recommendations could be appended to the decision and reasons sent out to the relevant parties. Unlike the decision itself, however, the recommendations, as such, would not be binding.

This frustration experienced by some panel members is one of the consequences of the appeal system having a disciplinary rather than a welfare focus (see also Monk 1999: 217), concentrating on acts of misbehaviour and their consequences rather than their causes. This needs to change and a more appropriate balance between these issues achieved. Children excluded from school often suffer from a variety of educational and social problems. An independent appeal hearing is an opportunity to take a broader look at the child's situation and needs. We feel that the criteria to be considered by the panel should be broadened to enable it to look at issues relating to the management of the child's possible reintegration into the school in assessing whether reinstatement should be ordered. The guidance addresses the issue of reintegration separately, as a matter to be considered by a multi-agency 'reintegration panel' on the basis that the exclusion stands (DFEE 1999b). We were impressed by the multi-agency case conference system we saw operating in a few areas and feel that it is beneficial in working out with parents how the child can be brought back within the school system. Even so, we feel that the question of possible reintegration ought also to be a matter for the appeal panel. The period during which the child is excluded has, despite its various negative consequences for children's education and social welfare to which we have referred, a positive effect sometimes on the child's behaviour and would make it possible for him or her to reintegrate into the school. Moreover, the appeal will have resulted in the assembling of a range of evidence relating to the child, which will be available to the panel. At present the panel is constrained by the two-stage approach specified by the guidance and, in particular, the second head, which requires it to look at whether the exclusion was a reasonable response to the child's conduct (DFEE 1999a: Annex D, para. 35). But there is an apparent conflict with another part of the guidance that states that the panel's remit is 'to decide if the pupil should be reinstated' (para. 34). The latter is consistent with the right of appeal itself, which relates to the governing body's (or the discipline committee's) decision 'not to reinstate'.[1] On that basis, the question whether reintegration in the school from which the child was excluded would be successful is surely a matter that it is relevant for the panel to consider. Indeed, it could be argued that at this point the onus of proof should be shifted onto the school to show why the pupil should not be reintegrated. Either way, the guidance needs to be amended accordingly, in our view. Lest it be thought that this broader focus would undermine the judicial role of the appeal panels, it has to be remembered that these are precisely the kinds of issues that the SENT has to consider when examining whether a child should attend a special school or be educated in a mainstream setting; and in some of those cases, the child's special educational needs relate to behavioural problems.

Too many parents who bring an exclusion appeal do so without having complete confidence in the fairness of the appeal system. In our view the evidence we have uncovered shows that, unfortunately, that lack of confidence is justified in many cases. We have suggested possible reforms that we believe could give more cause for confidence in the system. We would extend some of our recommendations – particularly better training for panels and clerks and proper guidance on handling witnesses – to the governors' reinstatement meeting stage. The negative experience of many parents at this stage clearly colours their judgement about taking their case any further. As far as the appeal panels are concerned, while most members approach their task conscientiously, too few of them appreciate the nature of the judicial task that confronts them. The predominant motivating reason they gave us for becoming a panel member was that they had an interest in education. Many said they wanted to do something useful with their time. Very few expressly indicated that they were motivated by the desire to perform a judicial role *per se*. There is a need for experienced laypeople such as these to be involved in the adjudication of education disputes. But it is important to ensure that they are able to act as competent adjudicators. Above all there is a need to ensure that the appeal system itself provides a fair and effective redress mechanism for parents and children. In several key respects it does not do so at present.

Appendix

Department for Education and Employment Guidance on Procedures for Excluding a Pupil (Including Appeals)

Annex D from DFEE Circular 10/99, Social Inclusion: Pupil Support (July 1999)
Reproduced with permission of the Department for Education and Employment, whose co-operation is acknowledged with thanks.

Procedures for Excluding a Pupil

Head teachers, governors, LEAs and appeal panels should have regard to this guidance in discharging their functions in relation to pupil exclusions (School Standards and Framework Act 1998) ('the Act')[1]. The guidance should be read alongside Section 6 of the Circular which explains the steps that should be taken before resorting to exclusion and when exclusion should be used.

Note: These procedures apply to all maintained schools and all pupils including those above or below statutory school age. The procedures do not apply to independent schools, city technology colleges, pupil referral units, free-standing nursery schools, or sixth form colleges which have no statutory duty to apply these procedures.

Responsibilities of the Head Teacher

Informing parents about the exclusion

1 A head teacher who excludes a pupil should make sure the parent is notified immediately, ideally by telephone, and that the telephone call is followed by a letter within one school day. An exclusion should normally begin on the next school day.

2 Letters about fixed period and permanent exclusions should explain:

- why the head teacher decided to exclude the pupil and the steps taken to try to avoid exclusion;

- the arrangements for enabling the pupil to continue their education, including setting and marking the pupil's work;
- the parent's[2] right to state their case to the Governing Body's Discipline Committee;
- who the parents should contact if they wish to state their case (usually the Clerk to the Committee);
- the latest date the parent can put a written statement to the Discipline Committee;
- the parent's right to see their child's school record[3];
- if the exclusion is for a **fixed period**, the length of the exclusion and the date and the time the pupil should return to school;
- if the exclusion is for lunchtimes only, the length of the exclusion (normally no more than five school days) and the arrangements for providing a meal for any pupil entitled to free school meals;
- if the exclusion is **permanent**, the date the permanent exclusion takes effect, and details of any relevant previous warnings, fixed period exclusions or other disciplinary measures taken before the present incident[4];
- the name and telephone number of a contact at the LEA who can provide advice on the exclusion process and the telephone number of the Advisory Centre for Education (ACE) helpline (020 7704 9822).

All correspondence should be in plain English and avoid unnecessary jargon. Exclusion cases should be treated in the strictest confidence.

3 A head teacher who extends a fixed period exclusion or, exceptionally, converts a fixed period exclusion into a permanent exclusion, should again write to the parent explaining the reasons and making the other points above. Where an exclusion is extended there is a new right for the parent to state their case to the Discipline Committee.

Informing the Discipline Committee and the LEA

4 The head teacher should inform the Governing Body's Discipline Committee and the LEA immediately of:

- all permanent exclusions
- all exclusions which result, separately or in total, in the pupil missing more than five school days in any one term, or which deny pupils the chance to take a public examination.

Short fixed period exclusions of one to five days school days should be reported termly, unless the LEA asks for more frequent reports.

5 For each exclusion reported the school should give:

- the name of the pupil;
- the length of the exclusion;
- the reason(s) for the exclusion;
- the pupil's age, gender, ethnicity, and whether they are on the SEN Code of Practice or have a statement of special educational needs;
- whether the pupil is looked after by the Local Authority.

Responsibilities of the Governing Body

The Discipline Committee

6 The Governing Body should set up a Discipline Committee made up of three or five governors (not including the head teacher), to review the use of exclusion within the school, including considering the views of the parent of an excluded pupil, and deciding whether or not to confirm exclusions of more than five school days or those where a pupil would miss an opportunity to take a public examination. The Governing Body should also appoint a clerk to the Discipline Committee to provide advice on the exclusions process and handle the administrative arrangements for considering exclusions. The Governing Body may nominate three or five governors to serve on the Discipline Committee or a pool of governors from which three or five will serve as the Discipline Committee to consider particular exclusions. The quorum for a meeting is three. If a governor has a connection with the pupil or the incident that could affect their ability to act impartially they should not serve at the hearing. If four members consider an exclusion, the chair has the casting vote.

7 If the exclusion is fewer than five days, the Discipline Committee cannot direct re-instatement, but should consider any statement from the parent. For exclusions of more than five days in a term, or where a pupil loses the opportunity to take a public examination, the Discipline Committee should consider the exclusion and decide whether the pupil should be reinstated. If the pupil has been excluded several times for fewer than five days each time, the Discipline Committee should meet once the pupil has missed more than five days in the term. If the same pupil is excluded again that term, they should meet again to consider the exclusion. Provided that the time limits are met (see paragraph 9 below), Discipline Committees may use a meeting to consider more than one exclusion.

8 If an exclusion for fewer than five days causes the pupil to miss sitting a public examination, the Discipline Committee should try to meet **before** the public examination. The normal minimum time limits do not apply. If, exceptionally, the chair of the Committee does not consider it practical

for the Committee to meet, the chair may consider the exclusion and decide whether to reinstate the pupil. Apart from this, the procedures for considering these exclusions are the same as the procedures for exclusions of more than five days in a term. The following paragraphs explain the procedures.

Setting up the meeting to consider exclusion

9 On receiving notice from the head teacher that a pupil has been excluded for more than five days, the clerk should:

- for an exclusion of between six school days and 15 school days in a term, set up a meeting between the 6th and 30th school days to consider the exclusion. (The minimum time limit allows the parent and the LEA time to put together their cases, and for a 'cooling off' period between the head teacher's decision and the governors' consideration.);
- for an exclusion of over 15 school days, set up a meeting between the 6th and 15th school day after that notice to consider the exclusion;
- invite the parent and the LEA to the meeting, at a time and place convenient to all parties, as far as possible within the time limits. The parent may be accompanied by a friend or a legal representative at their request;
- ask for any written statements in advance of the meeting;
- circulate any written statements, ensuring that the identity of the pupil is concealed, and a list of those who will be present at the hearing to all parties attending.

10 Unless there are strong reasons to refuse, the chair of the Discipline Committee should allow the excluded pupil to attend the meeting and present their case if the parent and pupil ask for this. But the parent formally remains the appellant unless the pupil is over 18.

Procedure at the meeting

11 If the pupil is back at school before the Discipline Committee meets, the meeting still enables the parent to give their views. The Discipline Committee can also consider whether more information should be added to the pupil's record (see paragraph 16).

12 If the pupil is still excluded when the meeting takes place, the Discipline Committee should decide whether to direct reinstatement. In reaching their decision the Committee should:

- consider the parent's and LEA's statements;
- have regard to the guidance on the appropriate use of the exclusion in Section 6 of this document, and consider whether the head teacher has tried sufficient approaches to improve the pupil's behaviour before resorting to exclusion, and whether any further strategies might be an alternative to exclusion;
- **for permanent exclusion**, the Discipline Committee should satisfy itself that all possible strategies to improve a pupil's behaviour were tried and failed. Strategies should include those in this guidance, including a Pastoral Support Programme. For children with statements of SEN, revising the statement might be better than resorting to exclusion;
- **if the head teacher has not used exclusion in line with this guidance, the Discipline Committee should normally direct reinstatement.**

13 If the Discipline Committee decide [sic] to direct reinstatement it should discuss with the LEA whether extra short term support would help to ensure successful reintegration. If the Discipline Committee confirms a head teacher's decision to exclude, it should be satisfied that there are satisfactory arrangements for the pupil to continue their education while away from school.

14 The Discipline Committee should notify the parent and the LEA of their decision, within one school day of the hearing, giving the reasons. The Committee may not attach conditions to the reinstatement of the pupil.

15 If the Discipline Committee uphold [sic] the head teacher's decision to exclude a pupil permanently, it should write within one school day to the parent:

- giving the reasons for the decision;
- explaining the parent's right to appeal to an independent appeal panel to which the parents can make oral and written statements;
- giving the name and address of the person the parents should contact if they wish to appeal, explaining that any notice of appeal should explain the grounds of appeal and stating the last date for giving notice (15 school days from the Discipline Committee's decision). The parent has the right to appeal to the panel even if they did not make a case to the Discipline Committee.

After the meeting

16 A note of the Discipline Committee's views on the exclusion should normally be placed on the pupil's record with a copy of the head teacher's exclusion letter.

Responsibilities of the LEA

Advising the Discipline Committee

17 The LEA's role is to give their view on the appropriateness of the exclusion. The LEA can make a statement to the Discipline Committee when they are considering whether to uphold an exclusion, for example about how other schools in the Authority have responded to similar incidents.

The Appeal Panel to hear appeals against permanent exclusion (Schedule 18 to the School Standards and Framework Act 1998)

18 The LEA must set up an appeal panel, appoint the members and a clerk, and choose the chair. The panel must have three or five members and:

- at least one member must have experience in education, have knowledge of educational conditions in the area of the authority, or be a parent of a registered pupil at the school; and
- at least one person must be a lay person, that is, someone without personal experience in the management of a school or the provision of education in a school (other than experience gained in a voluntary capacity or as a school governor).

19 A person may **not** serve as a member of an appeal panel if:

- they are a member of the local education authority, or of the Governing Body of the excluding school;
- they are an employee of the local education authority or the Governing Body, unless they are employed as a teacher;
- they have, or at any time have had, any connection with the authority or the school or with any person employed by the authority or the Governing Body (except as a teacher), or with the excluded pupil or with the incident leading to their exclusion, of a kind which might reasonably be taken to raise doubts about their ability to act impartially in relation to the authority, the school or the excluded pupil or if they have any connection with a school to which the parent might apply for the child's admission if their appeal were to be unsuccessful.

20 The local education authority should keep a list of suitable people who are eligible to serve on appeal panels and should establish a clear procedure for selecting potential panel members and for appointing the chair. The role of the chair is particularly important and in appointing them, LEAs should look

for people with prior experience in the conduct of appeal hearings, and where possible, with a legal background.

21 LEAs will wish to have in place appropriate mechanisms to recruit lay members. It is for the authority to determine whether a particular person is eligible to be a lay member. Where there is doubt, the authority should err on the side of caution and not appoint.

22 The LEA must indemnify the members of an appeal against any reasonable legal costs and expenses reasonably incurred by them in carrying out their functions.

23 It is important that the LEA makes arrangements for chairs, panel members and clerks to be given appropriate training. Apart from formal training courses this might include attendance at an appeal hearing as an observer.

24 A member of an appeal panel is entitled to receive allowance for financial loss[5] and for travelling subsistence.[6]

Arranging an Appeal Hearing

25 The letter from the clerk to the Discipline Committee should inform the parents of their right to appeal against the decision of the Discipline Committee not to reinstate the permanently excluded pupil, but the LEA should also write within three working days of the Discipline Committee meeting confirming the details of the appeal. The LEA's letter must tell the parent the last date on which an appeal may be made, which will be 15 school days from the date the parent receives notice. The letter should give the name and contact details for the clerk to the appeal panel and explain that the parent's notice of appeal must be in writing and set out the grounds of appeal.

26 The day on which the parent is given notice is taken to be the second school day after the date of posting by first-class post, or, where the notice is hand-delivered, the date of delivery (unless a different date of receipt can be demonstrated). No appeal may be accepted if it is made after the time for lodging notice of appeal has expired.

27 The appeal panel must meet within 15 school days of the date the parent lodges notice of appeal. Exceptionally, the LEA has discretion to extend the period where the parent asks for a delay; for example, if they ask for more time to prepare for the appeal hearing and there are exceptional circumstances which warrant this. Such requests should be considered on their own merits.

28 Those entitled to attend a hearing and present their case are:

- the parent, who may be represented by a legal or other representative;
- the head teacher, who may make oral representations;
- a nominated member of the Discipline Committee, who may make oral representations;

- a nominated LEA officer, who may make oral representations;
- a legal or other representative of the Discipline Committee.

29 The head teacher, governing body and LEA may also make written representations. Wherever possible, the clerk should make available all written evidence to the panel members and the parent four working days in advance of the hearing. The pupil, if they and their parents so request, should be allowed to attend the hearing and speak on their own behalf, unless there is good reason to refuse. Appeal panels should be sensitive to the needs of child witnesses to ensure that the child's view is properly heard. If the parent wishes to bring more than one friend or representative, the clerk should seek the panel's agreement in advance, having regard to a reasonable limit on numbers attending the hearing.

30 The law requires the LEA to take reasonable steps to find out when the parent and others entitled to attend the hearing would be available. The LEA must take account of these times when arranging the hearing and should ensure, so far as it is reasonably practicable, that all parties are able to attend the hearing.

Role of the Clerk

31 The appeal panel should have the services of a clerk who should serve as an independent source of advice on procedure for all parties to the appeal. Ideally, they should have received some legal training and have experience in the conduct of appeal hearings. They should not have served as a clerk to the prior Discipline Committee hearing.

32 When the panel withdraws, or invites the parties to do so, when it wishes to consider its decision, the clerk may remain with the panel, but only for the purpose of offering advice on procedure or law, helping by reference to notes of evidence and recording decisions and reasons.

Procedure at the Hearing

33 The appeal hearing should not be held at the excluding school. The appeal panel should do everything possible to establish an atmosphere of informality where the parties can present their cases effectively.

34 The remit of the appeal panel is to consider whether the pupil should be reinstated, not 'to clear the pupil's name'. An appeal hearing would not be appropriate if:

- it became clear that the parent did not wish the child to be reinstated. Parents may consider alternative schools in case their appeal fails, but should not have their child admitted to another school (if the opportunity rises) before the hearing of their appeal, unless they are content for their appeal to fail;

- reinstatement could not take place because the pupil had in the meantime come to the normal end of their career in the excluding school.

35 In considering an appeal, the panel should decide whether the pupil actually did what they are accused of doing. If more than one incident of misconduct is alleged, the panel should decide on each incident. If satisfied on the balance of probabilities that the pupil did what they are alleged to have done, then the panel should decide whether, considering all relevant factors, permanent exclusion is a reasonable response to that conduct. Relevant factors must include:

- whether permanent exclusion was used in accordance with the Secretary of State's guidance – where there is doubt the appeal panel should direct reinstatement;
- the broader interests of the other pupils and staff in the school, as well as those of the excluded pupil;
- the school's published discipline policy;
- where other pupils were involved in the same incident and were also disciplined, the fairness of the permanent exclusion in relation to the sanctions imposed on the other pupils involved.

36 To reach such a decision, the panel may need to hear evidence from those directly or indirectly involved, including the pupil. The Discipline Committee may not introduce new reasons for the exclusion. However, the parent and the LEA may put forward new information that may not previously have been available. If this happens, the Discipline Committee should be given an opportunity to respond.

37 The order of the hearing should be notified in advance to the parties. At the start of the hearing the chair or clerk should welcome the parties and introduce those present, pointing out that the panel is independent of the Authority and the governing body and that its decision is binding on them. The clerk should explain the order in which the parties entitled to be heard will state their case and that there will be an opportunity for questioning by the other parties afterwards. The panel members may also ask questions of the parties to the appeal or of any witnesses who appear, in order to clarify an issue or to elicit more information. So far as possible such questions should be reserved until the end of each party's statement and questioning by the other parties. The clerk may be called to give legal or procedural advice to the appeal panel during the course of the hearing and when they retire to consider their decision.

38 The chair should order proceedings and lead the panel in establishing the relevant facts. If the parent appears to be having difficulty in presenting

their case, the chair should intervene to assist them to ensure that their case is established and that factual matters not in dispute are clearly identified. The chair should assist parents who have English as a second language or who have literacy problems, and who may not have understood all the paperwork.

39 Appeals must be heard in private except where the LEA direct otherwise, which is unlikely to be appropriate in the majority of cases. However, a member of the Council on Tribunals may attend any meeting of an appeal panel as an observer.

40 The conduct of proceedings is at the discretion of the appeal panel itself and should be based on fairness coupled with informality. Informality is unlikely to be helped by the tape recording of the proceedings, a practice which should be avoided unless there is good reason for it and all parties agree.

41 The order of the hearing should be notified in advance to the parties. At the outset of the hearing the clerk should explain the order in which the parties who are entitled to be heard will state their case and that there will be an opportunity for questions after each presentation. If the appeal panel wish to vary the notified procedure, they should only do so after hearing the view of all the parties present and entitled to make representations.

42 Sufficient time must be allowed for each party to put its case. The panel should ensure that parents are given the opportunity to comment on relevant information obtained from the LEA or Governing Body. Care must be taken to ensure that no party attending the hearing is present alone with the appeal panel in the absence of the others.

43 The panel members may ask questions of the parties to the appeal or any witnesses who appear, in order to clarify an issue or elicit more information. Such questions should so far as possible be reserved until the end of each party's presentation.

44 In exceptional cases the panel may adjourn an appeal to a later date. If there is an adjournment, it is essential that no part of the proceedings takes place other than in the presence of all the panel members.

Combined Appeals

45 The Act provides that two or more appeals may be combined and dealt with in the same proceedings if the appeal panel consider that it is expedient to do so because the issues raised by the appeals are the same or connected. In potential cases of combined appeals the panel should seek to ascertain that the appellants have no objection to the combining of appeals.

Evidence and Witnesses

46 Where the school's case rests largely or solely on physical evidence, and where the facts are in dispute, then the physical evidence, if practicable, should be retained and be available to the panel, if they wish to see it. Where there are difficulties in retaining physical evidence, photographs or signed witness statements are acceptable as evidence.

47 The appeal panel cannot compel witnesses to attend and any witnesses must therefore appear before it voluntarily. The Discipline Committee may wish to call witnesses who saw the incident or behaviour which gave rise to the exclusion(s). They may also wish to call a teacher or teachers (other than the head teacher) who investigated the incident and interviewed pupils. The head teacher has the right to make written representations to the panel and to appear and make oral representations.

48 Where adult witnesses are unwilling to appear in person or are unavailable, the panel must rely on their written statements, copies of which will have been circulated to all parties by the clerk before the hearing. In the case of witnesses who are pupils of the school, it will generally be appropriate for the panel to rely on their written statements. Pupils may, however, appear as witnesses in person if they do so voluntarily and their parents consent. All written witness statements must be authorized and signed, except in cases where the school has good reason to protect the anonymity of pupils. In such cases the statement will not be attributed and some names may be blanked out. The general principle remains that someone accused of something is entitled to know the substance and the source of the accusation. If any witnesses are going to appear in person, all parties need to know the details in advance of the day of hearing.

49 The calling of character witnesses is at the discretion of the panel, but should be allowed unless there is good reason to refuse. It is for the panel to decide whether any witness, having given evidence, should remain for the remainder of the presentation of the case. On some occasions this would help the informality of the proceedings but there could also be objections which the panel will need to consider.

50 If any of the parties intend to raise matters or produce documents at the hearing which are not covered by the statement of decision or the notice of appeal, these should be submitted to the clerk to the appeal panel in good time before the hearing. If substantial new issues are raised for the first time at the hearing, an adjournment may be necessary to allow all parties to consider the issues,

51 An appeal panel, when directing reinstatement, may specify a future date rather than an immediate return; perhaps, to allow for support arrangements to be put in place. But the date of reinstatement should not be more than five school days from the decision date, without a compelling reason.

In case of dispute, the test will be what is reasonable to expect of the panel. The appeal panel can not attach conditions to the reinstatement of a pupil.

52 Under no circumstances can an appeal continue if the number of panel members drops below three at any stage during the appeal. Once an appeal has begun, no panel member may be substituted by a new member for any reason. In the case of a five member panel, if any member dies or is taken ill, the panel may continue, provided the two categories of member are still represented on the panel.

Record of the Proceedings of an Appeal Panel

53 In addition to notes taken during appeals to help the panel's decision-making process (including a record of the Discipline Committee's decision and the reasons for it) the clerk to an appeal panel should keep brief notes of the proceedings, the attendance, the voting and the decision in such forms as the Local Education Authority deem appropriate.

After the Hearing

54 The decision of the appeal panel is final and binding on all parties. The Act requires the panel to communicate its decision to all parties by the end of the second school day after the appeal hearing. Where a hearing is held on the last day of a term or outside term-time, the panel should endeavour to notify all parties by the end of the second working day after the conclusion of the hearing.

55 If the appeal panel upholds the permanent exclusion, the clerk should immediately report this to the LEA. The clerk should also advise the parent to contact the LEA about arrangements for their child's continued education. The head teacher should remove the pupil's name from the school roll the day after conclusion of the exclusion appeal. Where the appeal panel direct reinstatement they should immediately inform the head teacher of their decision and specify the date on which the pupil must be readmitted.

56 As the remit of the appeal panel does not include 'clearing the pupil's name', details of an exclusion may not lawfully be deleted from the pupil record, if an exclusion is a matter of fact. The Governing Body must, however, comply with any parental request to append their appeal statement to the pupil's record. It will be for the Governing Body to decide what details of the exclusion are included in the pupil's school record: copies of the principal correspondence might be included and possibly the minutes of the Discipline Committee and appeal panel hearings, if the Discipline Committee and appeal panel respectively agree to this.

Further Remedies Available to the Parent

Complaint to the Commissioner for Local Administration (the Local Government Ombudsman)

57 Only a parent can complain to the Local Government Ombudsman. The grounds of complaint would be maladministration by the appeal panel. The ombudsman has no powers to direct a pupil's reinstatement. The Ombudsman can only make recommendations if they find that there has been maladministration. The Ombudsman might recommend a fresh hearing, if this were practical, and the LEA would normally comply.

Judicial review

58 If any party to the appeal – the parent, the Governing Body or the LEA – considered that the decision of the appeal panel was legally flawed, any one of them could apply for a judicial review. If judicial review were granted, the Court would consider the lawfulness of the panel's decision. If it found the panel's decision to be unlawful or unreasonable (in the narrow legal sense, i.e. irrational or perverse), it could quash the decision. If expedient, it could order the LEA to set up a fresh appeal hearing before a newly constituted panel.

The role of the Secretary of State

59 The role of the Secretary of State is to provide, from time to time, guidance on the use of exclusions. But the Secretary of State cannot intervene in the proceedings or decision of an appeal panel.

Notes

1 Introduction

1 *Hansard*, House of Commons, Standing Committee B, 1 July 1986, *per* Mr C. Patten, Minister of State for Education.
2 See the School Standards and Framework Act 1998 (Commencement No. 7 and Savings and Transitional Provisions) Order 1999 (S.I. 1999, No. 2323), Schedule 6.
3 Tribunals and Inquiries Act 1992, Schedule 1, para. 15, as amended by the SSFA 1998, Schedule 30, para. 47.
4 SSFA 1998, s. 67 and Schedule 18. The terminology has changed under the 1998 Act. Formerly these bodies were referred to as appeal committees; now they are referred to as appeal *panels*.
5 SSFA 1998, Schedule 16, para. 8.
6 DFEE 1999d.
7 Reported in *The Guardian*, 15 May 1996.
8 Reported as *R v South Tyneside Education Department and the Governors of Hebburn Comprehensive School ex parte Cram* [1998] E.L.R. 508 (Ognall J).
9 *Hansard*, House of Commons, Standing Committee B, 1 July 1986, cols 375–376, *per* Mr A. Bennett MP.
10 *R v East Sussex County Council ex p. T* [1998] E.L.R. 251 at 258G–H.
11 SSFA 1998, s. 67(3).
12 The Act will be fully operational in October 2000. It is currently in operation in respect of powers devolved to the National Assembly of Wales and the Scottish Parliament.
13 This caveat forms the basis to the UK reservation to this part of the Convention.
14 See above and Chapter 4, showing that many children do not receive a proper education once excluded from school.
15 Such a right is now to be included in the Standards in Scotland's School Bill: see Scottish Executive 2000.
16 The new Bill in Scotland (ibid.) will also contain this duty.
17 *Campbell and Cosans v United Kingdom* (1982) 4 EHRR 293; *Costello-Roberts v United Kingdom* [1994] E.L.R 1; *A v United Kingdom* (Case 100/1997/884/1096), 23 September 1998, ECHR.
18 This particular Convention relates to 'family proceedings' and is taken not to apply to actions by teachers and school authorities, so that when it refers to the issue of 'protection from cruel and degrading treatment' it is concerned with mistreatment by parents 'rather than, say, children's treatment by teachers or the police' (Sawyer 1999: 154).
19 SSFA 1998, ss 65(5) and 67(1).
20 Via regualtions: see Scottish Executive 2000.

21 Ibid., Schedule 18, paras 10 and 17.
22 Ibid., s. 110(5).
23 The government refused to support an amendment to the School Standards and Framework Bill in 1998 that would have conferred this right.
24 *R v Governors of St Gregory's RC Aided High School and Appeal Committee ex p M* [1995] E.L.R. 290 at 297H; *R v Governors of Bacon's City Technology College ex parte W* [1998] E.L.R. 488 at 498C–D; *R v Head Teacher and Independent Appeal Committee of Dunraven School ex parte M* (1999) 24 September (unreported). See further Chapter 9.
25 [1998] 2 W.L.R. 604 at 609.

2 Education and Redress of Grievance

1 Local Government Act 1974, s. 26(6). The problem of overlapping jurisdiction is discussed later in this chapter.
2 See Education Act 1996, s. 497(3).
3 Parliamentary Commissioner for Administration (1999): 52.
4 Sections 496 and 497.
5 In *Secretary of State for Education and Science v Metropolitan Borough of Tameside* [1976] 3 All ER 665 the House of Lords (*per* Lord Wilberforce) defined 'unreasonably' in the context of s. 68 of the Education Act 1944 (the forerunner of Section 496 of the present legislation) as meaning acting in a way that no other reasonable body would act – involving an objective test of unreasonableness – applied to the particular circumstances surrounding the relevant body's decision, action or inaction.
6 See note 6.
7 *R v Inner London Education Authority ex parte Ali and Another* (1990) Admin LR 822 and *R v South Tyneside Education Department and the Governors of Hebburn Comprehensive School ex parte Cram* [1998] E.L.R. 508
8 This would fall to be interpreted in the *Tameside* way (see note 5 above) by virtue of the link between s. 409(4) and s. 496.
9 Education (Special Educational Needs) (Information) Regulations 1994 (S.I. 1994 No. 1048), Schedule 1, para. 12.
10 [1989] 1 All ER 1033.
11 Section 269.
12 Local Government Act 1974, s. 26(6).
13 *R v Local Commissioner for Administration for the North and East Area of England ex parte Bradford Metropolitan City Council* [1979] 2 All ER 881, *per* Lord Denning MR.
14 SSFA 1998, ss 65 and 66.
15 *R v Cambridge University ex parte Beg* (1999) 11 Admin LR 505 at 514c–d.
16 *Per* Brooke J in *R v Fernhill Manor School ex parte A* [1994] E.L.R. 67 at 79E. See also *R v Board of Governors of the London Oratory School ex parte R* (1988) *The Times*, 17 February.
17 *R v London Borough of Camden and the Governors of the Hampstead School ex parte H* [1996] E.L.R. 360; *R v Solihull Borough Council ex parte W* [1997] E.L.R. 489; and *R v Northamptonshire County Council ex parte W* [1998] E.L.R. 291.
18 *R v Inland Revenue Commissioners ex parte Preston* [1985] 1 AC 835 at 862C, *per* Lord Templeman. See further Harris (1997) at 8.
19 *R v Governing Body of the Rectory School and the London Borough of Richmond ex parte WK (A Minor)* [1997] E.L.R. 484. For another exceptional case, see *R v London Borough of Newham and Another ex parte X* [1995] E.L.R. 303.
20 SSFA 1998, s. 68.
21 *R v Northamptonshire County Council ex parte W* [1998] E.L.R. 291; *R v Roman Catholic Schools ex parte S* [1998] E.L.R. 304; *R v South Tyneside Education Department and the Governors of Hebburn Comprehensive School ex parte Cram* [1998] E.L.R. 508.

22 e.g. *R v Secretary of State for Wales ex parte Williams* [1997] E.L.R. 100.
23 *R v East Sussex County Council ex parte T* [1998] E.L.R. 251.
24 *R v Leeds Metropolitan University ex parte Manders* [1998] E.L.R. 502.
25 *R v Essex County Council ex parte EB* [1997] E.L.R. 327; *R v Kent County Council ex parte C* [1998] E.L.R. 108
26 [1994] E.L.R. 67. See also *R v The Incorporated Froebal Educational Institute ex parte L* [1999] E.L.R. 488 (QBD).
27 *R v Head Teacher and Independent Appeal Committee of Dunraven School ex parte M* (1999) 24 September 1999 (unreported). The quotations are taken from the official transcript published by Smith Bernal, p.33.
28 See also note 7 above.
29 *R v Head Teacher of Fairfield Primary School and others ex parte W* (1997) 18 July (QBD) CO/541/97.
30 *Per* Moses J in *R v Roman Catholic Schools ex parte S* [1998] E.L.R. 304 at 317E.
31 See now SSFA 1998, Schedule 18, para. 5 and Schedule 24, para. 7.
32 See Harris (1997).
33 The government refused to back a proposed amendment to the School Standards and Framework Bill in the House of Lords in 1998 that would have granted such a right: see *Hansard*, H.L. Debs, Vol. 590, cols 698–699, 8 June 1998.
34 *S v Special Educational Needs Tribunal and the City of Westminster* [1996] E.L.R. 226.
35 *Price v Wilkins* (1888) 58 LT 680; *Fitzgerald v Northcote* (1865) 4 F and F 656.
36 See note 26 above.
37 *R v Cobham Hall School ex parte S* [1998] E.L.R. 389.
38 *R v Governors of Haberdashers' Aske's Hatcham College Trust ex parte Tyrell* [1995] E.L.R. 350.
39 *Hunt v Damon* (1930) 46 TLR 579. See further Chapter 5.
40 *Sharp v The Governors of Sheene School* (1996) (unreported).
41 [1995] E.L.R. 404.
42 [1998] E.L.R. 587.
43 [1998] E.L.R. 38.
44 [1999] 3 W.L.R. 79 (HL).
45 [1999] E.L.R. 356 (CA).
46 (1999) *The Times* Law Report, 23 November.

3 Discipline in Schools: Social Theory and Law

1 There are varying theories concerning the application of Marx's theories to education. This is partly explained by the changes between Marx's earlier and later works. For a detailed discussion and critique of the various Marxist theories of education see Sarup 1978. The discussion here of Marxism and education aims to provide a mere overview of his views on education.
2 According to Foucault enclosure is not needed in all institutional settings.
3 An interesting example of such an agreement is cited in Clark (1998: 75–76). It is the behaviour agreement used in the Ridings school at the time of the controversy surrounding the school. It read:

> I wish to be re-admitted to the Ridings School. I agree that the problems I have had in school are because of my behaviour and that if I wish to continue coming to the Ridings School I must: follow all instructions given to me by a member of staff – without argument; be well mannered and polite to other pupils and staff; never threaten or touch other pupils and staff; never use foul or obscene language or gestures; conform to the school's behaviour code, and code

of school dress.

The agreement also contained a section 'committing the school staff to dealing with the youngster in a fair manner' and 'developing appropriate programmes to take account of any special circumstances'.

4 See School Inspections Act 1996, s. 10(5).
5 s. 2, introducing a replacement s. 154 of the 1996 Act.
6 SSFA 1998, s. 61(2).
7 Ibid.
8 Ibid., s. 61(4).
9 1996 Act, s. 154(7), as amended by 1997 Act, s. 2.
10 SSFA 1998, s. 61(7).
11 Education Act 1997, s. 13.
12 SSFA 1998, s. 110(2)(d).
13 Ibid., s. 111(6).
14 Ibid., s. 111(5).
15 Ibid., s. 110(5).
16 *Hansard* H.L. Debs, Vol. 590, col. 1098, 10 June 1998, *per* Baroness Maddock.
17 SSFA 1998, s. 15.
18 See further DFEE (1998a) Circular 1/98 *Behaviour Support Plans.*
19 1996 Act, s. 550B, added by the 1997 Act, s. 5.
20 1996 Act, s. 550A, added by the 1997 Act, s. 4.
21 *Hansard*, H.C. Debs, Vol. 289, cols 84–87, 27 January 1997, *per* Mr E. Forth MP.
22 SSFA 1998, s. 131, introducing a new s. 548 into the 1996 Act.
23 Sex Discrimination Act 1975, s. 22 and Race Relations Act 1976, s. 17.
24 As, for example, to some extent reflected in the principles within, and the aims of, the 1996 Act, s. 351.

4 Exclusion in Practice: The Social Context to School Exclusion

1 SSFA 1998, s. 68.
2 Education Act 1996, s. 431.
3 *Hansard*, H.C. Standing Committee A, cols 548–549, 19 February 1999, *per* Ms E. Morris.
4 *R v East Sussex County Council ex parte T* [1998] E.L.R. 251.
5 DFEE Circular 11/99, p. 13, borrowing from section 19(6) of the Education Act 1996.
6 See now Education Act 1996, s. 9.
7 Regulations were to be made under the new provisions, but the Secretary of State has decided not to make them but merely to advise PRUs to have a management committee.
8 See also SSFA 1998, s. 113.
9 Ibid., s. 112.

5 School Exclusion: The Legal Framework

1 For examples, see the decisions in *Cleary v Booth* [1893] 1 Q.B. 465; *Ryan v Fildes* [1938] 3 All ER 517 and *R v Newport (Salop) Justices ex parte Wright* [1929] 2 KB 416.
2 *Cleary v Booth* and *R v Newport (Salop) Justice ex parte Wright* (note 1).
3 *R v Solihull Borough Council ex parte W* [1997] ELR 489.
4 *R v London Borough of Newham ex parte X* [1995] ELR 303 at 306H–307A.

5 *Hunt v Damon* [1930] 46 TLR 575
6 Children Act 1989, s. 2(9).
7 See, for example, *R v Rahman* (1985) 81 *Crim App Rep* 349.
8 See *A v United Kingdom* (1998) 23 September 1998, ECHR.
9 Ibid., s. 3(5).
10 See, in particular, ss 24 and 25 of the 1986 Act.
11 Ibid., s. 23.
12 Education Act 1993, s. 261(1)(a) and (3)(a).
13 *Hansard*, H.L. Debs, Vol. 547 col. 173, *per* Baroness Blatch.
14 Education Act 1993, s. 261(1)(b).
15 Ibid., s. 262. The Education (Amount to Follow Permanently Excluded Pupils) Regulations 1994 (S.I. 1994 No. 1697) provided the detail of the funding adjustments to be made. These regulations have since been replaced. See, at present, the 1999 regulations of the same name (S.I. 1999 No. 495) and Education Act 1996, s. 494 which, when substituted by SSFA 1998, Schedule 30, para. 128, will provide for recoupment of funds for excluded pupils by LEAs.
16 Circular 8/94 *Pupil Behaviour and Discipline*; Circular 9/94, *The Education of Children with Emotional and Behavioural Difficulties*; Circular 11/94, *The Education by LEAs of Children Otherwise than at School.*
17 Nevertheless, in general exclusion is more prevalent in schools where a high proportion of pupils are in receipt of free school meals: OFSTED 1996a: para. 28.
18 Section 17, read with section 1, outlaws direct or indirect discrimination in the context of subjecting a pupil to exclusion or 'any other detriment'.
19 [1983] 1 All ER 1062.
20 (1860) F & F 202.
21 [1996] E.L.R. 360.
22 At 378B.
23 *R v Northamptonshire County Council ex parte W* [1998] E.L.R. 291.
24 At 301C.
25 At 302A-B.
26 Education Act 1997, s. 6, amending sections 156 and 307 of the Education Act 1996.
27 The Education Act 1997 (Commencement No. 3 and Transitional Provisions) Order 1998 (S.I. 1998 No. 386).
28 *Hansard*, H.C. Debs, Vol. 578, col. 14, 10 February 1997, *per* Lord Henley, Minister of State.
29 Education Act 1997, s. 9, inserting s. 527A into the 1996 Act. See also DFEE (1998).
30 Section 7(4), inserting para. 12A into the Schedule 16 to the 1996 Act. A parallel amendment was made in relation to grant-maintained schools by s. 8 of the 1997 Act (inserting s. 307A into the 1996 Act).
31 Ibid.
32 *R v Governors of St Gregory's RC Aided High School and Appeal Committee ex p. M* [1995] E.L.R. 290.
33 Note 30 above.
34 *R v Head Teacher and Independent Appeal Committee of Dunraven School ex parte M* (1999) 24 September (unreported) CO/1794/99, manuscript p.33.
35 SSFA 1998, s. 68.
36 s. 64(4).
37 [1997] E.L.R. 489 at 502B–C.
38 Ibid.
39 See also *R v Board of Governors and Appeal Committee of Bryn Elian High School ex parte Whippe* [1999] E.L.R. 380, where Kay J confirmed the relevance of this factor.
40 *R v Neale and Another ex parte S* [1995] E.L.R. 198.

41 *R v Staffordshire County Council Education Appeals Committee ex parte Ashworth* (1997) 9 Admin. L.R. 373 at 395F-G.
42 *R v London Borough of Newham ex parte X* [1995] E.L.R. 303 at 307A–B.
43 *R v Governors of Bacon's City Technology College ex parte W* [1998] E.L.R. at 500B–D (author's emphasis).
44 *R v Head Teacher and Independent Appeal Committee of Dunraven School ex parte M* (1999) 24 September (unreported) CO/1794/99, per Nigel Pleming QC (deputy High Court judge).
45 *R v Laurelhill High School ex parte K* (1997) 6 February (unreported).
46 419 U.S. 565; 95 S.Ct 729 [1975].
47 Ibid., at 568 and 732 respectively. See Lawrence 1998: 147–148.
48 *R v Roman Catholic Schools ex parte S* [1998] E.L.R. 304
49 This was essentially the view of the Court of Appeal in *R v London Borough of Camden and the Governors of the Hampstead School ex parte H* above.
50 See also Chapter 9. In *R v Board of Governors and Appeal Committee of Bryn Elian High School ex parte Whippe* [1999] E.L.R. 380 (QBD), however, Kay J accepted that the child's behaviour in storming out of the room meant that the head teacher was deprived of an opportunity to hear from her. The court found that he already had a clear view of the facts in any event.
51 *R v Head Teacher and Independent Appeal Committee of Dunraven School ex parte M* (1999) 24 September (unreported) Co/1794/99, *per* Nigel Pleming QC (deputy High Court judge).
52 *R v Governors of St Gregory's RC Aided High School and Appeals Committee ex parte M* [1995] E.L.R. 290.
53 *R v Governors of Bacon's City Technology College ex parte W* [1998] ELR 488 at 498D–E.
54 S.I. 1989 No. 1261.
55 The guidance suggests that membership might include EWOs, social workers, educational psychologists, staff from pupil referral units or other non-school providers, admissions and special educational needs policy staff, head teachers and representatives of ethnic minority communities: see DFEE 1999b: para. 5.4.
56 Education Act 1996, ss 431 and 432.
57 See note 45.

6 The Governing Body's Reinstatement Meeting

1 See ss 65 and 66.
2 SSFA 1998, Schedule II, para.4; and the Education (School Government) (England) Regulations 1999 (S.I. 1999 No. 2163) and (Same) (Wales) Regulations 1999 (S.I. 1999 No. 2242), in both cases regs 42(3), 48 and 51. The head teacher may not be a member of this committee: reg 51. All these provisions came into force on 1 September 1999.
3 The Academic Development Fund of the University of Leeds was crucial in supporting the research – in particular, in securing the assistance of Richard Skelton, who provided valuable input into the process of designing the questionnaire and in its administration.
4 SSFA 1998, s. 66(2).
5 Ibid., s. 66(6)(b).
6 *R v Governing Body of the Rectory School and the London Borough of Richmond ex parte WK (A Minor)* [1997] E.L.R. 484.
7 *R v The Board of Governors of Stoke Newington School and Others ex parte M* [1994] E.L.R. 131 at 137G.

8 Interestingly, there was no steady increase across the LEAs over this period and in the largest LEA there was a significant reduction in the number of permanent exclusions, whilst the number of fixed-term exclusions over five days rose considerably . In broad terms, the urban authorities seemed to deal with similar rates of exclusion and the rural authorities were also broadly comparable with each other, with slightly lower exclusion rates.
9 But note that the head teacher and governor surveys were conducted in only four of these areas.
10 SSFA 1998, Schedule 11, para. 7(b), replacing the Education Act 1996, Schedule 8, para. 20.
11 SSFA 1998, s. 67(1).

7 The Exclusion Appeal Panels

1 *Hansard*, H.C. Debs, Vol. 973, col. 39, 5 November 1979.
2 *Hansard*, H.C. Standing Committee B, 1 July 1986, col. 376, Mr A. Bennett MP.
3 Ibid., cols 390 and 400–401.
4 See the Education (Lay Members of Appeal Committees) Regulations 1994 (S.I. 1994 No. 1303).
5 Education Act 1980, Schedule 2 para 4A, added by the 1993 Act.
6 *Hansard*, H.L. Debs, cols 757–758, 8 June 1998.
7 Ibid., at col. 761, *per* Baroness Blackstone.
8 Persons employed by the authority as teachers are not to be taken, by reason only of that employment, as having such a connection with the authority: para. 2(8).
9 Education (Lay Members of Appeal Committees) Regulations 1994 (S.I. 1994 No. 1303).
10 *Hansard*, H.L. Debs, Vol. 590, col. 762, 8 June 1998, *per* Baroness Blackstone.
11 Ibid.

8 Bringing Appeals: Access to the Arrangements

1 SSFA 1998, Schedule 18, para. 7.
2 Although reference is made here to appeals by parents, a pupil aged 18 or over has an independent right of appeal (as noted in Chapter 1). Very few pupils aged over 18 are excluded permanently from school, so for the sake of simplicity reference to appeals by these pupils is omitted from the discussion. All rights and duties applicable to parents here do, however, apply to pupils aged 18 or over.
3 SSFA 1998, s. 66(6).
4 Education Act 1996, Schedule 16.
5 Above note 1.
6 Ibid.
7 See for example, the Social Security Decision-Making and Appeals Regulations 1999 (S.I. 1999 No. 991), as amended.
8 Special Educational Needs Tribunal Regulations 1995 (S.I. 1995 No. 3113), reg. 7.
9 Ibid., reg. 41. See Harris 1997: 93–94.
10 Reports 92/A/3573, 7 July 1994 and 93/C/3220, 6 June 1995.

9 Exclusion Appeal Hearings

1 SSFA 1998, s. 67(3).
2 Ibid., Schedule 18, para. 8(3).

3 Education Act 1996, Schedule 16, para. 7A (added by the Education Act 1997, s. 7(2)), now incorporated in the SSFA 1998, Schedule 18, para. 9.
4 This change was also made by s. 7 of the Education Act 1997. The duty is now to be found in the SSFA 1998, Schedule 18, para.10.
5 SSFA 1998, Schedule 18, para. 10.
6 Ibid., read with S.65(6) and regulations made under schedule 11, para. 4 (see S.I. 1999 No. 2163 and S.I. 1999 No. 2242).
7 SSFA 1998, Schedule 18, para. 11.
8 Ibid.
9 Ibid., para.12.
10 *R v Governors of Bacon's City Technology College ex parte W* [1998] E.L.R. 488 at 493C–E.
11 Times here do not include the panel's deliberations or breaks in hearings.
12 See note 10.
13 Ibid., at 498C–D.
14 *R v Governors of St Gregory's RC Aided High School and Appeals Committee ex parte M* [1995] E.L.R. 290, at 297H. See also *R v Head Teacher and Independent Appeal Committee of Dunraven School ex parte M* (1999) 24 September, CO/1794/99 (unreported).
15 *Hansard*, H.L. Debs, Vol. 590, col. 706, 8 June 1998, *per* Lord Whitty.
16 Report 97/C/5075, 29 October 1998.
17 As was noted in Chapter 5, the courts have held that regard should be had to the guidance and this has now become a statutory requirement under SSFA 1998, s. 68.
18 Each side's case includes their final summary, for this purpose.
19 See note 10.
20 *R v London Borough of Camden and the Governors of the Hampstead School ex parte H* [1996] E.L.R. 360 and *R v Roman Catholic Schools ex parte S* [1998] E.L.R. 304. See further Chapter 5 for discussion of other exclusion cases.
21 Report 96/C/729.
22 SSFA 1998, Schedule 18, para. 13.
23 Ibid., s. 67(4).
24 Ibid., Schedule 18, para. 14. The guidance states that where the hearing is held on the last day of term or outside term time, the decision should be communicated within two working days: para. 54.
25 Education Act 1996, Schedule 16, para. 14.
26 See note 1.
27 *R v Staffordshire County Council Education Appeals Committee ex parte Ashworth* (1997) 2 Admin L.R. 373 at 397D.
28 [1994] E.L.R. 530 at 537F.
29 *R v Lancashire County Council ex parte M* [1994] E.L.R. 478 at 483A.
30 *R v Northamptonshire County Council ex parte W* [1998] E.L.R. 291 at 295C–F.
31 At 296A–E.

10 Conclusion

1 See SSFA 1998, s. 67(1). See also s. 66(6).

Appendix

Author's note: Notes 1–6 below are the original ones included in the Circular.

1 Section 68 of the School Standards and Framework Act 1998.
2 Or, in the case of a pupil aged over 18, the right of the pupil.

3 Under the School Records Regulations, heads should comply with the parent's written request for access to their child's record within 15 school days. However, head teachers should respond promptly where the request is linked to exclusion.
4 This may take time to collate. Rather than delaying the letter notifying the exclusion this information could, if necessary, be contained in a prompt follow-up letter.
5 In accordance with section 173(4) of the Local Government Act 1972.
6 In accordance with section 174 of the Local Government Act 1972.

References

ACC/AMA (1992) *Education Appeals: Code of Practice on Procedure – Seminar Report* (London: ACC)

ACE (1992) 'Exclusions', *ACE Bulletin* 45 Jan–Feb:11–16

Archer of Sandwell, Lord (1996) 'Cutting humility down to size' (social security appeal tribunals training paper) (unpublished)

Association of County Councils (1992) *Education Appeals: Admissions, Exclusions, Reinstatements, Special Educational Needs. Code of Practice on Procedure* Revised edition (London: ACC)

—— (1994) *Revised Code of Practice for Appeals under the Education Act 1980 and the Education (No. 2) Act 1986* (London: ACC)

Audit Commission (1996) *Misspent Youth* (London: Stationery Office)

Bainham, A. (1996) 'Sex education: a family lawyer's perspective', in Harris, N. (ed.) *Children, Sex Education and the Law* (London: National Children's Bureau), 22–44.

—— (1998) *Children: The Modern Law* 2nd edn (Bristol: Jordans)

Baldwin, J., Wikeley, N. and Young, R. (1992) *Judging Social Security* (Oxford: Clarendon Press)

Barton, C. and Douglas, G. (1995) *Law and Parenthood* (London: Butterworths)

Bayliss, S. (1982) 'Rise in suspensions for playground fights', *TES* 15 October

Bell, K. (1975) *Research Study on Supplementary Benefit Appeal Tribunals. Review of Main Findings. Conclusions. Recommendations* (London: HMSO)

Blair, A. and Waddington, M. (1997) 'The home–school "contract": regulating the role of parents', *Education and the Law* 9 (4): 291–305

Blyth, E. and Milner, J. (1993) 'Exclusion from school: a first step in exclusion from society?', *Children and Society* 7 (3): 255–268

——(1994) 'Exclusion from school and victim blaming', *Oxford Review of Education* 293–306

—— (eds) (1996) *Exclusion From School: Inter-Professional Issues For Policy and Practice* (London: Routledge)

Bourne, J. Bridges, L. Searle, C. (1994) *Outcast England: How Schools Exclude Black Children* (London: Institute of Race Relations)

Bowles S. and Gintis H. (1976) *Schooling in Capitalist America* (London: Routledge and Kegan Paul)

Bradley, A. (1999) 'The implications of the Human Rights Act 1998 for schools', *ELAS Bulletin* 23: 2–13

Bridges, L., Meszaros, G, and Sunkin, M. (1995) *Judicial Review in Perspective* (2nd edn) (London: Cavendish)
Brown, Sir S. (1998) 'Justice for children', *New Law Journal* 510
Carlen, P. (1992) *Truancy – The Politics of Compulsory Schooling* (Milton Keynes: Open University Press)
Carvel, J. (1996a) 'Heads seek full expulsion rights', *The Guardian* 12 September
—— (1996b) 'Third of boys aged 15 "carry arms" ', *The Guardian* 15 May, p. 6
—— (1997) 'Violence in schools "not being tackled" ', *The Guardian* 1 September, p. 13
Charter, D. (1997) 'Teachers may strike over pupils caught with gun', *The Times* 4 April, p. 2
—— (1998) 'Teachers to strike over laser pen', *The Times* 13 January
Children's Society, The (1997) 'Exclusion epidemic hits primary schools: charity calls for action at project launch', Press Release 24 September
CIPFA (1998) *Education Statistics 1997–98 Estimates* (London: The Chartered Institute of Public Finance and Accountancy)
Citizen's Charter Complaints Task Force (1993) *Effective Complaints Systems: Principles and Checklist* (London: HMSO)
CLA (1992) *Devising a Complaints System* (London: Commission for Local Administration in England)
—— (1995) *Local Government Ombudsman Annual Report 1994/95* (London: CLA in England)
—— (1998) *Local Government Ombudsman Annual Report 1997/98* (London: CLA in England)
Clark, P. (1998) *Back from the Brink. Transforming the Ridings School and Our Children's Education* (London: Metro)
Cohen, R. and Hughes, M. with Ashworth, L. and Blair, M. (1994) *School's Out: The Family Perspective on School Exclusion* (Essex: Family Service Unit)
Council on Tribunals (1988) *Annual Report 1987/88* (London: HMSO)
—— (1992) *Annual Report 1991/92* (London: HMSO)
—— (1993) *Annual Report 1992/93* (London: HMSO)
—— (1995) *Annual Report 1994/95* (London: HMSO)
—— (1996) *Annual Report 1995/96* (London: HMSO)
—— (1997a) *Annual Report 1996/97* (London: HMSO)
—— (1997b) *Digest of Training: Education Appeal Committees, England and Wales* (London: Council on Tribunals)
—— (1997c) *Tribunals, Their Organisation and Independence* Cm 3744 (London: The Stationery Office)
—— (1998) *Annual Report 1997/98* (London: HMSO)
CRE (1985) *Birmingham LEA and Schools: Referral and Suspension of Pupils* (London: CRE)
—— (1996) *Exclusions from School: The Public Cost* (London: CRE)
—— (1997) *Exclusion from School and Racial Equality: A Good Practice Guide* (London: Commission for Racial Equality)
Delamont, S. (1999) 'Gender and the discourse of derision', *Research Papers in Education* 14/1, 3–21
DES (1985) *Better Schools* (London: DES)
—— (1987) *Education (No. 2) Act 1986: Further Guidance* (London: DES)

—— (1989) Circular 1/89 *Education Reform Act 1989: Local Arrangements for the Consideration of Complaints* (London: DES)

DFE (1992) *Exclusions – A Discussion Paper* (London: DFE)

—— (1994a) *The Education by Local Education Authorities of Children Otherwise than at School. Circular 11/94* (London: DFE)

—— (1994b) *Exclusions From School. Circular 10/94* (London: DFE)

—— (1994c) *Pupil Behaviour and Discipline Circular 8/94* (London: DFE)

—— (1995) *Final Report to the Department for Education National Survey of Local Education Authorities' Policies and Procedures for the Identification and Provision for Children who are out of School by Reason of Exclusion or Otherwise* (London: DFE)

DFEE (1997a) *Excellence in Schools* Cm 3681 (London: The Stationery Office)

—— (1997b) *Framework for the Organisation of Schools* (London: DFEE)

—— (1997c) *Permanent Exclusions from Schools in England in 1995/96* (London: DFEE)

—— (1997d) *School Security. Dealing with troublemakers: protecting pupils and staff using the law* (London: DFEE)

—— (1998a) Circular 1/98 *Behaviour Support Plans* (London: DFEE)

—— (1998b) *Permanent Exclusions from Schools in England in 1996/97 and Exclusion Appeals Lodged by Parents in 1996/97* (London: DFEE)

—— (1999a) Circular 10/99 *Social Inclusion: Pupil Support* (London: DFEE)

—— (1999b) Circular 11/99, *Social Inclusion: The LEA Role in Pupil Support* (London: DFEE)

—— (1999c) *Draft Guidance: Pupil Support* (London: DFEE)

—— (1999d) *Permanent Exclusions from Schools in England in 1997/98 and Exclusion Appeals Lodged by Parents in 1997/98* (London: DFEE)

DSS (1998) *Social Security Statistics 1998* (Leeds: Corporate Document Services)

Durkheim, E. (1968) *Education and Sociology* (London: The Free Press)

Elton, Lord (1989) *Discipline in Schools. Report of the Committee of Enquiry Chaired by Lord Elton* (London: HMSO)

Fortin, J. (1998) *Children's Rights and the Developing Law* (London: Butterworths)

Foucault, M. (1991) *Discipline and Punish: The Birth of the Prison* (London: Penguin)

Franks Committee (1957) *Report of the Committee on Administrative Tribunals and Enquiries*, Cmnd 218 (London: HMSO)

Freeman, M. (1998) 'The next Children's Act', *Family Law* 28: 341–348

Galloway, D. (1982) 'A study of pupils suspended from schools', *British Journal of Educational Psychology* 52: 205–212

Garner, P. (1996) 'A la Recherche du temps perdu: case-study evidence from off-site and pupil referral units', *Children and Society* 10: 187–196

Genn, H. et al. (1999) *Paths to Justice: What People Do and Think About Going to Law* (Oxford: Hart).

Genn, H. and Genn, Y. (1989) *The Effectiveness of Representation at Tribunals* (London: Lord Chancellor's Department)

Gill, M. and Hearnshaw, S. (1997) *Personal Safety and Violence in Schools* DFEE Research Report No. 21 (London: DFEE)

Goriely, T. and Williams, T. (1997) *Resolving Civil Disputes: Choosing Between Out-of-Court Schemes and Litigation. A Review of the Literature* (London: Lord Chancellor's Department)

Hamilton, C. (1997) 'Rights of the child: a right to education and a right in education', in Bridge, C. (ed.) *Family Law Towards the Millennium: Essays for P.M. Bromley* (London: Butterworths), 201–233

Harris, M. (1999) 'The place of formal and informal review in the administrative justice system', in Harris, M and Partington M. (eds) *Administrative Justice in the 21st Century* (Oxford: Hart), 42–54

Harris, N. (1983) 'Reform of the Supplementary Benefit Appeals System', *Journal of Social Welfare Law* 5: 212–227

—— (1992) *Complaints About Schooling* (London: National Consumer Council)

—— (1993) *Law and Education: Regulation, Consumerism and the Education System* (London: Sweet and Maxwell)

—— (1995) *The Law relating to Schools* 2nd edn (Croydon: Tolley)

—— (ed.) (1996) *Children, Sex Education and the Law – Examining the Issues* (London: National Children's Bureau)

—— (1997) *Special Educational Needs and Access to Justice* (Bristol: Jordans)

—— (1998) 'Judicial review and education', in Buck, T. (ed.) *Judicial Review and Social Welfare* (London: Pinter)

—— (1999) 'The developing role and structure of the education appeal system in England and Wales', in Harris, M. and Partington, M. *Administrative Justice in the 21st Century* (Oxford: Hart), 296–325

Hayden, C. (1994) 'Primary age children excluded from school: a multi-agency focus for concern', *Children and Society* 8 (3): 257–273

—— (1996) 'Excluded from primary school', *Representing Children* 9 (4): 199–209

Herman, M. (1972) *Administrative Justice and Supplementary Benefits: A Study of Supplementary Benefit Appeal Tribunals* (London: Bell)

HM Government (1991) *The Citizen's Charter* Cm 1599 (London: HMSO)

HM Government (1999) *United Nations Convention on the Rights of the Child. Second Report by the United Kingdom* (London: The Stationery Office)

Hyams-Parish, A. (1995) 'Banished to the exclusion zone: a guide to school exclusions and the law', *Childright* May/June No. 116: 11–15

—— (1996) *Banished to the Exclusion Zone – School Exclusions and the Law from the Viewpoint of the Child* (Colchester: Children's Legal Centre)

Labour Party (1995) *Diversity and Excellence – A New Partnership for Schools* (London: The Labour Party)

Lawrence, R. (1998) *School Crime and Juvenile Justice* (New York: Oxford University Press)

Lee, A. (1997) 'Parents threaten revenge for primary school rape', *The Times* 9 May, p. 5

Lewis, N. and Birkinshaw, P. (1993) *When Citizens Complain. Reforming Justice and Administration* (Buckingham: Open University Press)

Lord Chancellor's Department (1999) *The Community Legal Service. A Consultation Paper* (London: Lord Chancellor's Department)

Lowe, R. (1997) *School and Social Change 1964–1990* (London: Routledge)

MacLeod, D. (1996) 'Head closes pupil-row school', *The Guardian* 29 October, p. 1

Macpherson, Sir W. (1999) *The Stephen Lawrence Inquiry: Report* Cm 4262-I (London: The Stationery Office)

Masson, J. and Oakley, M. W. (1999) *Out of Hearing. Representing Children in Care Proceedings* (Chichester: Wiley)

McAvoy, D. (1996) 'Why discipline laws behave badly', *TES* 11 October

McCarthy, M. (1993) 'Dispute over "disruptive" 10-year-old closes school', *The Times* 21 May

McManus, J. R. (1998) *Education and the Courts* (London: Sweet and Maxwell)

Meighan, R. (1981) *A Sociology of Educating* (London: Holt, Rinehart and Winston)

Melrose, M., Barrett, D. and Bodie, I. (1999) *One Way Street? Retrospectives on Child Prostitution* (London: The Children's Society)

Monk, D. (1999) 'Failing children. Responding to young people with behavioural difficulties', in King, M. (ed.) *Moral Agendas for Children's Welfare* (London: Routledge), 214–229.

Mulcahy, L. (1999) 'Sliding scales of justice at the end of the century – a cause for complaints', in Harris, M. and Partington, M. *Administrative Justice in the 21st Century* (Oxford: Hart), 66–82

NASUWT (1996) 'NASUWT reaction to government plans to improve school discipline', Press Release, 10 October (London: NASUWT)

—— (1997) *Conference Resolutions, The Pavilion Theatre, Bournemouth, 31 March 1997 to 4 April 1997* (Birmingham: NASUWT)

National Consumer Council (1992) *When Things Go Wrong at School: Redress Procedures in the Education Service* (London: National Consumer Council)

OFSTED (1993a) *Education for Disaffected Pupils 1990–92* (London: OFSTED)

—— (1993b) *Exclusions – A Response to the Department for Education Discussion Paper* (London: OFSTED)

—— (1996a) *Exclusions from Secondary Schools 1995/96* (London: The Stationery Office)

—— (1996b) *Recent Research on the Achievements of Ethnic Minority Pupils* (London: OFSTED)

—— (1999) *Special Education 1994–98. A Review of Special Schools, Secure Units and Pupil Referral Units in England* (London: OFSTED)

O'Leary, J. (1996) 'Education chiefs call for laws to prevent pupils from suing schools', *The Times* 2 December

Page, A. (1999) 'The Citizen's Charter and administrative justice', in Harris, M. and Partington, M. *Administrative Justice in the 21st Century* (Oxford: Hart), 85–98

Parliamentary Commissioner for Administration (1999) *Annual Report 1998/99* (London: The Stationery Office)

Parsons, C. (1996) 'Permanent exclusions from schools in England in the 1990s: trends, causes and responses', *Children and Society* 10: 177–186

Parsons, C., Benns, L., Howles, J., Howlett, K. (1994) *Excluding Primary School Children* (London: Family Policy Studies Centre)

Parsons, C., Castle, F., Howlett, K. and Worrall, J. (1996) *Exclusion from School: The Public Cost* (London: Commission for Racial Equality)

Petrie, A. J. (1992) 'The provision and monitoring of education for all children not in school', paper presented at the British Comparative International Education Society Conference, York, September, 1992

—— (1993) 'Education at home and the law', *Education and the Law* 5 (3): 139–144

QCA (Qualifications and Curriculum Authority) (1998) *Education For Citizenship and the Teaching of Democracy in Schools – Summary* (London: QCA)

Rawlings, J. (1998) 'Recruiting school appeal panel members', *Tribunals* 5 (2): 4–6

Sainsbury, R. (2000) 'Social security decision making and appeals', in Harris N. et al. *Social Security Law* (Oxford: Oxford University Press), 207–230

Sarup, M. (1978) *Marxism and Education* (London: Routledge and Kegan Paul)

Savage, J. and Rae, M. (1994) 'Children's participation in education', unpublished conference paper, May 1994

Save the Children (1996) *All Together Now – Community Participation for Children and Young People* (London: Save the Children)

Sawyer, C. (1999) 'One step forwards, two steps back – the European Convention on the Exercise of Chidren's Rights', *Child and Family Law Quarterly* 11 (2): 151–170

Scottish Executive (2000) *Improving Our Schools* (Edinburgh: Scottish Executive)

Secretary of State for Social Security (1999) *Opportunity for all. Tackling poverty and social exclusion* Cm4445 (London: The Stationery Office)

SEN Website statistical bulletin 2/98 *Special Educational Needs in England: January 1997*. http: www.DFEE.gov.uk/sen/

Sewell, T. (1997) 'Towards solutions: black boys escaping the cycle of exclusion', *Children UK* Winter issue 15: 4–5

Sherwin, M. (1996) 'The law in relation to the wishes and feelings of the child', in Davie, R., et al. *The Voice of the Child* (London: Falmer), 15–26

Sinclair, R. (1996) 'Children's and young people's participation in decision-making: the legal framework in social services and education', in Hill, M. and Aldgate, J. *Child Welfare Services: Developments in Law, Policy, Practice and Research* (London: Jessica Kingsley), 90–102

Smith R. (1998) *No Lessons Learnt: A Survey of School Exclusions* (London: The Children's Society)

Smithers, R. (1997) 'Weapons carried at 1 in 10 schools', *The Guardian* 7 October, p. 4

Social Exclusion Unit (1998) *Truancy and Social Exclusion. Report by the Social Exclusion Unit* Cm 3957 (London: Stationery Office)

Spencer, J. R. (1998) 'Competency: children and witnesses with learning disabilities – Part 1', *New Law Journal* 1,472 and 1,491

Street, H. (1975) *Justice in the Welfare State* (London: Stevens)

Sutherland, M. (1988) *Theory of Education* (Harlow: Longman)

Taylor Committee (1977) *A New Partnership for Our Schools* (London: HMSO)

Thomas, P. (1999) 'Defining the relationship between the courts and a public sector Ombudsman', in Harris, M. and Partington, M. (eds) *Administrative Justice in the 21st Century* (Oxford: Hart), 141–144.

Thompson, B. (1999) 'Administrative justice: towards the millenium. Towards integration?', in Harris, M. and Partington, M. *Administrative Justice in the 21st Century* (Oxford: Hart), 463–481

Thornton, K. (1998) 'Grown-up victims of classroom bullying', *The Times Education Supplement* 26 June

UN Committee (on the Rights of the Child) (1995) *Eighth Session. Concluding observations of the Committee on the Rights of the Child: United Kingdom of Great Britain and Northern Ireland* (New York: United Nations)

Williams, T. and Goriely, T. (1999) 'A question of numbers: managing complaints against rising expectations', in Harris, M., and Partington, M. *Administrative Justice in the 21st Century* (Oxford: Hart), 99–111

Wright, J. (1989) 'How black pupils are losing out', *Childright* No. 62, December

Index

www.ingramcontent.com/pod-product-compliance
Ingram Content Group UK Ltd.
Pitfield, Milton Keynes, MK11 3LW, UK
UKHW040855180926
475701UK00001B/9
9780415230810